Archaeology, Economy and Society
England from the fifth to the fifteenth century

Pages 105 – 120 missing.
A.C. 11-12-97.

Archaeology, Economy and Society

ENGLAND FROM THE FIFTH TO THE FIFTEENTH CENTURY

David A. Hinton

Seaby

London

© David A. Hinton 1990
First published 1990
Second impression 1993

Photoset by Enset (Photosetting), Midsomer Norton, Bath
and printed and bound in Great Britain by
Biddles Ltd, Guildford and King's Lynn
for the publishers
B A Seaby Ltd
7 Davies Street
London W1Y 1LL

British Library Cataloguing in Publication Data
Hinton, David A. (David Alban);
Archaeology, economy and society: England from the
fifth to the fifteenth century.
1. Great Britain. Archaeology
I. Title
936.1

ISBN 1-85264-049-9

Contents

Acknowledgements for Illustrations

In collecting the illustrations used in this book, the author has amassed debts of gratitude not only to old friends but also to several archaeologists not known to him personally who have gone to great trouble to locate photographs and drawings. The author and publishers are grateful to the following who have supplied illustrations and given permission for their reproduction:-

M. Aston and C. J. Bond (8,1); B.S. Ayers, Norfolk Archaeological Unit (4,2; 6,3); K. Barclay, Winchester Excavations Committee (4,3); B. T. Batsford Ltd. (6,2; 9,1); G. Beresford and English Heritage (6,1); G. Beresford and Society for Medieval Archaeology (7,5); J. Blair and Monumental Brass Society (8,5a); M. Brisbane, Southampton Museums Service (8,4); British Museum Publications Ltd. (1,1); R. Brownsword and Monumental Brass Society (8,5b); T. C. Champion (2,3); R. I. H. Charlton, A. Jackson and the Visitors of the Ashmolean Museum, Oxford (1,3; 2,1; 2,4; 4,5; 4,6; 5,5; 6,2; 6,5; 7,2; 7,4; 7,4; 7,7; 9,3; 9,4; and cover photographs); S. M. Davies, Trust for Wessex Archaeology (8,2); A. Down, Chichester District Archaeology Unit (2,5); D. A. Edwards, Norfolk Archaeological Unit, and *East Anglian Archaeology* (5,1); P. J. Fasham, Trust for Wessex Archaeology, and Hampshire County Museums Service (7,6); F. M. Griffith, Devon County Council (7,5); R. A. Hall, York Archaeological Trust (5,3); Historic Buildings and Monuments Commission for England (3,1b); C. M. Heighway and R. Bryant, Past Historic (5,6); C. G. Henderson, Archaeological Field Unit, Museums of Exeter, and Society for Medieval Archaeology (8,3); J. W. Huggett (2,2); S. E. James (5,4; 6,4; 7,5); R. McNeil and Rescue Archaeology Unit, University of Liverpool (7,3); D. M. Metcalf (3,2a; 3,2b; 3,3); D. Miles and N. Palmer, Oxford Archaeological Unit, and Council for British Archaeology (1,2; 7,8; 9,2); National Maritime Museum (5,2); N. Palmer, Warwickshire Museum (9,5); Royal Commission on the Historical Monuments of England (3,1b); R. Shoesmith, City of Hereford Archaeology Unit, and Council for British Archaeology (4,4); H. M. Taylor and Royal Archaeological Institute (3,1a); J. R. Watkin, Yorkshire Museum, and Society for Medieval Archaeology (4,1); and M. J. Watkins, City of Gloucester Museum and Art Gallery, and Society for Medieval Archaeology (7,1).

Introduction

The purpose of this book is to examine the contribution that archaeology can make to an understanding of the social, economic, religious and other developments that took place in England from the Migration period to the beginning of the Renaissance. It does not provide detailed descriptions of archaeological material which are available elsewhere, but takes a chronological approach in order to emphasize the changes that can be observed in the physical evidence and some of the reasons for them that can be suggested.

The difficulty of setting some of the archaeological material into a very precise time-scale or ascribing it to particular people means that it is usually general trends rather than exact moments in time and the deeds of particular individuals that become apparent through physical change. This is not therefore a book to please current government thinking, which promotes the view that history should be about great people and great events – provided of course that the great people were British and the great events British victories. History, however, should seek to explain the processes which shaped past societies and caused individuals to behave as they did. Archaeology can reveal the physical environment in which people functioned and how they expressed themselves through it – in their cooking-pots, houses, quern-stones or burial practices. There are occasional names of individuals in this book, because their ambitions affected other people, and they were themselves constrained by social customs and economic pressures. But castles and palaces are not more important than peasants' tofts and crofts: all are symbolic of the behaviour patterns and aspirations of different social classes.

The scope of the book is severely limited geographically to present-day England (with two exceptions: Hen Domen, for instance, is too important not to mention). Other areas settled by English people or ruled by English kings, whether briefly or not, have been excluded. This insularity is not desirable, merely practical, as the book had to have some limits of time and space. For similar reasons, many possible discussion topics have had to be curtailed. Indeed, I should like to think that inside this rather thin book there is a fat one wildly signalling to be let out.

Another purpose of the book is to try to show how new archaeological data, usually recovered in 'rescue' excavations, stimulate discussion and provide material for fresh interpretations. On occasions an already established hypothesis has been demonstrated by reference to a newly published site, to show that new evidence can also serve to bear out contentions originally based upon what is now well-known material. Thus some familiar site names may not occur as frequently as they might be expected. But some familiar names do not appear, or appear infrequently, because the evidence from them has not yet been published in sufficient detail for it to be evaluated: the remedy for anyone who feels slighted thereby lies in their own hands!

Many of the references in the foot-notes are to primary sources such as excavation reports, so that many important secondary works appear in them rarely if at all, although the ideas and information that they contain are fundamental. Of these, J. Campbell (ed.), *The Anglo-Saxons* (Oxford, Phaidon, 1982) has pride of place for the early Middle Ages. D. M. Wilson (ed.), *The Archaeology of the Anglo-Saxons* (Cambridge University Press, 1976) has many valuable syntheses. A University of Southampton graduate, R. Hodges, opened many people's eyes to archaeologists' claims to provide explanations rather than merely raw data, in *Dark Age Economics* (London, Duckworth, 1982). For the later Middle Ages, two recent books should be used for thematic descriptions: H. Clarke, *The Archaeology of Medieval England* (London, British Museum, 1984) looks closely at some of the issues, while J. M. Steane, *The Archaeology of Medieval England and Wales* (London/Sydney, Croom Helm, 1985) is wider in its coverage. My colleague at Southampton, C. Platt, in *Medieval England* (London/Henley, Routledge and Kegan Paul, 1978) was the first to look at post-Conquest archaeology chronologically, thereby giving the subject a new depth. My own *Alfred's Kingdom: Wessex and the South 800–1500* (London, Dent, 1977) seems in retrospect a slightly unhappy mixture of the two different approaches.

The first draft of this book was written in the summer vacation and winter term of 1987, during a sabbatical for which I am grateful to my employers, the University of Southampton. It was rewritten during the summer vacation of 1988, and was typed during the winter. Inevitably there are things that have been published in that time of which I have not been able to take full account: G. Astill and A. Grant (eds), *The Countryside of Medieval England* (Oxford, Blackwell, 1988) makes exactly the sort of use of both archaeological and documentary evidence that is needed when particular – and fundamental – questions are addressed. I was sorry only to be able to refer in foot-notes to the essays in D. Hooke (ed.), *The Anglo-Saxon Settlements* (also published in 1988 by Blackwell), and I am writing this introduction with an unopened copy of E. King, *Medieval England* (London, Phaidon, 1988) beside me: I am sure that it will be as useful as was his *England 1175–1425* (London/Henley, Routledge and Kegan Paul, 1979).

I should like to thank various people who have answered my questions, knowingly or otherwise, in the preparation of this book: I hope that they will find their names in the foot-notes. Nick Bradford helped with illustrations, as did many others named in the Acknowledgements. I am grateful to Mrs Sandra Williams for her exemplary typing.

Chapter One

THE FIFTH AND SIXTH CENTURIES

Reorganisation Among the Ruins

Two of the most informative categories of archaeological evidence are pot sherds and coins, and nothing shows more clearly the extent to which the economic system of the fourth century had changed by the middle of the fifth than that mass-produced vessels ceased to be made in the British Isles, and that there were not enough coins to sustain the circulation of an officially-recognised currency.

Coins had been used to pay the Roman army and to maintain the Empire's bureaucracy, to collect tax and to facilitate the exchange of goods; without them, no large-scale organisation could operate. Early fifth-century coins are found at various sites, but there were no new supplies to maintain a coin-using economy – although the extent to which coins were used in Britain even in the fourth century for marketing rather than for paying the army is not clear. In the same way, the army had created a substantial demand for pottery; without the troops, long-distance transport of pottery was not economic. It was probably also increasingly difficult to carry goods as roads and waterways became overgrown or silted up without the regular maintenance that a central authority could insist upon; consequently production centres could only hope to supply their own immediate hinterlands. Such restricted circulation was unable to justify the scale of production of earlier periods, so the industries came to an end, their workforces presumably merging into the general population. The coarse, hand-made pots of the fifth and sixth centuries, many tempered with farmyard dung, seem to owe nothing to the wheel-thrown products of the specialist late Roman industries.[1]

Within the span of what for some could have been a single life-time, the structure of the economy and society in those parts of the British Isles which had been under the governmental control of the Roman Empire greatly changed. The nature of the changes was not necessarily uniform: differences in soil types, ease of access to other regions, possession of natural resources, the weight of inherited traditions and external pressures would all have been factors creating wide diversity. Some contrasts between the fourth and fifth centuries can be exaggerated by modern values; that stone buildings were widely in use in the former may hinder proper appreciation of the quality of timber buildings that can be inferred from post-holes and beam-slots in the latter. It may, however, have been a contrast in standards of which contemporaries were themselves well aware. Timber buildings erected within the walled area of Wroxeter, Shropshire, were solid and substantial, but were they regarded as highly as the partly still-standing stone baths alongside, or were they seen as a feeble attempt to keep up appearances?[2] Those who had enjoyed the trappings of power, wealth and luxury would not willingly have given up all pretence of them or have lost hope that revival might occur. Even those who had not shared in them could still aspire to what they had offered.

Few agricultural workers or artisans need have felt much sense of loss. For producers, as opposed to entrepreneurs and merchants dealing in finished articles, the breakdown of the market and taxation systems, and of the social structure which went with them, probably meant some relaxation of ties that forced dependence. A family might have the opportunity to take up land, perhaps keeping up a craft skill as a limited part-time activity. Those who worked the land could expect to benefit from the weakening of the state's support for land owners in their exploitation of the production capacity of their slaves and tenants, just as state-imposed tax burdens were reduced, removing some of the pressures on land owners in areas where they managed to remain in possession of some vestiges of their former rights. If there were slaves, their legal servility might be relaxed, equating them with other producers whose role was to support their own families and to create some surplus for their lords.[3]

One of the problems in this period is to assess the extent to which a land-owning class continued to exist, a problem exacerbated by the difficulty of reconstructing the complete settlement pattern in any area, and of recognising any hierarchy both within individual settlements and within the overall pattern. In the south and east, excavations of rural domestic sites have not produced evidence that much social differentiation was physically expressed in the fifth and sixth centuries, but this may be because settlement sites are still far from common, and the most fully excavated and published site, West Stow in Suffolk, may not be typical. But there was at any rate no house-complex there which, from the size of its buildings or from the quality of the contents of the rubbish deposits closest to it, can be claimed as that of a 'headman' surrounded by his dependents.[4]

West Stow was practising a mixed agricultural economy. There was evidence for a range of cereals: wheat, barley, rye and oats. Because pollen samples could not be obtained from the site, evidence of the use of peas and beans is all but absent, but animal and bird bones survived well, and are further evidence of mixed farming: cattle, sheep, pigs, a few goats, and domestic fowl and geese.[5] A small number of horses were kept. The bones of some red and roe deer, and of wild birds, were so few that they show plainly that domestic stock was what mattered; anything hunted was an incidental addition to the basic diet. Bones from all parts of the animals were found, so carcasses were not brought to the site already partly jointed, an indication, if any were needed, that they had been locally produced. The quality of the stock is a reflection of agricultural standards; the animals were in general not noticeably smaller or scrawnier than animals from earlier sites. Although changes in the economic pattern destroyed the potteries and took money out of circulation, they did not also cause a collapse of the rural base. Meadowland must have been maintained, with a hay crop that could sustain cattle through the winter, since about half the animals were allowed to live until fully grown. Many cows were five years old or more when slaughtered, an indication that they were kept largely for their milk. The pigs on the other hand were nearly all slaughtered while still young, which is good husbandry: only a few breeding sows were allowed to continue to live and feed, since the only point of a pig is its pork. A site with the bones of old pigs is often one with woodland near it, where the swine could range freely and were difficult to recapture. If there were no great woods close to West Stow, however, it was still possible for its inhabitants to acquire timber plentifully, as they used it liberally in their buildings. They may therefore have had gathering rights in woodland quite distant from their homes.

The sheep at West Stow were being killed at an earlier average age than on most later sites, which implies that their main function was to supply meat and milk rather than wool. This suggests that wool was not being produced in quantity for commercial reasons, as it was to be in the rest of the Middle Ages. Weaving was certainly taking place, as clay loom-weights and bone tools attest the use of vertical looms (5,4) – as indeed they do on most residential sites before about 1100. This was probably basic domestic production, with each household supplying its own needs; certainly the evidence for weaving was not concentrated in particular zones of the site, which would have suggested specialised craft workshop areas. There may have been some production of a surplus, but the sheep bones do not indicate pressure to concentrate upon wool at the expense of other crops.

Other evidence of craft activity that a self-reliant settlement site might produce includes pottery. Over 50,000 sherds were recovered from West Stow, a huge quantity in comparison to most contemporary sites, even though no more than two or three farms may have been operating there at any one time. All the fifth- and sixth-century pottery was made in the locality, since none of the fabrics contained minerals other than what can be found within a ten-mile radius. None was made on a wheel, none was glazed, and all could have been fired in bonfires which would usually leave no trace in the ground. No structural evidence of pot-making can therefore be expected. There was, however, a 'reserve' of raw clay found on the site, although this could have been intended for use in wall-building. There were also, near the clay, five antler tools cut so that their ends could be used as stamps, possibly on leather, but more probably on pots. The sheer quantity of pottery found at West Stow, and the care that went into the burnishing and other decoration of at least some of it, suggest a high demand, and perhaps therefore production by people for whom it was a special activity, albeit part-time or seasonal, rather than production by each household just for its own immediate needs. Presumably therefore the pot-makers were turning out a surplus which they could exchange with their neighbours, perhaps in other settlements.

The direct evidence of other crafts is no less scanty. Fragments of worked bone and antler can be assumed to be the waste discarded during the production of some of the tools, such as the five antler dies, and combs. Again, these could all have been produced on the site, but both the quantities and the decoration suggest that those making them had particular skills. Similarly, iron could have been smelted, in small bowl hearths difficult to locate archaeologically, as superficial ore deposits probably existed locally; but only someone with a blacksmith's skills could have produced knives, reaping-hooks and other tools and weapons, and a little slag indicates that at least some smithing did take place. Some raw materials, such as glass, could have been scavenged from earlier, abandoned sites, but the iron objects are too numerous all to have been made from such scrap, nor were any distinctively pre-fifth-century iron objects found awaiting recycling at West Stow, whereas earlier glass rings, and copper-alloy coins, brooches, spoons and other miscellanea were quite common. The glass beads found there may well have been made by melting down such detritus, as could the copper-alloy and silver objects, although no crucibles or moulds were found. Analyses at other sites are showing that considerable care went into the selection of metal for the alloys used in particular objects, although scrap was certainly utilised.[6] Amber, used like glass for making beads, could have been collected on occasional forays to the coast, just as shed antlers could have been found in the woods. The West Stow dwellers could therefore have been very self-reliant in producing objects for their everyday needs, just as they were in food; but the range of materials in use, and the variety of skills needed to produce the objects made from them, suggests a more complex system than one in which each household consumed only what it produced, and indicates a greater range of expertise than the known size of West Stow seems likely to have been able to accommodate.

Some of what was found at West Stow cannot have come from the immediate area. Fragments of lava quern-stone could only have come from the Rhineland. Four fragments of glass claw-beakers datable to the sixth century would almost certainly have been made either in Kent or in the Rhineland. West Stow must, therefore, have been involved in some exchange transactions, many of which, such as the need to acquire salt to preserve foodstuffs, would not have left any archaeological trace. Such exchanges may have been fairly infrequent, perhaps little more than annual. Nevertheless, despite the absence of evidence that the site's economy was geared to producing an exportable wool surplus, there was an ability to acquire objects that were status-supporting as well as life-supporting. Even the apparently prosaic Rhenish quern-stones should perhaps be thought of in status terms, for it would have been possible to use local 'pudding stones' for grinding, and a few examples were indeed found. Lava may have been more efficient, but it was also more eye-catching.

The range of objects recovered from the West Stow settlement can be compared to that from a cemetery half a mile away. Certain types of object were found at both sites, but whereas some, such as beads, are directly comparable, others, such as brooches, seem far grander at the cemetery and were presumably specially selected for burial. Because it is so elaborate, the ornament on many of the brooches can be likened to that on brooches from a myriad of other sites, in England and abroad. They probably arrived in a variety of ways – such as with spouses from other communities, as spoils of war, or in exchange for other goods or services. Some may have been made on the spot by an itinerant bronze-smith, who did not stay long enough to have to replace his moulds, leaving his old ones or his broken crucibles behind him. Some were probably new when buried, others heir-looms. Although they are not paralleled at the settlement, they are not really discordant with what was found there in terms of wealth, allowing for the inevitable discrepancy between accidental loss and deliberate deposit. The only silver pin, for example, was from the settlement, where there were also a silver-gilt buckle fragment and a silver pendant; in terms of precious metal, the settlement site holds its own against the cemetery.

Nowhere near to West Stow has been recognised as a local market centre where such goods were regularly available; only a mile away is a site at Icklingham which was large enough to have functioned as a small town in the fourth century, and where coins show use into the early fifth, but no later material such as pottery is recorded from there, nor was West Stow acquiring goods of types recognisable as developing out of the traditions of the fourth century, which would have been the case if there had been trade between two co-existing communities. Instead, the reused scraps at West Stow are of all centuries from the first onwards, which suggests that they were collected randomly from abandoned places. The local fifth-century economy must have functioned without the use of established market centres such as Icklingham, nor is there any evidence that new ones were created; instead, exchanges in basic materials must have been effected by visits to or from producers, or during occasional assemblies held for religious, administrative or social reasons. Family and personal relationships may have been the modes by which many goods went from one person to another, and barter must have played an important part where no such interdependence existed. But the Rhenish quern-stones and the glass claw-beakers had to come from too far away for a system relying on face-to-face negotiations between producer and user, and promises of future requital. Any merchant bringing such things – and their provenances suggest that wine may have been coming in as well – would not have been satisfied with three dozen eggs and a day's hay-making next summer. Similarly, the objects could not have been sent directly as presents to a family member or to someone whose friendship or service was sought, for personal alliances can only operate over such a long distance amongst the rich and powerful, not at the social level of the West Stow farmers. It may be significant that the claw-beakers all date from the later part of the sixth century – the quern-stones cannot be so precisely dated – by which time it may be that a system of exchange was developing in the area between an élite group of merchants, supplementing an existing, local system based on personal knowledge and contact. Some imported and other goods may then have been passed on by the élite to their dependents.

Icklingham has not been excavated, so the history of its abandonment is not fully known. It may have been a gradual process, as it was in a comparable small town at Heybridge, Essex, in which buildings have been found with pottery of various fifth-century types; initially some of this was coming from Oxfordshire and from the Nene valley some eighty miles away, but those supplies had dried up by the middle of the fifth century and only locally-made wares were available. Occupation in Heybridge did not last until the end of the century, although the site was on the coast and potentially a port. There are very few fourth-century towns of this scale which are likely to have had a very different history, even if they survived at all into the fifth century; the re-emergence of some of them as the sites of markets later in the Middle Ages could simply be because they were well-placed on communication lines, or it might possibly be because in a few cases they continued as occasional meeting-places, even if not as occupation sites. Exodus from them in the fifth century was inevitable if they were not to be market or production centres – building debris would have hindered their use even for agricultural purposes.[7]

A rather different picture is emerging from excavations within the walled towns. The extent to which these had operated as market places and artisan centres in the fourth century, as well as administrative, religious, defensive and leisure foci, is not well understood. Wroxeter is not the only one with standing buildings surviving into the fifth century, and in York and Gloucester collapsed tiles sealing later levels show that some structures at least remained partly roofed for several generations.[8] This is not proof of continuous use, however, any more than is topographical evidence that gates or certain street lines were kept open or were re-opened. In many such towns, thick deposits of soil have been found, the compositions of which suggest that they did not accumulate slowly from rotting timbers and other inert debris, and were not washed in as flood silts, but occasionally result from rubbish dumping, sometimes from deliberate attempts to level up uneven ground. In either case, they indicate a lot of abandoned building space, but paradoxically also a considerable human involvement in their accumulation, although many seem insufficiently humic to have been cultivated.[9]

One possibility is that some at least of the walled towns were being used into the fifth century as centres for the collection of agricultural products. Grain driers in Exeter, Devon, and in Dorchester, Dorset, could indicate large-scale processing, just as a building in Verulamium, Hertfordshire, interpreted as a barn, may indicate a need for storage of large quantities of agricultural supplies. A function of this sort for the towns could have lasted only for so long as there was an authority which could enforce the collection of the produce, and so it is symptomatic of the changing nature of that authority that there is no sign of storage and processing after the end of the fifth century, and in most towns much earlier. It is as though a system initiated during a period of strong government operating a complex structure of control and distribution was temporarily sustained by a few opportunists who were able to usurp authority locally despite the disintegration of centralised state power.[10] Their inability to redistribute large volumes of produce into a wide market might cause them only to seek to maintain that part of the system which brought them what they required for their own consumption. For this, direct supply from the producers to the residences of the powerful was more effective than collection in and redistribution from some formerly urban centre.

The loss of central authority inevitably affected different areas in different ways, as a unified state broke down into discordant parts. In Suffolk's Lark Valley, for instance, there is no known site which would seem to be 'superior' in status to West Stow. If Caistor-by-Norwich had been the centre of the local area in the fourth century, its decline in the fifth seems to have left a vacuum, or it may be that it is difficult to locate the aristocratic site or sites that succeeded it. At Gloucester, by contrast, there are fifth-century timber buildings inside the walls, and the town may have remained as a focal point in the area. Authority, however, probably resided just outside in the Roman fort at Kingsholm, where the burial of a man within an already existing small stone structure, and the objects buried with him, mark him out as someone of distinction who died early in the fifth century. Although there is nothing else of that date from Kingsholm, it was later to be the site of the royal palace, of which substantial timber buildings identified in excavations may have formed part.[11]

The precise status of the Kingsholm man is not indicated by the objects buried with him, but it may be significant that nothing about the grave suggests an intention to denote that he had been a warrior. He had a small iron knife, but it is not a weapon distinctively for use in battle, as a sword would have been. The man appears to have been wearing shoes with silver strap-ends, rather than boots, and the rest of his surviving costume fittings are not associated with specifically military dress. It was obviously not considered important to associate him in death with a warrior's life. His accoutrements and his place of burial suggest however that he was at least an aristocrat, if not an autocrat.

A site which shows how an aristocrat's life-style might have been maintained in the fifth and sixth centuries is in the far north at Yeavering, Northumberland, an inland promontory – though not hill-top – site. Timber buildings, some very large and using very solid posts and planks, were replaced at various times in a period of occupation which ended during the seventh century **(1,1)**.[12] The site's initial use was in the Bronze Age as a cemetery, and recognition of this religious use in the past may have been a reason for reoccupation, if association with such antiquities was considered to give some claim to ancestral links, and rights of inheritance to land and authority. The reuse probably started in the fifth century as no mass-produced pottery or other fourth-century artefacts were found. The very few objects that were recovered included an elaborate bronze-bound wooden staff in a grave aligned on the largest building; its purpose is unknown, but its importance must have been clear to those who deposited it in such a prominently-placed grave.[13]

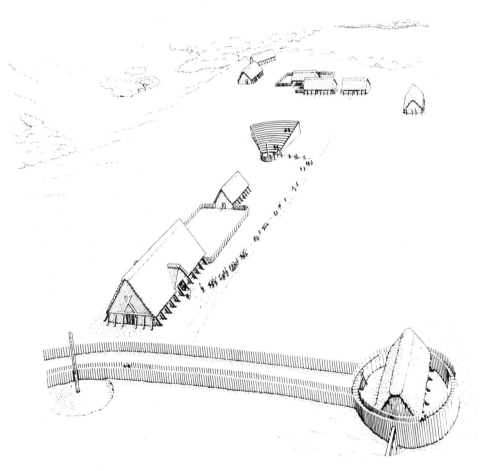

1, 1. Reconstruction drawing by S. James of one of the phases of the use of Yeavering, Northumberland. In the foreground is part of the 'great enclosure' and one side of its entrance, a fenced circle enclosing a building. If animals were brought here as tribute to the palace's owner, it is difficult to see how they could have been prevented from trampling the barrow mound (emphasised here by a totem-like post). The great hall, joined by an open enclosure to a small annexe building, would have been the focus of feasts and entertainment. Beyond, the reconstruction of the post-holes and slots as staging suggests a setting for decision-making by the leader and his people. One of the buildings in the background may have been used as a temple, as human burials and deposits of ox bones and skulls were found associated with it.

Ceremonial and ritual at Yeavering are also suggested by a timber structure, the fan-like ground-plan of which has generally been accepted as the remains of wooden staging, for use during assemblies. These occasions were presumably enlivened by feasts and sacrifices, which the ox skulls overflowing from a pit alongside one building seem to attest. Before their slaughter, the animals were probably kept in a great enclosure on one side of the site. Sheep were also taken to Yeavering, and at least one building may have been used specifically for weaving since loom-weights were found in it.

Yeavering suggests a site to which large numbers of animals came, presumably brought as tribute owed from the surrounding area to its chieftain. The feasts that were held after their slaughter would have confirmed this leader's status as one whose authority brought wealth which could be conspicuously, even recklessly, consumed; the high proportion of young calf bones suggest a profligate disregard for the need to maintain breeding herds. The meeting-place was where decisions were announced and agreed; the biggest of the buildings is interpreted as a hall where the feasts took place and oaths were sworn. These occasions were used to reinforce social ties that bound people together, as lord and dependent. Nor is Yeavering unique, since there is a site not far from it at Sprowston which seems to have most of the same features, except for the assembly-place, and at Thirlings, also in Northumberland, a complex of rectangular buildings, one some twelve metres long, has been investigated.[14] Dating is not precise at any of these, but that the Yeavering staging was enlarged from its original size could be an indication that a larger group of people was becoming involved in the affairs conducted there as time passed, as though the authority of the ruler was becoming extended over a wider area.

Nowhere that has been excavated in the south of England has shown evidence comparable to Yeavering's. In the south-west, and possibly further east in a few cases, hill-top sites may have been used by the aristocracy, but it is difficult to establish the precise functions of those places where some evidence of activity has been found. Glastonbury Tor, Somerset, was initially interpreted as a chieftain's residence, on the basis that animal bones suggested food inappropriate to the religious life, but that is now seen as too exclusive an interpretation.[15] Activities there included metal-working; crucibles were found, and copper-alloy residues and a fine little head. Dating depends upon Mediterranean and Gaulish pottery imported into the south-west in the fifth, sixth and seventh centuries, bowls and dishes being recognisable as having been made in the East Mediterranean and North Africa between *c.* 450 and 550.[16] Most such sherds are from amphorae, which were probably reaching the south-west as wine containers, so their presence at Glastonbury Tor suggests drinking of an exotic rarity at the feasts of those who managed to obtain it. But the bones found there do not suggest such high-quality consumption; most of the beef and mutton came from elderly animals, not young stock which would have provided the most succulent joints, as at Yeavering.

The meat consumed on Glastonbury Tor was nearly all brought there already butchered and prepared, which is hardly surprising on such a small site where there would have been no room to do the slaughtering. At Yeavering, the great enclosure and the ox skulls suggest that animals were brought on the hoof; only one quern-stone was found, however, which could indicate that most of the grain arrived already ground into flour. A good standard of agriculture would have been necessary to supply Yeavering and the other residences used by a chief and his entourage as they progressed round their territory. Various pollen studies from the north of England show no decrease in meadowland and cereal plants in the fifth century, though some show regeneration of scrub and bog during the later sixth; but these analyses have to be made on sites which, being prone to wetness, have low agricultural potential and are inevitably therefore marginal and not necessarily representative of what was happening everywhere. It is even possible that poorer land was being farmed in preference to better, because the latter tended to be in less remote areas and was therefore more vulnerable in troubled times to slave raiders and other disrupting agents.[17] Nevertheless, the evidence from the north seems to support that from West Stow in the east, of reasonable standards being kept up.

The extent to which actual fields and field systems were maintained, abandoned, or allowed to revert from arable to grazing land is not easy to evaluate. On the one hand, there are areas like the high chalk downs in Hampshire, where field boundaries of the fourth century or earlier have been found in what is now thick woodland, and so may never have been used again. In north Nottinghamshire, field boundaries can be seen to have grown over, and to have had no later use. The opposite has happened elsewhere, however; from Wharram Percy, in the Yorkshire wolds, and other sites has come evidence of ditches which were filled up during the third and fourth centuries, but which remained as boundary lines into the Middle Ages and are identifiable as furlong boundaries in strip-field systems. Such cases may only mean that the ditch created a conveniently visible line for later farmers to follow – or one which still affected drainage so that it could not be ignored – and there may have been an intervening period of disuse.[18] There is also Nature to consider; flooding and raised sea-levels certainly affected parts of northern Europe, such as the Low Countries, and some low-lying land was probably lost in England as well, creating the Isles of Scilly, for instance, though some of the fens and marshes may have resulted as much as from failure to maintain drainage systems. Certainly flood deposits recorded in some towns are more plausibly attributed to the collapse of sewers than to increased rainfall or rising sea-levels.

It is proving very difficult to find field systems that can be directly associated with the rural settlements that have been located. Around West Stow, for instance, there are no surviving field boundaries or scatters of pottery resulting from manure spreading to indicate whether an infield/outfield system was operated, with arable fields adjacent to the site and rough grazing further away, or with all the land available to the settlement being ploughed at least periodically. It is now established that strip-fields with their ridge and furrow, characteristic of many areas later in the Middle Ages, were not yet introduced, as no such strips and furlongs underlie sites that came into use in the seventh century as they do under some sites of the eleventh, nor can they be seen to radiate out from any fifth- or sixth-century settlements later abandoned. It can also be assumed, from the locations of most of these last, that light soils such as river-gravel terraces, sands and chalks were in use: place-names attributed to the fifth, sixth and seventh centuries show a strong sense of terrain and topography. That leaves unresolved the problem of whether heavier soils such as clays were still ploughed, perhaps from existing sites, or were allowed to revert to rough grazing or scrub and woodland. The Lark Valley again provides an example of the problem: if people were still living in the fifth century at sites where pottery scatters suggest that they had been in the fourth, they have left no trace of themselves, which is not impossible if they did not adopt new burial customs, were no longer acquiring the types of objects available to them before, and eschewed the use of crude, hand-made pottery in favour of wood and leather. Such an aceramic situation can arise: in Gloucester, various sites had been excavated and little pottery found, yet a previously unknown ware was discovered in some quantity in a recent excavation close to the wall of the Roman town. In the Lark Valley, re-emergence of enamelling on metalwork in the sixth century could be evidence for the survival of knowledge of that craft among people for whom its use was traditional, unlike those buried in the cemetery near West Stow.[19] Nevertheless, abandonment of many settlement sites in favour of those on lighter soils does seem the most likely pattern in most areas, and would have been facilitated by any weakening of the legal restrictions that tied people to their homesteads. Decline in population, through plague, migration, or falling birth-rates – often a demographic response to adversity – may have been another factor, but one that is extremely difficult to measure in a period of rapidly fluctuating change. There seem to have been fewer large cemeteries in the sixth century than the fifth, but there are also more smaller ones, so that the change may reflect changes in ideas about appropriate burial-places, not in population totals.

Some rural sites used in the fourth century were also used in the fifth. Although the stone buildings at Barton Court Farm, Oxfordshire, were demolished, activity in and around them continued into the sixth century, with timber buildings and burials, the latter not necessarily of people who had lived on the site, since the objects with them suggest a mid sixth-century context, by which time the timber buildings may have been abandoned (**1,2**).[20] Connections between the fourth and fifth centuries are hard to evaluate, but nearly all the latter's buildings were outside the former's enclosure, and the pottery and other objects used were very different in kind. The culture was different, even if the land area utilised may have been the same. Other sites have reported a comparable pattern, such as Orton Hall Farm in Cambridge-

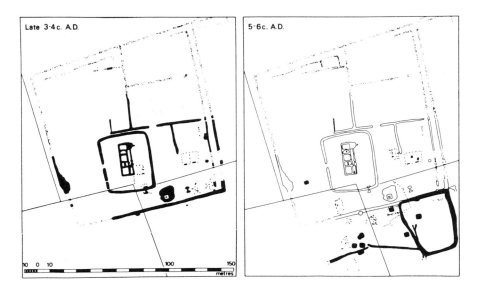

1, 2. Romano-British and later phases at Barton Court Farm, Oxfordshire, excavated by D. Miles. An eight-roomed stone house was demolished after *c.* 370, other buildings surviving a little longer. Sunken-featured structures, fence-lines and burials followed, but not in arrangements which suggest that they had any direct connection with the previous use of the site. The new enclosure emphasises this break: it is almost as though for most purposes the earlier lay-out's effect was a negative one, and its structures were avoided except for burials - which could be later than the sunken-featured buildings.

shire. At Rivenhall, Essex, a stone complex had a timber structure built over it, and there were then burials before the area was used for a Christian church and cemetery. Although the dating is uncertain, this could indicate an élite site remaining in use through from the fourth century so that its owners eventually became the owners and builders of the church, a sequence that could be more common than has been realised.[21] Field patterns in Essex also suggest the continuing importance of existing boundaries.[22]

Cultural differences seem to be even more clearly revealed in studies of burial practices. In Essex, there are considerably fewer cemeteries in which people were buried with grave-goods than there are in other eastern counties. Yet even in areas in which objects are found in quantity, there is little uniformity. An analysis of two cemeteries some twelve miles apart has shown the subtlety of variation that can occur. The artefacts in the graves at the two sites were not significantly different in type, but there were differences in the ways in which they were deposited. In Holywell Row, near Mildenhall, Cambridgeshire, knives were found in most of the graves of both males and females, as though they were primarily a symbol of adulthood, whereas in Westgarth Gardens, near Bury St Edmunds, Suffolk, knives were found much more frequently in men's than women's graves, as though there they usually signified specifically male adulthood. There were also differences in the way that the cemeteries were arranged – children were kept more separate from adults at Westgarth Gardens, but male and female adults were more intermingled.[23] Differences like these are at least as important as differences between the objects, particularly since they held good for several generations, which suggests surprisingly stable communities retaining variations in their burial customs despite the intermingling with neighbours through marriage and other social alliances that must surely have taken place. In times of stress, even quite small groups of people may be tenacious of their customs, to emphasise their sense of community.[24] With localized differences like these, it becomes difficult to put too much weight upon grave-goods as an indication of wealth. A cemetery in which there are many elaborate brooches may be the burial-place of people richer than those in a cemetery with few such exotica: or it may just be that one group thought it appropriate to festoon their dead, while another did not.

In many parts of the south and east, cremation as well as inhumation was practised. Only a mile from West Stow and its adjacent cemetery, though separated from it by the River Lark, is a totally contrasting cemetery which contained, so far as is known, nothing but cremations. Was Lackford for people of particular distinction, or particular infamy, or race, or family? At another predominantly cremation cemetery, Spong Hill, Norfolk, excavations are making it possible to observe variations in the contents, fabrics, sizes, shapes and locations of burial urns. From this it may be possible to suggest that particular kin-groups can be identified, and to reveal attitudes to age and gender. Children were often distinguished from adults by placing them in smaller pots, as though to acknowledge that they had not attained full membership of the community; women usually have more accompanying objects than men, as they do in contemporary inhumations; taller pots with what seem to be 'higher status' objects such as playing-pieces may notify the resting place of those higher in the social hierarchy.[25]

Identification of the sex of cremated bones is usually very difficult, but even bone from inhumation does not always survive in good enough condition to be fully analysed. At Sewerby, East Yorkshire, the sex of several adults could not be recognised, and some uncertainty is created amongst the rest by two identifications of bones as being those of males although they were accompanied by objects normally associated with females, which may indicate aberrant behaviour if it does not indicate the limitations of sexing criteria.[26] No-one seems to have been buried in this small assemblage who was aged less than seven or over forty-five; presumably the former were disposed of elsewhere – but did the community have no venerable elders, or were they also given special burial treatment?[27] One man had had a bad injury or wound which had damaged his forehead, but it had partly healed, and other bones did not have the sort of breaks and cuts that a violent society, or one regularly engaged in warfare, might be expected to show. Similarly at Portway, near Andover, Hampshire, only a single wound could be recognised.[28] At that site, infants as well as youths and adults were buried, though baby bones had mostly rotted away if they were ever present. Childhood and youth were vulnerable periods, with a one-in-three chance of dying before the age of fifteen; the three years from fifteen to eighteen were relatively safe; the death-rate then rose steadily to the end of about the fortieth year, reached by fewer than a quarter of the population. A small number of people older than forty-five were buried at Portway, however, which shows that some reached a greater age than Sewerby would have suggested possible.

The approximate age-at-death of a reasonably well-preserved skeleton is not difficult to estimate; nor is the average height. Some graves have produced 'giants' over 6ft 6ins, but Portway produced no-one over 5ft 11ins and Sewerby's tallest was only 5ft 8ins; 5ft 1in was the smallest recorded there even for a female, however. The heights measured in these cemeteries are of well-grown people, which is some indication that adequate food supplies were available for the whole population. There are occasional signs of deficiency-related problems in the bones, such as *cribra orbitalia* which can result from insufficient iron in the food, but this was recognised in only two of the Portway skeletons. Many more such investigations are needed before the population's true profile can be established, but there is at present no evidence that some people were consistently deprived of access to a sufficient share of the food resources, or were particularly protected from strains of manual labour. This is not quite in keeping with what might have been expected from the quantities of objects in cemeteries where grave-goods occur; the number of objects varies from grave to grave, with many having nothing at all in them. This could be taken to suggest a wide range of status variation, even within small communities, but it may actually reflect differences in ideas about goods-deposition during the time that a cemetery was in use; there seems to be an increase in quantities generally in the sixth century.

Grave-goods are usually taken to indicate that the people responsible for providing them believed in some sort of after-life, or perhaps a world of gods and spirits running concurrently with the human world. Since tools are infrequent, goods do not seem to have been meant for 'use' but may have been symbols – weapons to identify the status, or brooches the family, of their possessor. Occasionally, it is possible to go further; some of the designs are recognisable as being the same as symbols associated with particular gods whose names and deeds are recorded in north European sagas written down in later centuries, and the use of other motifs on both pots and brooches may signify that they are family emblems. In the west, both a hill-top site at Cadbury-Congresbury, Somerset,[29] and Wroxeter have had finds that may indicate a skull or head cult, which could have Celtic antecedents. Is the Glastonbury Tor copper-alloy head another example? Several western temples or shrines have produced evidence that a site was still used in at least some way after the fourth century; near that at Brean Down, Somerset, burial seems to have continued into the seventh century, and at Uley, Gloucestershire, there is evidence of a shrine completely remodelled at the end of the fourth century that remained active for a long time thereafter, possibly converted to Christian usage.[30] There is no archaeological, as opposed to documentary, evidence that Christianity, which had been widely though not exclusively practised in the fourth century, was still practised anywhere in the fifth, until the appearance of memorial stones. The earliest of these, such as one from Wroxeter of the late fifth to mid sixth century, may not be Christian, as they record simply the names of fathers and sons; distinctively Christian formulae such as '*Hic iacet*' do not occur until the sixth century. Their distribution in England is then confined to Cornwall and Devon, with outliers in the extreme south-west of Somerset and at Wareham, Dorset.[31]

Also exclusive in its distribution is the imported Mediterranean and south Gaulish pottery, found at various sites in Cornwall, Devon and Somerset, but nowhere further east. Some of the 'A' ware bowls of *c.* 450 to 550 have incised crosses, and so were at first thought to have been for use in the Christian Mass with the wine that would also have been needed at such services, but the quantity of this imported pottery that has now been found at a variety of sites indicates that it did not have exclusively religious use. The difficulty of establishing the real nature of those sites has already been referred to in relation to Glastonbury Tor, and is well illustrated by Tintagel, Cornwall, where excavations on the peninsula in the 1930s produced evidence then interpreted as identifying a Celtic monastery. More recent work has recognised that that part of Tintagel has no burials or other proof of Christian use. The quantity of imported pottery could be because there was a landing place, and the goods arriving there may not have been consumed at Tintagel. There are, however, timber structures and hearths which show that there was occupation, and mounds in the graveyard of the present church on the mainland suggest the possibility of barrow-burials of people of high status. It therefore seems that Tintagel was a residential complex, perhaps visited seasonally by a wealthy element who controlled the resources of the local territory.[32]

Tintagel is not apparently a very good harbour, though usable; an example of a site which may have been more inviting as a coastal trading-station is at Bantham, South Devon, where middens, rubbish pits, hearths and traces of structures have been found. A variety of objects, including a number of knives and other iron and bone tools, suggests crafts being practised, and animal as well as fish bones were found in some quantity, indicating that this was not simply a site specialising in the exploitation of marine resources for food. There were also imported pottery sherds, mostly 'B' wares, particularly handles of amphorae, suggesting breakages. Bantham may well have been a landing place, therefore, perhaps a 'beach market' only used seasonally, as it is too exposed to make a comfortable winter residence.[33] Goods landed there were probably passed on to consumers elsewhere. That Devon and Cornwall possessed an aristocracy able to command such things is suggested by the memorial stones with their formulae stressing the male line of family descent, which presumably enhanced claims to inherited rights and property. They were in a good position to control the peninsula's trade, particularly perhaps the p

duction and export of its valuable metals, notably tin; ingots at Praa Sands, Cornwall, where radiocarbon dates centring on the seventh century have been obtained, may indicate the whereabouts of another landing place like that at Bantham. Gwithian, Cornwall, may be another, but it also served as an agricultural site, since there are traces of scratch-ploughing associated with it. Its small, drystone-footed huts do not suggest high-status use, but there is a quantity of imported pottery from it. If that was not being passed on up the line to a superior site, it suggests a remarkably high standard of living for ordinary farmers.[34]

Pottery found at some south-western sites indicates where the local aristocrats were probably living. In Cornwall there are enclosures called 'rounds', such as Trethurgy, where much 'A' ware has been found. These 'rounds' were not necessarily new sites in the fifth century, and suggest less disruption to settlement patterns than occurred further east. Their surrounding banks would have distinguished them, and thus their owners, from their neighbours. Such sites have not been identified in any other county, even Devon; the best candidate there for a place of comparable status is High Peak, on the coast near Sidmouth, where 'B' ware has been found, but in circumstances that do not explain its context. The site is a prehistoric hill-fort, with a stone wall revetting the banks, but it is unlikely that this was contemporary with the pottery. In Somerset, the Iron-Age hill-fort at South Cadbury was certainly given a stone and timber wall on its existing top rampart, and there is evidence for timber gates and wall-walks. 'B' wares were among the finds from it.[35]

The cultural differences between the four most south-westerly of England's later counties are worth stressing because they illustrate how divergent were different areas: only Cornwall has 'rounds'; it also has stone-lined cist graves, unknown in Devon, whereas both Dorset, at a cemetery at Ulwell, and Somerset at Cannington, have them.[36] Devon and Cornwall have memorial stones, otherwise found only in the extreme south-west of Somerset, and in Dorset only at Wareham, where there is a group of five, none necessarily earlier than the later seventh century. At Poundbury, outside Dorchester, is a cemetery which probably had some use after the fourth century. There is no trace at Maiden Castle or at any of Dorset's other hill-forts of the sort of reuse found at South Cadbury in Somerset. All that is firmly datable to the sixth century is a small cemetery excavated at Hardown Hill, near Bridport, where the objects are like those found in counties to the east.[37]

No 'A' or other such imported wares have yet been found in Dorset, or anywhere east of Somerset. Their distribution is clearly owed to contacts that some, but not all, parts of the south-west had with the Mediterranean and, into the seventh century, southern Gaul. Further east, different overseas contacts can be demonstrated; there are sufficient objects that must have originated in the areas on the Continent controlled by the Franks for it to be possible to argue that they signify not only the importing of prestigious material, but actual immigration of Frankish people.[38] So similar to cremation urns in the area of north Germany around the rivers Elbe and Weser are some in certain cemeteries in Norfolk that it seem impossible that they should not have been made by potters from that area who had settled in East Anglia.[39] There are bracteates, brooches and other objects which suggest strong contacts between Kent and modern Denmark. Further north, in Humberside and East Anglia, wrist-clasps indicate contact with Norway. But some of the wrist-clasps were buried in England in positions which suggest that they were not all worn on the ends of sleeves, and almost all were worn by women, whereas in Norway a significant proportion were also worn by men.[40] Slight though these differences may be, they underline the difficulty in knowing how far objects can be used to measure direct migrations of people, rather than links created through trade, through formation of family and political alliances, or through exchanges created by the unknown demands of some religious cult. Similarly, to trace the internal distribution of a particular type of brooch or pot may be to trace the settlement progress of immigrants who used it, but is as likely to be to identify a particular local custom not directly associated with an ethnic group, and the appearance of the object may owe more to burial rites and any changes to them than to an actual spread of the object's use.

Many objects in use in the fifth century, such as the distinctive quoit-brooches, cannot be associated with any particular continental area, because they are heavily influenced by styles of costume and decoration that originated in the fourth century in the Roman provinces.[41] Contacts between those who lived on the two sides of the formal frontier led to a fusion of 'classical' Imperial and 'barbarian' Germanic tastes. Consequently objects cannot usually be used to indicate the precise origins of those who made or owned them. Some brooches, such as simple discs with ring-and-dot ornament, are common to a number of areas in England, whereas some, like square-headed brooches, can be grouped into sub-divisions which are geographically confined. These may not indicate significant cultural divisions, however, so much as the area in which a particular family dominated, or even where a single craftsman's output circulated. They do not even make clear-cut frontiers between 'British' of native descent and 'English' immigrants; penannular brooches were certainly made by the former, but are frequently found deposited as grave-goods in the manner assumed to be characteristic of the latter.[42] Such things suggest a great deal of interaction between peoples of different origins, and much acceptance of others' fashions and modes of behaviour. It is likely that it was not just superficialities that were accepted; many burials in the cemeteries of eastern England may be of predominantly indigenous people who had accepted new customs, willingly or not. Similarly there may well be English stock in at least the latest phases of unfurnished cemeteries like Cannington, which had come into use long before migration is likely to have reached so far west. In some areas, distinctions may have been carefully retained if co-existence was uneasy. The upper Thames Valley has many cemeteries with fifth- and sixth-century grave-goods, yet outside Dorchester and at Beacon Hill, Lewknor, Oxfordshire, are large graveyards with virtually no objects, but fifth- and sixth-century radiocarbon dates show that they were in contemporaneous use.[43]

It is not only objects used and funerary rites practised which are studied to try to distinguish between peoples of different origins. As an increasing number of buildings is revealed, they too can be considered. The most distinctive fifth-century and later structure has a sunken area, sometimes apparently floored over, as can be demonstrated in one or two of the seventy-odd examples at West Stow, but more usually using the lowered ground surface as the floor. Because they would have been cool and moist inside, they are thought especially suitable for craft activities such as spinning and weaving, as thread and yarn must not become dry and brittle. They have been found as far apart as Yorkshire and Hampshire; there are even a couple as far west as Poundbury at a late, probably seventh-century stage in that site's use, after it had ceased to be a cemetery.[44] There are also examples on the Continent, in the Low Countries and Germany. Many larger, rectangular timber buildings are now known. Their origin is uncertain, for whereas their plan is like that of Roman buildings, such details of their construction as can be postulated from the traces of timbers in the ground suggest that they were not built in the Roman manner, but had external buttresses, ridge-beams and pairs of opposed doors. They suggest a fusion of 'British' and 'Germanic' modes, widely spread; building styles seem less geographically confined than many artefacts.[45] It is also worth noting the absence of any features in the buildings at Yeavering to mark any point at which ownership passed from one cultural group to another. Either fusion there was complete, or the place was owned by 'Germanic' people from the start, even though it is in an area well to the north of those in which fifth- and sixth-century 'Germanic' cemeteries are found.

Certain types of buckle and strap-end of the later fourth and the first half of the fifth centuries are thought originally to have been issued by the Roman authorities to barbarian warriors brought over for defence against pirates, and later by those 'British' who were trying to maintain Romanised authority. One British writer, Gildas, knew the word *foederati* that had been applied in the Roman Empire to barbarian troops used on the frontiers in the hope that they would defend it against other barbarians.[46] The claim that examples found in England in fifth-century contexts must have been associated with 'mercenary' soldiers assumes a continuity of practice that runs counter to the general evidence of the speed of fifth-century change; a buckle type originally issued as military wear might quickly become an item of dress not specific to a soldier. Furthermore, as organisation broke down, specialisation of that sort would have disappeared, as defence became a preoccupation of all holders of land. It is also sobering that the best-known graves in which early 'Germanic' objects were found, outside Dorchester, Oxfordshire, did not certainly have weapons with what is thought to have been the one male burial; but iron objects were reportedly thrown away, so he may have had at least a knife or spear.[47] Those graves are the only ones of their kind known, so they do not establish a pattern.

Because so much of the *Anglo-Saxon Chronicle* and other sources are written in terms of warfare, it has usually been assumed that confrontation between different groups of people, particularly natives and immigrants, was the norm. Archaeological material is used to try to prove or to disprove the conquest of a particular area by a particular group at a particular time (e.g. **1,3**). But most of the dates in the documents are no less problematical than those that can be attributed to the archaeological record, and it is not until the end of the sixth century that a clear narrative framework begins to emerge. As

1, 3. Old Sarum, Wiltshire. The Iron-Age ramparts might have sheltered an army when 'Cynric fought against the Britons at the place which is called Salisbury' in 552 - but even if the *Anglo-Saxon Chronicle* is correct about site and date, the record need not mean more than that Sarum was a landmark close to where the battle took place. Cemetery evidence suggests that people using English burial customs were already established in the area: a victory for Cynric may have been a stepping-stone in the progress of his dynasty, but not in that of the Saxon settlement. In the early eleventh century, Sarum became a place defended against Viking raiders, but the castle ruins and the outline of the cathedral attest its Norman use. As a town, Sarum was replaced by Salisbury in the early thirteenth century: its numerous inhabitants, intra- and extra-mural, have left no visible trace, a reminder of the difficulty of recognising many sites even from the air.

the end of the formal administration of *Britannia* by the Roman Empire removed from the province the stability of an imperial system based on taxation and a standing army, so the economic system of big estates, perhaps associated with 'plantations' of slaves, and the wide distribution of bulk products and of money could not be maintained. The eastern side of the island was both closer to the Continent and had been more Romanised than the west; consequently its social and economic structures were more complex and more liable to collapse, and it was more open to migrant peoples. Yet even Essex and Kent, on the two sides of the Thames, seem to have varied in their patterns of settlement. Some areas retained more ability to resist change than others, but the unity of *Britannia* broke down into parcels of separate elements, in some of which more signs of élites and power structures are recognisable than in others. Some of these separate elements may be thought of as no more than bands of kin-groups in loose alliance with or actively hostile towards their neighbours; others may be classified as tribal confederacies, though probably ethnically mixed; and others, in the north and west at least, may have evidence of chieftains. What the lack of uniformity shows certainly to have been lacking in this plethora of human conditions was the overriding authority of a centralised state.

Chapter Two

THE LATER SIXTH AND SEVENTH CENTURIES

Christianity and Commerce

During the course of the sixth and into the seventh century, both the quantity and the quality of what is found in the cemeteries of Kent, especially the gold, silver and garnet jewellery (2,1), increasingly contrast with what is found elsewhere in England. Proximity to the Continent, and particularly to the powerful Franks on the opposite side of the Channel, enabled people in Kent to establish a network of inland and overseas contacts.[1] Objects recognisable as made in England but found in France may indicate exchanges of gifts, which would have created or confirmed family or political alliances. The tangible wealth of Kent seems to be more than could be accounted for by this sort of reciprocal gift-giving alone, however. Some of it could have been sent over to Kent just to buy friendships, but the Franks cannot have stood to benefit much from establishing as clients in this way neighbours who offered them little threat. They may have thought it prestigious to be seen to dispense patronage, since they were themselves obtaining subsidy payments from the Empire, much of it in the form of gold coin, in order to purchase a peaceful alliance. Such alliances may sometimes have been cemented by marriages, and Frankish jewellery styles found in England have often been seen as the result of brides bringing dowries. But the position on skeletons in Kentish cemeteries of much of the jewellery shows that it was not always worn in the Frankish mode and some continental fashions, such as the use of elaborate earrings, are hardly ever in evidence in England.[2] It seems unlikely, therefore, that many Frankish women were being buried in Kent, as they would have had no reason to abandon their habits of dress. The marriage of King Aethelberht of Kent to the Frankish Bertha may therefore have been exceptional, nor should its significance be overstressed, since she was not a very important princess.

It was not only Frankish jewellery that was coming into Kent. There were imported gold coins, Byzantine *solidi* and Gaulish *trientes*, known in England as 'thrymsas' or 'tremisses'. Copper-alloy 'Coptic' bowls and other items originally made in Egypt and elsewhere in the Eastern Mediterranean and routed through Italy, across the Alps, along the Rhine and across the Channel are found in such quantities in Kent as to suggest that they were being deliberately directed there. A few of these things are found outside Kent and,

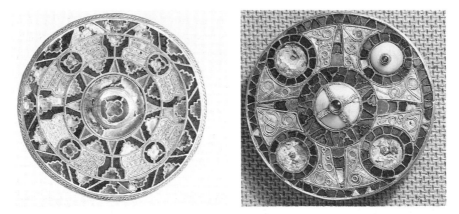

2, 1. The Amherst and Monkton brooches, both from Kent: shown actual size. Both are 'jewelled composite disc brooches', a distinctive Kentish type making lavish use of imported gold and red garnets: but to achieve greens and blues, glass or paste had to serve; paste, cuttle fish shell or, if obtainable, shell from the Indian Ocean was used for whites. Analysis of the gold in the Amherst brooch (left: see also colour picture on cover) has shown that it is 83% fine, whereas that in the Monkton brooch (right) is only 55% fine, a difference visible even in a black-and-white photograph because silver alloyed with the gold makes the colour much paler. The Amherst brooch's cells (*cloisons*) holding the stones are made of gold, but those of the Monkton brooch are copper alloy, originally gilded to try and deceive the eye. This sparing use of gold, and the smaller garnets, are probably not because the Monkton brooch was made for a less wealthy owner, but because gold, garnets and other exotica became harder to obtain as north-western Europe's contacts with the East broke down in the seventh century: on analogy with the gold content of contemporary coinage, the Amherst brooch was made before *c.* 620, the Milton brooch in the 640s.

when they are not stray finds without recorded associations, they are found in the richest graves or similar élite surroundings—a *triens* was one of the very few objects found at Yeavering. They suggest Kent's ability to supply social leaders in other areas with status-enhancing goods – a different pattern from that of many other imports, such as crystal and ivory, which are more widely spread and have no marked Kentish ties, as though they circulated more generally by reciprocal exchange between equals and with less obvious political intent (**2,2**).[3] If Kent was indeed distributing a restricted supply of exotica to élites elsewhere, it was presumably because those people's friendship was worth buying, to secure both peace and the material goods which they were in a position to supply. Kent was helping to upset any equilibrium that may have existed, by encouraging the development of a small number of people who, if they could win and hold control of a territory, could exploit its resources to gain for themselves the trappings of power.

What did Kent, and from Kent the rest of Europe, want that England could supply? There is little in the archaeological record, though lead from Derbyshire and perhaps the Mendips became more important as church building increased again. The former's rôle is suggested by the large number of rich objects in Peak District graves of the seventh century.[4] Hunting dogs are mentioned in both earlier and later documents, and there are certainly dog bones in settlement sites like Barton Court Farm: occasionally they are recognisably 'long-legged and well exercised',[5] but was anyone breeding them for export? Wool, cloth and hides are similar enigmas. Then there are the potential producers of such agricultural products, slaves. Pope Gregory could buy *Angli* in Rome in the sixth century, and slavery was one of the main catalysts for long-distance exchanges, linking the northern economy into that of the Mediterranean and the growing Islamic worlds. There are no pathetic trails of dropped debris to chart the forlorn passage of slave caravans, nor do sudden outbreaks of strange funerary rites mark where some of them found their ultimate destiny. The native culture of slaves is usually totally submerged by that of their owners, since it would be spurned not only by those who had their freedom but probably also by those who had not, whose new conditions would have made them ashamed of their own gods and customs, which had failed to protect them.[6] Consequently it is unsurprising that there is nothing tangible to show that there were slaves from the British Isles on the Continent, but perfectly credible that some of the profits of those benefiting from the trade should be manifest in Britain.

If it is correct to identify slavery as being particularly important, not only the quantity of imported objects becomes more explicable, but also the nature of many of the objects chosen for burial. Ultimately, slaves had to be obtained by fighting for them, and weapons in graves may symbolise such ideas as the success of the warrior who had won great booty, and the success that he had had in protecting himself, his kin and his land from despoliation and slavery. Weapons might also symbolise power and rank at a time when family dynasties were not yet well enough established to bestow inherited status. A spear, or a spear and shield, might symbolise merely a man who had reached adulthood.[7] The iron swords are certainly more likely to be symbolic than anything else, since their edges were made of such low-carbon iron that they would not have been hard enough for practical use.[8] Despite this, swords were often given elaborate hilts and scabbards that are beyond what was accorded to other weapons, and their scarcity and frequent association with other valuable objects suggest the importance attributed to certain males. Hit-and-run booty-seeking raids are also an inference that can be drawn from horse bones or riding equipment. A horse-burial with a bit has recently been reported from Heslerton, North Yorkshire;[9] horse bones found in urns at Spong Hill are all with the cremations of adult males; they occur at Sutton Hoo in Suffolk. Settlement sites like West Stow yield horse bones, but in very small numbers. So horses — ponies by today's standards — were available, but their numbers and size suggest that they were for riding and pack transport rather than cart or plough haulage.

Another sign of the emergence of a social élite who were not engaged in agriculture, but who could more easily dominate those who were, is the grow-

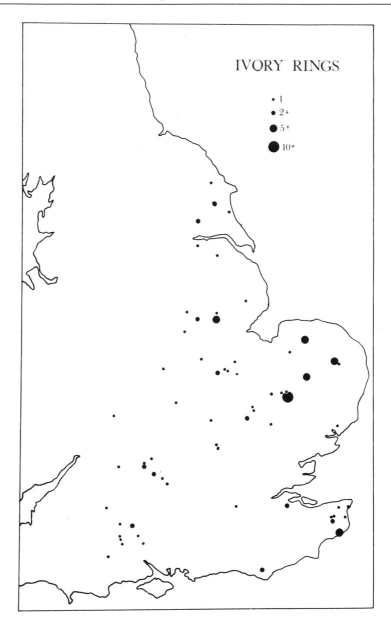

2, 2. Maps by J.W. Huggett showing the contrasting distributions of ivory rings (left) and wheel-thrown pottery (right) found in early Anglo-Saxon cemeteries. Both were imported, but whereas the ivory rings are found over most of the areas where graves occur, the wheel-thrown pottery is predominantly from Kent. Furthermore, there are several cemeteries in which more than one ring has been found, suggesting that they travelled inland in some quantities and were distributed from more than one centre; only single exam-

ples of the pots are known outside Kent, suggesting that they were allowed to leave that kingdom very sparingly and were not available elsewhere for redistribution. Three of the non-Kentish pots are from parts of the Continent with which Kent did not have many links, though some of the richer people in other kingdoms were trying to establish their own sources of supply. From such information, ideas about the different ways in which objects may have changed hands can be formulated.

ing sixth-century practice of distinguishing some graves by placing them in small enclosures such as penannular ditches, or in barrows.[10] Barrows may also have emphasized rights to property, through physical association with a claimed or actual forebear. Outside Kent in the seventh century, high status seems to have become even more clearly signalled by burial within isolated barrows, rather than in cemeteries that contain a range of differently-provided graves. Many barrows also yield evidence of elaborate burial-rites – what seems to have been a bed draped with textiles at Swallowcliffe Down, Wiltshire, or the ships at Snape and Sutton Hoo in Suffolk. In some cases, this wealthy élite's members enhanced their claims to land of which their possession was in fact fairly new by being buried in existing, usually Bronze Age, barrows as though to associate themselves with the peoples who had lived in the area long ago, rather in the manner of Victorian industrialists who not only bought country houses but also acquired old portraits which might be mistaken for their ancestors.[11] At Sutton Hoo, traits such as the ship-burial rite indicate Scandinavian connections; the personal names of the ruling Wuffinga family suggest that they had originated in Sweden, and their funeral practices might well have served to emphasize their separateness of identity from their East Anglian subjects.[12] In the most complete ship-burial, the objects are not only from a wide geographical range, but they seem to emphasize three aspects in particular of an élite life-style: weapons for war, horns, cups and other vessels for feasting, musical instruments and gaming-pieces for relaxation. The last category frequently marks out an aristocracy, whose members alone have the leisure to indulge in such pursuits, and gaming-pieces were often buried in barrows and other rich burials, as they had been in the taller pots at Spong Hill.

The people in the rich graves may have felt a need to emphasize their pre-eminence because they were under particular pressure to preserve their new positions, against both internal and external challenges. The social conditions which produced them could also have caused them to be supplanted. It is also sometimes suggested that the disposal of goods in burials was a way of getting rid of treasure, so as to prevent over-accumulation and thus ensure that societies did not become too stressed by having to support extremes of wealth and power. Increasingly to be set against this interpretation, however – and perhaps even a corrective to over-emphasis upon the exceptional wealth of the few – is the growing record from settlement-site excavations. The gold coin and a silver-inlaid iron buckle are stray-find losses that seem to emphasize the seventh-century distinction of Yeavering, but West Stow had its glass and silver fragments, and objects from other sixth- and seventh-century occupation sites include the central part of an originally highly complex gold and garnet brooch from Swindon, Wiltshire, a hanging-bowl escutcheon from Chalton, Hampshire, and a cowrie-shell, imported from the Persian Gulf or the Red Sea, at Puddlehill, Bedfordshire.[13] There is nothing to suggest that these sites were exclusively for the élites, yet they could acquire more than just subsistence necessities. The objects in graves may therefore have been surplus drawn off from a considerable stock, and the funerary rites may have been more important than the intrinsic value of the grave-goods in giving distinction to particular people. Elaborate burial displays may also have to be seen in the context of the spread of Christianity, and the culture of the Frankish and Mediterranean worlds, leaving people on the margin of those developments resisting the erosion of their own culture and the status that it conferred upon them, and using more and more elaborate ceremonial to try to maintain their sense of tradition and separateness.

The social stratification that seems to be indicated by barrow-burials now seems to be becoming visible also within seventh-century settlements. It is only in the seventh century that the West Stow site became internally more formalised, with drainage ditches suggesting the possibility of property boundaries. Until then, it seems that relocation of building sites was possible, accounting for the widely-spread occupation of the area by what was probably never more than three or four households. Sites in Oxfordshire, at Cassington and New Wintles, apparently suggest a similar absence of barriers to internal movement. At Chalton, however, where there is no evidence that occupation began before *c.* 600, the buildings seem to have been formally arranged, with an open space between them that could have served as a village green, a formal plan which limited rearrangement of the site. Some of the buildings clearly relate to lines of post-holes which imply fenced enclosures – gardens and yards (**2,3**). Similar enclosures have been excavated at another Hampshire chalk site, Cowdery's Down, where occupation also centred on the seventh century. At a late stage in the site's use a larger, slightly isolated building up-slope of the others may indicate that social stratification had become more complex, the new structure being for a 'chieftain's' use.[14] At Cowage Farm, Wiltshire, a building complex identified by air photography has been tested by excavation, producing material broadly contemporary with Chalton and Cowdery's Down; one structure there appears to be very similar to the large one at the latter.[15] Again, however, a correction to over-emphasis on emerging chieftains and their warring, raiding lifestyle may be in order: it is remarkable that none of these sites was defended with an earthwork; none has even yet produced evidence of a substantial perimeter fence.

It may be that some of the linear earthworks that litter the map of England belong to this era, and were intended for the defence of particular territories. Since they are all virtually undatable, however, the most important point about them is that they show some corporate management in their construction, which in turn probably means that someone was able to compel a labour force to perform a communal service rather than that everyone turned out by mutual consent. Certainly it is in the sixth century that territorial units under dynastic leaders begin to be recognisable from documentary sources, some more clearly than others; most obvious is Aethelberht of Kent, who was able to use the title of king. It was a mark of his and his kingdom's importance that it was to him that St Augustine went for support in 597.

Canterbury became the centre of Augustine's mission. His cathedral

0   50 m

2, 3. Plan of the complex of structures excavated at Chalton, Hampshire, by P.V. Addyman and T.C. Champion. The rectangular structures seem to be disposed around a central open space: the further they are from that area, the less clearly aligned to it they seem to be. Some sort of formality of lay-out at the centre is indicated. On the north side, a building seems attached at its gable end to a fenced enclosure: another of a different period is to its south. Were these the houses of the more important members of the community? Although Chalton was in use in the seventh century and perhaps into the eighth, none of the buildings can be positively identified as a church, and no burials were found.

was built within its walls, his abbey immediately outside them: some of the surviving traces of structures in the latter can confidently be ascribed to Augustine and his immediate successors. The city was probably already a centre, although not necessarily the main centre, of Kentish royal authority. It may be that there was little or no domestic use of the city, but pottery, jewellery and a coin found within it date from the fifth and sixth centuries and show that it had not been completely and permanently abandoned after the end of

Roman imperial administration, even if its use was only sporadic. The way that some of the streets now ignore the Roman topography but lead towards the central amphitheatre has led to the suggestion that this remained in use for occasional assemblies at which the king and his people convened, as they probably did in the timber structure at Yeavering. The extra-mural site of the abbey may have been chosen because a Roman cemetery was known to have existed there, and perhaps Christian associations with it were remembered, or burials had continued to take place within it. St Pancras, one of the line of small church buildings there – a line which is a feature of several early Christian foundations – may have a Roman structure at its core, as may the church some distance east of the abbey which was dedicated to St Martin. Bede says that this was used by Bertha, Aethelberht's already-Christian queen, and it was presumably therefore on a royal estate.[16]

After Canterbury, several other Roman towns were to become Christian centres, partly to associate the new Christianity with the urbanised structure of the Roman church as it had existed in the fourth century and still did in Rome, partly because their walls gave an appropriate sense of enclosure, and partly also because there were others like Canterbury which had retained some sort of central rôle. This hypothesis is sometimes based on internal finds, such as quantities of sixth-century glass in Winchester, and the possibility of the existence there of an aristocratic presence represented by a small group of graves, one of a lady with seventh-century jewellery, including a necklace with gold pendants, a new fashion in the seventh century which ultimately derived from Mediterranean cultures.[17] Sometimes, the proximity of several nearby fifth- to seventh-century cemeteries may suggest that a city had remained a focal centre, but such clustering may simply reflect geology – good local farming conditions would often have been the original stimulus of the town. As not all the Roman cities were to have major churches founded within them, there was no overall revival strategy effected by Augustine and his successors. Where a city was in a poor agricultural area, or was remote from communication lines, or was in a frontier zone between kingdoms, its re-emergence was unlikely to occur. Thus Silchester, Hampshire, was eventually supplanted in its region by Reading, Berkshire, and Caistor, Norfolk, by Norwich: both the new places were on navigable rivers and did not rely solely on road transport like their predecessors.

Reasons for the precise locations of the churches founded in Roman towns are not yet established. At Canterbury, where the amphitheatre was perhaps still used for assemblies, the cathedral was positioned at some distance from the focal point that that should have created. In York, no trace of the earliest minster has been discovered below the present cathedral, so its physical relationship to anywhere which was being used in an attempt to preserve or restore something of the Roman power-structure is uncertain: excavations there have shown that some of the buildings of the Roman legionary fort still stood, albeit ruinous, but a few burials are the only indication that King Edwin's seventh-century church may be close to the site of its Norman successor.[18] Previous religious, not administrative, use of sites is more often revealed as the probable reason for the choice of a church's location. Canterbury's cathedral has recently been shown to overlie a large Roman building which might have been thought to have had earlier Christian use, rightly or wrongly. In Exeter, the present cathedral is immediately east of the Roman forum – but this was also the site of a basilica demolished in the fifth century and then used as a cemetery, which came back into use in the seventh. There is no evidence that the basilica had been a Christian one, but the cemetery may well have been converted to serve Christianity. [19] There is also a spring near the site, which could have been important for baptism: churches in Leicester and Lincoln near or on Roman bath sites may have been located there for their water supply, and the church at Bath, Somerset (Avon), may have benefited from the hot springs.[20]

Relationships between early churches and pre-existing burial sites have been shown most graphically at Wells, Somerset, where a stone mausoleum of late Roman type had burials around it by the eighth century and became the core of a chapel. The burial which had occupied the mausoleum was removed, perhaps so that the bones could be venerated in a new shrine. A similar process is perhaps the reason why the great abbey of St Alban is outside Roman Verulamium. Excavations have yet to discover the body of Britain's first martyr, but they have justified the claim that there was a late Roman cemetery on the site, where his tomb might have been. Such extra-mural burial-sites could also explain what happened at both the Dorchesters; the Dorset Dorchester's principal medieval church was certainly extra-mural, in Fordington, and at Dorchester-on-Thames the later medieval abbey may be on a site that was used by St Birinus in the seventh century even though it may never have been enclosed by the wall of the small Roman town.[21]

Also significant is the association between church sites and Roman forts. Often the extant structures date from well into the Middle Ages and so may not be early foundations, but many are known from documents to have been used in the seventh century.[22] Physical evidence has also been found in some, but it is not always demonstrably ecclesiastical: excavations at Portchester, Hampshire (2,4), produced occupation of all centuries from the third onwards, but nothing that can be used to claim Christian church use before the eleventh, even though there may have been a 'minster' within the walls. At Bradwell, Essex, a seventh-century church – but probably not the main church – survives in the fort that is usually taken to be the *Ythancaestir* given to Bishop Cedd by a king of Essex. At Burgh Castle, Norfolk, however, long thought to be the site of the *Cnobeheresburg* given to Bishop Fursa by King Sigeberht *c.* 630, early claims that traces of ecclesiastical buildings had been found have been discounted, though there was a cemetery with radiocarbon dates not inconsistent with foundation by Fursa. Walled sites like these provided convenient ready-made enclosures, but the choice of particular cases suggests that there may have been other reasons as well.

Even more difficult to discuss with certainty is the significance of the

2, 4. Portchester Castle, Hampshire. The walls of the Roman shore fort are now known from excavation to have enclosed activity in all subsequent centuries, although the earliest visible evidence of such use is the Water Gate on the left, the lower part of which is early Norman. The keep was built in three stages, although from the exterior only the final two can be recognised, the break marked by where the buttresses stop. Behind the keep, the ruined hall with its two-storey porch provided the context for the palatial entertainment and display expected of a fourteenth-century king. In the left corner, the tall, square 'Assheton's Tower' was a late fourteenth-century innovation for gunnery. The church is what remains of the twelfth-century Augustinian priory: the long white lines to its west show where there were barrack blocks in the eighteenth and early nineteenth centuries. The twentieth-century's contributions are the tennis courts and, in the other quadrant, a cricket pitch.

association between individual Roman structures and subsequent Christian churches. In a few cases, such as Stone, Kent, standing Roman walls were reused;[23] in rather more, a church directly overlies a Roman building. The church of St Helen, in York, was found to be the successor of a building in which there was a mosaic pavement depicting a female head, perhaps associated with a Roman cult site for the mother of the Emperor who established Christianity and who was subsequently believed, wrongly, to have been born in York.[24] Any stone building where ruins were visible was likely to accrue legends and the belief that it had once been a church.[25] Some Roman villas had indeed witnessed Christian worship, and some churches may well have been built on Roman sites by people thinking that they were thus re-creating an earlier Christian use. The more prosaic sequence is of Roman sites remaining as the administrative centres of land-units and thus becoming residences where wealthy landowners would build their churches, since the 'proprietary church' was an accepted institution, as has been suggested for Rivenhall. Examples of churches on or very close to known Roman sites may, of course, merely reflect the frequency with which Roman sites were reutilised without actually proving any thread of continuity. Nor is the sequence known to be all that frequent; even in Essex, where more examples have been found than in other counties, it is only about one church in five where the juxtaposition has been found. The later the church, the less likely is the sequence.

Although nominal conversion to Christianity had been achieved through-out England within a hundred years of Augustine's arrival, the old religions could be very tenacious: in Sussex, despite its proximity both to Kent and to the Continent, the positively anti-Christian ceremony of cremation was still occasionally practised in the second half of the seventh century, as excava-tions at Up Marden in the far west of the county are showing (**2,5**).[26] Whether genuine Christians would have been anything but extremely reluctant for their bodies to be buried in a graveyard where pagan practices like that con-tinued might be doubted, but it does now seem that there was not always a very immediate change of burial location upon conversion. What are called 'final-phase cemeteries', usually with West-East inhumations and few or no grave goods, and sometimes close to others which are well-furnished and not always uniformly aligned, may contain burials of people who remained pagan even though their aristocracy had accepted Christianity and were being buried elsewhere. Or they could be new Christian cemeteries located to dis-tance converts from old gods, but which were superseded if a church with a graveyard was built somewhere else. At the same time, location of some ap-parently pagan-period cemeteries close to churchyards, as at Sancton, York-shire, and discovery of objects inside some churchyards that might have accompanied pagan burials on the site before it came into Christian use, do not suggest any absolute necessity for new cemetery sites to separate converts from pagans. The richly-furnished barrow-burial at Taplow, Buckingham-shire, is actually within the perimeter of a churchyard. This could be because a church was subsequently built at the site, conceivably by a ruler who wished to bestow posthumous conversion upon a predecessor, perhaps with the intention that his family could then still be buried at the site which testified to their claims of heredity and property descent; or it may be that a church had already been built (by 'Tappa' himself?) and that the burial was not of a pagan. There was nothing specifically anti-Christian about either grave-good deposition or the raising of a barrow: they were simply irrelevant to Christian-ity. The priest may have winced a little as he bestowed his blessing, but it was better to bear with old customs than to upset a patron.[27]

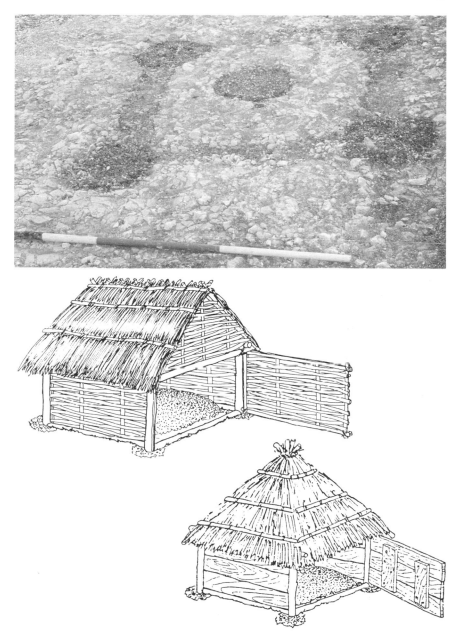

2, 5. Compton Appledown, Sussex. Excavation photograph by A. Down of a four-post mortuary structure with a small pit in the centre which contained human cremations, buried without a pottery urn. The two drawings, by M. Wholey, show two possible reconstructions of how this structure might have appeared, with a low earth mound over the cremation. It would have been surrounded by a shallow ditch, now filled with soil and visible in the photograph linking the four post-holes at the corners. Such post-holes at this site have often been found to contain cremated human bone, as though the structures were small shrines to which burials were added from time to time.

'Final-phase' cemeteries may also be seen as part of the frequent process of relocation which seems to have characterised the first centuries of the millennium generally. Sites like West Stow can be examined because they were abandoned and left for agriculture. This process could have been because of deliberate decisions of landowners to move tenants, in the interests of improving control over them and over the surpluses which they produced; or by agreement of all those involved, since it can be desirable to move habitation sites and then plough over land which has become well fertilised by a sustained concentration of human and animal manure; in some areas such as the high chalk-lands, abandonment may have been for the opposite reason, that the rather thin soils had been exhausted by over-utilisation even by the relatively small numbers of farmers involved; or a falling water-table may have made the higher sites inoperable; or clay soils may have been becoming manageable through the use of heavier ploughs, and rising population and new institutions such as the Church may have led to a demand for more intensive production.[28] Direct evidence for any one of these reasons is lacking. Some sites may have stayed in use, unrecognised below later building: Raunds, Northamptonshire, has now produced evidence of successive use at least of contiguous areas, and Walton, Buckinghamshire, has evidence that runs from the fifth century, with concentration of activity periodically shifting within the immediate area, rather as it probably did at West Stow, Cassington and elsewhere before their total abandonment.[29]

One complex problem which these abandonments raises is that of the extent to which they would have been concomitant with rearrangement of estate holdings. The land charters which begin to appear with the advent of Christianity increasingly list the boundaries of the estates with which they are dealing, boundaries frequently recognisable in the landscape today as prominent hedge-lines or other physical survivals. They are sometimes still the boundaries of modern estates: more often they are the lines of ecclesiastical parish boundaries, as revealed for the first time on nineteenth-century tithe maps or other sources. Consequently it can be supposed that many parishes originated as estate units. How early these estate units were formed presumably varied: some correlations between churches, parish boundaries and Roman villa sites may indicate that an estate once run from a villa was maintained as a unit whether or not administered from the Roman centre any longer. It used to be thought that post-Roman cemeteries were to be found close to parish boundaries, and that this showed that burial-sites were chosen to define the edges of a community's territory, and at a distance from settlements to keep the spirits of the dead away from the living. Although some cemeteries are indeed close to boundaries, statistical methods show that there is no demonstrable, regular association between them, except in the seventh century and then perhaps in particular areas such as Wiltshire where barrow-burial and reuse of Bronze Age sites may have had a particular vogue. Furthermore, settlements are not necessarily far from cemeteries: West Stow is a case in point with both settlement and cemetery close to a parish boundary. If a settlement had its land all round it, the probability is that that land was re-distributed when the site was abandoned, and that its territory was split up. Consequently parish boundaries cannot be presumed to fossilise early Saxon estates, only those of the seventh century and later, a more fluid picture than that implied by the possibility of Roman estate-unit survival. The implication is that abandonments were caused by owners of large areas of land which they could parcel up and sub-divide as it suited them, shifting their tenantry at the same time; agriculturalists acting on their own initiatives would not have been able to rearrange their land boundaries without conflicting with their neighbours.[30]

The proximity of settlements and cemeteries, and their abandonment in many cases, shows that communities could be persuaded to leave their traditional religious foci and the burial-places of their ancestors. The change to a new religion would have helped to reduce any resistance to this in the seventh and eighth centuries, but thereafter a church and graveyard could become a factor militating against the desertion of one settlement site in favour of another, and be one reason why there are many fewer known abandonments after the end of the seventh century. Even so, it was not overriding, as the demolition of a church and the redevelopment for building of the churchyard at Raunds in the twelfth or thirteenth century shows. Some early churches may not have had burial grounds. Cowage Farm has one building unlike any so far recognised at the other abandoned settlements, being rectangular with an eastern apse and contained in its enclosure slightly apart from the rest of the complex. The obvious interpretation is that this is a Christian church: there was some human bone in its enclosure ditch, but no graves were located in the trench dug through it, and none are visible in the air photographs. This argues that it was not a high-status church, such as the monastery which is recorded as having existed in the immediate area in the second half of the seventh century. If it was a church, it would seem to have been one which had not yet acquired burial rights, but had been built as a proprietary chapel by the landowner, not long before the site was abandoned.

If Cowage Farm really did have a church, it is a demonstration of the relative speed with which Christianity came to be accepted. This was by no means inevitable, for there were many barriers. One was that its official acceptance by one kingdom would have been a reason for its rejection by another, since acceptance would have involved overtones of subjection. Another was that a rival internal faction might espouse the old religion when a king accepted the new, so that Christianity could be divisive. Nor did it directly bolster the king's position, by endowing him with priestly authority: rather, it introduced what could become a competing authority, although that was a strain which the Church normally sought to avoid. The Church also affected the social structure, since many of its members came from outside the kingdom, and so were not part of any existing kin network, the normal agent of control of social relations. The Church as a landowner removed property from potential ac-

quisition by the laity, which caused stress and undermined traditional aspirations, especially if a donor's kin felt that they had been deprived of estates
which properly belonged to their family. Indirectly, however, the Church had
much to offer. Royal prestige might be regarded as enhanced by connections
with Rome, putting English kings on a par with those on the Continent. The
written word offered an appearance of authority to law codes. In funding
church buildings, kings and aristocrats were creating monuments to themselves which allied them to a religion that promised eternal life rather than
merely an eternal fate, and permanent commemoration by name in prayers,
not rapid anonymity in a barrow. Churches could be mausolea, as was demonstrated from the first when King Aethelberht was buried in a *porticus* (or
side chapel) of the church dedicated to St Peter and St Paul at Canterbury.
Because many priests were outside a kin, they needed royal protection, so the
Church had a vested interest in maintaining – and preaching – the authority
of a just king. A successful king would also offer protection through keeping
his kingdom secure, and the Church needed peace in which to operate. It also
wanted him to guarantee the secure tenure of its lands.[31.]

The Church probably also encouraged kings to take new initiatives as they
came to see themselves as more than just tribal leaders and chieftains. One
object discovered outside Canterbury is a circular gold pendant, apparently
struck in the manner of continental coins with a head and the inscription
'Leudardus Ep[iscopu]s', i.e. Bishop Liudhard, who can only be the priest
known to have been in Kent with Queen Bertha. This churchman's interest
in something that has many of the attributes of a coin suggests that it may well
have been Church influence which encouraged the first attempt to produce
coins in England. The earliest is probably one found near Folkestone, Kent:
it is a 'thrymsa' or 'tremissis', similar to a type produced in south-western
France but with a runic name on it that no French coin would have ever
borne. Even more definite is one in a Frankish style of *c.* 595–612 which includes the Latin name for Canterbury in its inscription. These early experi-
ments may have been intended to create a currency but were more likely
meant to show that the king of Kent could emulate continental kings by having a coinage. It was perhaps not until the 620s or even the 630s that anything
more systematic was produced. Continued Kentish power is shown by their
King Eadbald's name on a coin struck also with the name of London, demonstrating his claim to control that city. There are signs of production also
in areas not subject to Kentish domination, such as the upper Thames Valley
(at Dorchester?) and in York, indicating that other rulers were prepared to
challenge Kent's supremacy.[32]

A hoard found at Crondall, Hampshire, deposited by *c.* 650, shows that
English gold coins were never plentiful. It contained ninety-seven coins, and
had been made up to a round number with three blanks. It may have been
used as a 'wergild' payment – a compensation for an injury – rather than in
any commercial transaction. Most of the English coins in the Crondall hoard
were struck from dies that were also used to make other coins in it: there

would not be nearly so many such 'die links' if the coins had been taken from a large and widely-circulated currency. It seems unlikely that gold coins could ever have changed hands on an everyday basis, although they were probably used as more than merely prestigious items: very few are found with loops or in mounts after the first quarter of the seventh century, so they were not being worn as though they had special value as amulets. They are, however, still often found in graves, perhaps to symbolise some special payments. They may have been units of account, stamped with devices which implied issue by an authority which guaranteed their value in weight and alloy purity. The growing importance of such units is further suggested by the scales and weights that are occasional though slightly more frequent grave finds; although often taken as evidence of dealings for which barter was insufficient and ascribed to merchants, such things may also have been needed by leaders distributing largesse and spoils of war according to some proportional system.[33] They might also have been needed by smiths involved in the alloying of different metals.

For reasons beyond the control of the Franks, the supply of gold from Byzantium and the Mediterranean world dropped away after *c.* 600; consequently the purity of gold coins in northern France fell from 80 per cent fineness to as little as 18 per cent. The English coins could not eventually but do likewise, and by the 660s their gold content was down to 30 per cent. This had a visible effect on contemporary Kentish jewellery, as the amount of gold used in brooches and other ornaments also fell away; an increase in gilding over silver or even copper alloy seems to have been an attempt to disguise the growing scarcity of the most precious metal (**2,1**).[34] Garnets, amethysts and other exotica may also have become much harder to obtain.

Decline in availability of trade goods from the Mediterranean, eastern Europe and beyond is made difficult to measure because of the changing archaeological record. Although deposition of objects in graves did not cease – even coins were still occasionally deposited in the later seventh century, and perhaps in the early eighth – the custom was waning. It may have died out as much because of the difficulty of getting suitably prestigious objects, however, as from the influence of Christianity. The change has the effect of disguising how land owners disposed of the surplus that they had from their tenants, or warriors of what they won in booty. It may, for instance, have led to even greater emphasis upon the ownership of land as large estates, and the big retinues of followers which they could supply, became a more attainable ambition than the acquisition of hoards of treasure. The reorganisation of estate units therefore should be seen partly in the light of growing territorial aspirations, and a need to extract more from the land as other sources of income, in the form of war spoils and subsidies, became harder to win.

Another aspect of changing attitudes to land and its ownership is the documentary evidence for the emergence, usually during the sixth century, of dynasties who increasingly claimed to rule particular territories, rather than over tribes or groups of tribes. The importance of loose-knit federations and of family and kinship was slowly overtaken by kingship based on a ruler's ability to control an area of land. That, at any rate, is the implication of references to *provinciae, regiones* and shires. Material evidence is not usually tightly confined within political units, so that archaeological distributions do not usually reveal the limits of a kingdom. Political barriers can have an effect, however, particularly if tolls are being extracted at frontier points, or if a political authority is actively seeking to exclude a rival's products, as often happens with coins. The former process may be demonstrated by a type of pottery being made in Ipswich from *c.* 630, which is found widely but not uniformly in south-eastern England. It is found in Suffolk and south Norfolk, though not much in north Norfolk. To the south, it is rarely found in Essex, except at one site, Wicken Bonhunt, but there are then small quantities in London and in Kent, at least in Canterbury. It is also found as far west as Northamptonshire. Much of this is a normal distributional 'fall-off' from its place of manufacture, quantities decreasing as transport difficulties increased. Its virtual absence from Essex, however, does not conform to the same pattern: perhaps no demand for pottery existed there, but more probably it was excluded by toll barriers, or even by active prevention of trade, for Ipswich was in East Anglia, ruled by a different dynasty from Essex.[35]

The clarity of this picture is obscured by Wicken Bonhunt, where some quantity of Ipswich ware is reported. Similar obfuscation usually occurs with any attempt to establish internal divisions within the kingdoms by using archaeological evidence: in Essex, for instance, kingship was not unique to an individual but was often shared between concurrent rulers. Some may have had particular control of a sub-unit within the kingdom, and the Dengie peninsula has been suggested as one area which could have been a *regio* of that sort because its field systems are different from those of the rest of Essex. But if this difference had arisen originally because of geography and Roman, perhaps even Iron Age, settlement patterns, and was not a seventh-century creation, its different identity may by then have had no cultural or administrative recognition. Few other potential *regiones* can be postulated from strictly contemporary evidence, even though they may be recognisable from documentary sources or from boundaries whose early history may be deduced but is nowhere explicitly stated.[36]

Ipswich-ware pottery was made with the use of a slow wheel, and of kilns rather than simple bonfires. These technological innovations suggest craft workers with specialist skills, who could establish a sufficient demand for their output to justify methods of production which involved 'plant' and a considerable investment of time. Since the types and the shapes of the vessels that they made were not noticeably different from what was already on offer, the potters were presumably English, not continental emigrants creating a demand for new styles and fashions. The Ipswich potters seem to have infiltrated and slowly added to existing, localised systems of production and distribution over the course of the next two hundred years.

The establishment of a pottery industry at Ipswich is almost certainly contemporaneous with development at that site of other activities, taking advantage of a sheltered landing place on a navigable river, although on what scale is not yet clear. During the second half of the seventh century, similar sites on other river estuaries came into being. On the south coast, part of what is now Southampton was already flourishing by the end of the century, with metalled roads apparently forming some sort of grid pattern, building plots, and a ditch enclosing an area of some forty hectares (a hundred acres). Such rapid development and apparent planning on a site with no previous occupation since the Iron Age seems to indicate a deliberate decision to create an industrial and commercial centre. Since the site's emergence is coeval with the establishment of control by the kings of Wessex over southern Hampshire and the Isle of Wight, its main catalyst was probably the enlargement of their territory and authority. Direct evidence of such involvement is hard to come by, however: nowhere within Saxon Southampton has yet produced an enclave which might be claimed as a royal palace, for instance.

Recent discoveries have suggested that similar sites were founded at London and York, in neither case within the Roman walls. In London, occupation around the Strand up-river of the city confirms theories formed from earlier stray finds and from the significant name Aldwych – the 'old *wic*': *Hamwic* was a mid Saxon name for Southampton, and York is referred to as *Eoforwic*. The site of the latter may well be a large zone of activity on the River Ouse about a kilometre downstream from the Roman fort, first revealed in 1985. Other *wic* sites may yet be found: Fordwich and Sandwich in Kent are two possibilities. They have counterparts on the Continent.

If Hamwic is to be related to the establishment of the enlarged kingdom of Wessex, Ipswich may be seen in the context of the power of the East Anglian kings, and York in that of the Northumbrian. London, however, seems to have been involved in a fluctuating power struggle. The gold coins show that Kent claimed an interest in it, but charters show that the Essex and West Saxon kings were prepared to dispute for its control. Documentary mention of 'citizens' at the very beginning of the seventh century suggests that London already existed as a significant place, and it cannot at present be claimed as the deliberate creation of any particular king or kingdom, which cautions against the assumption that royal interest was necessarily what lay behind these new trading-stations. No doubt they could not have flourished without the protection of kings, but that does not mean that they were set up exclusively to supply those kings with the prestigious goods which their position demanded. So far as can be seen, such things had been arriving for two centuries without the need for large trading-stations; instead, they were presumably landed up river-mouths and creeks at a variety of small sites which needed no permanent facilities, probably much like those in the south-west at Bantham and perhaps Praa sands. Roman shore-forts like Portchester (**2,4**) which are known to have been occupied may also have been used in this way.[37]

Two factors which affected trade in the seventh century and may also have been instrumental in the establishment of trading-stations were the decrease in availability of Mediterranean goods and the growth of the Church. The former may have meant that there was a considerable decrease in the per-item value of any goods being traded: instead, imports to England may increasingly have concentrated on silver from central Europe rather than gold and on bulkier goods like wine that northern Europe could supply and which required storage and handling facilities at permanent sites. English exports, if they were slaves, wool, cloth, certain metals and hides, could also be more efficiently handled through fixed entrepôts. This may have been the primary reason why traders found trading-stations to be in their interests. They may also have felt better protected within them: certainly from the kings' point of view it would be easier to oversee merchants from there, and to offset losses to royal control of resources that the decline in the east Mediterranean supply may have involved by ensuring that tolls were extracted.[38]

Because of the inability to maintain supplies of exotica from the east Mediterranean, there may have been an overall decrease in the value of commerce, despite the apparent buoyancy that the trading-stations suggest. Certainly imported pottery suggests that the second half of the seventh century was not really a very thriving period for trade. Seventh-century 'E' ware, probably made in south-west France, is found in some quantity in sites in Cornwall, Devon and Somerset, but not further east. This implies that the English kings' achievement of political control over the latter two counties later in the seventh century did not mean that traders from Aquitaine were able to set up new markets in Wessex, or that Wessex traders ventured to Bordeaux. If anything, it suggests that conquest broke off such contacts as already existed. On the other side of the country, the Scandinavian connections shown by jewellery or at Sutton Hoo did not develop into large-scale trade with the Baltic. Instead, England's overseas commerce seems to have been confined almost to the immediately opposite shores, from Normandy to the Low Countries, the territory of the Franks and Frisians. It was probably in imitation of these peoples that a silver coinage was introduced into limited parts of England towards the end of the seventh century, after a brief 'pale gold' currency had proved that even alloys which contained much silver and little gold could not be used satisfactorily.[39]

The other major new factor in seventh-century commerce was the Church, whose houses needed regular supplies of food, wine, building materials and the means to produce books, altar embellishments and the like. By establishing itself as a landowner, a church could grow its own food and produce its own vellum and it might be possible to get stone for the walls, and even lead for the roofs, from Church-owned quarries. Houses which did not have their own supply could hope for a comradely gift to make up the deficiency. Gifts might be erratic, however, making purchase the only reliable means of acquisition. Lead is one product which might be obtained by donation or exchange between churches, but the rich Peak District burials suggest that at least in the seventh century it was individuals who profited from and thus probably controlled the mines. The area's wealth after the Conversion is shown by the elaborate carved stone slab in the church at Wirksworth, Derbyshire.

The Church in England would have needed to obtain some of its requirements from overseas, particularly wine, and its members had to maintain their communications with continental houses and with Rome. This may explain their interest in trade and trading-stations, as revealed in charters, and some houses may have directed their own shipping. Ironically, the renewal of intellectual and spiritual contacts with Rome coincided with the declining availability of east Mediterranean goods which had largely been routed through Rome and north Italy.

Chapter Three

THE LATER SEVENTH AND EIGHTH CENTURIES

Princes and Power

The eighth century's main problem for the archaeologist is that there are few things that can be dated confidently within it. Without the classificatory sequences derived from grave-goods, and with a paucity of objects that can be attributed to dates derived either from associated material or from continental parallels, it is difficult to establish a chronology. Furthermore, historical sources are less forthcoming for this century than for either its predecessor or its successor: no historian was to write about the period of the Heptarchy as Bede did about the Conversion, while the *Anglo-Saxon Chronicle* gives a sketchy outline of events in Wessex, and says little about the rest of England, for which charters, ecclesiastical records and such-like scattered documents are all that survive. A figure like King Offa of Mercia (759-96) can therefore assume exaggerated importance although little is known about him, because even less is known about his contemporaries.

The linear earthworks that effectively divide much of England from Wales were being attributed to King Offa at least within a hundred years of his death, since Asser, the biographer of King Alfred, says that this '. . . vigorous king . . . had a great dyke built'. There is no immediately contemporary record, however, and recent work suggests that the dyke system is more piecemeal than was once supposed. There is a long stretch in the southern part where none can be traced at all, and further north there is no single, unitary line: for part of the way, two earthworks run roughly parallel to each other, and only one, Wat's Dyke, continues to the coast. A disconnected dyke, now call 'The Whitford Dyke' has been shown to have been constructed differently from all the rest, having ditches on both sides, not just on the west side, of its bank. In other places, a preliminary 'marker' bank and ditch were dug along the line that the main bank was to follow, but elsewhere there are no such initial works to be recognised – perhaps a series of posts was sufficient. Only the Rowe Ditch near Hereford has so far produced any dating evidence, and that has yielded Roman pottery. A Roman site may have been disturbed here, but actual Roman construction of the ditch cannot be ruled out. As a result of all these discoveries, it is not possible to be confident about which lengths of dyke were constructed or in use at the same time: Wat's Dyke may be the predecessor or contemporary of what is now called Offa's, or even its successor. That 'Offa's' does not actually run a full course from coast to coast may be an indication that the king was not able to fulful his original purpose, or was pushed back by Welsh enemies, or was too pre-occupied with events elsewhere to see his western frontier work carried through to its conclusion. What was it all for? That it marked an agreed frontier, so that Welsh and English could dwell in peace on their respective sides, is borne out neither by contemporary records of raids nor by political likelihood at a time when a treaty was as likely to be taken as a sign of weakness as of strength or prudence. There could have been a marcher area to its west, to be patrolled by mounted Englishmen for whom the Dyke was a barrier upon which to fall back: later records of riding services have been used to justify this. Or it may have been a straightforward boundary line, whether or not intended to be defensible.[1]

But whatever their military role, the dykes' social role should also be stressed. Although it was not a colossal effort of expense or organisation to create an earthwork, it nevertheless represented a leader's ability to demand service from his people and a visible testimony to his power. England's other undated linear banks can be presumed to have been the creations of rulers able for a brief time to mobilise men to build them, but whose prowess was soon forgotten as political adjustments made most of their territorial demarcations irrelevant. Much of the dyke that bears his name may not have been built by Offa, but by others whose names have not survived because their successes were overshadowed by his in later tradition and folk memory. What was undertaken between England and Wales was on a larger scale than anything done previously. Nevertheless, calculations based on the *Tribal Hidage* tax list and the Wessex *Burghal Hidage* suggest that later eighth-century Mercia could have raised the man power to complete a line from coast to coast in only two seasons of 40 working days. Much would of course have depended on the amount of clearance work required – pollen analyses have shown extensive burning – and whether a wall or palisade was built along the crest of the whole bank, for remains of stone walling, presumably contemporary, have been found in places. This all seems to point to a political authority with a greater territory and a greater scale of resources than had existed in England before, an authority which expressed itself in grandiose monumental display, and one which was also perhaps claiming parity with continental kings such as whoever was able to construct the great Danewirke at the base of the Jutland peninsula, the first phase of which can now be dated to *c.* 737 from dendrochonological evidence of the sort unfortunately irrecoverable in English dykes systems.

Although the dyke systems are the most obvious of earthwork constructions, others are now being discovered. Associated with the south end of Wat's Dyke, for instance, is the Morda Brook which seems to have been canalised, presumably at the time that the dyke was being built. On the opposite side of the country, in Essex, the half-mile long causeway that links Mersea island to the mainland has been shown by dendrochronology to have been constructed between *c.* 681 and 702. At Oxford, a causeway across the

Thames has been dated to the eighth century by a combination of conventional and scientific techniques. A different form of water control is shown by the discovery at Tamworth, Staffordshire, of a ninth-century mill building, with a timber wheel-race and clay-built dam. Tamworth has also produced evidence of an enclosure surrounded by an earth bank and ditch, its precise circuit not yet established, but presumed to be associated with the Mercian palace site first recorded in the eighth century. Tamworth's is the earliest post-Roman mill found in England, and its location adjacent to a known palace and enclosure means that it was probably built to serve the royal estate.[2]

That a king should have been among the first to be provided with a water-driven mill is a further example of royal ability to invest in new construction. It may have been seen as prestigious to control such a marvellous engine, though this should not be overstressed as there were many operating in Ireland at this time. It may also show increasing agricultural production, the grinding of large amounts of grain into flour being more efficiently achieved than by processing with hand-querns. A mill usually testifies to a landlord's ability to force his tenants to use it, so that he can extract a toll from them, but initially such considerations may have been less important than a king's ability to extract large tributes in kind from his people, which had to be made ready for consumption. The Church was probably as interested as the kings in getting the best returns from their estates. Two grain-drying ovens found in Hereford (**4,4**) dated by radiocarbon to the eighth century, may have been on the bishop's estate, since the see had been established in the later seventh century.[3] Grain-driers are like mills, large and permanent ones only being worth building if large quantities are to be processed. Also suggestive of increased attention to efficient exploitation is the fish-weir of this period found at Colwick, Nottinghamshire, in the River Trent, although its ownership is not known.[4]

The growing importance of the centres of large estates and administration units is suggested at Ramsbury, a site in Wiltshire where evidence of iron-smelting and the making of iron tools has been found. Within quite a small area several furnaces were located, and stone found there suggests that some untreated ores may have been brought from up to twenty miles away, as well as from more local deposits. Ramsbury is not recorded in documents until it was chosen as a diocesan centre in 909, but there are sculptures preserved in its church which suggest its importance before then, and the likelihood is that in the eighth century it was a major royal estate. Radiocarbon dating shows that, probably before the end of the century, specialist iron-workers were being employed, presumably to serve the needs of the estate and perhaps to produce goods which enhanced their patron's prestige if he distributed them as gifts, although a small strap-end with silver inlay was the only object actually found which was more status-boosting than a frying pan or a pot hook.[5]

The extent to which many of these sites rely on radiocarbon for their dating evidence is disturbing, since it is not a very accurate medium and seems to be subject to distortion by acid soils and other contaminants. A complex of buildings at Northampton has a sequence which starts with sunken-featured buildings like those on many fifth-century and later sites, and traces of ground-level structures.[6] There is then the plan of a most impressive rectangular timber building with two end annexes, carefully laid out so that the main part is a module of two 'twenty-seven foot' squares (the actual unit of measurement used need not have been the modern foot) and two 'twenty-one foot' squares. Originally attributed to the seventh century on the basis of similarity to structures at Yeavering and Cowdery's Down, it is now ascribed to the mid-eighth century, because radiocarbon dates centre on the ninth century for the mortar and bone associated with its demolition, immediately prior to the construction of an even larger stone building on the same site. Unfortunately, there are no datable pottery sherds or other artefacts from the timber structure to give the radiocarbon plausibility. But a coin associated with its stone successor, found in the bottom of an adjacent post-hole, is certainly eighth-century, perhaps of *c.* 750; although this could be residual, its relatively unworn condition does not suggest that it had been kicked around in the dirt before being scuffed into the post packing by an unobservant labourer. Basically, the coin can be used to question whether the stone structure is not of the second half of the eighth century, and therefore its timber predecessor perhaps a century earlier, maintaining the seventh-century parallels cited for it. Only some ninth-century pottery in extensions added to the stone structure supports the radiocarbon, but there is no evidence for the overall duration of use of this building before its demolition towards the end of the ninth century.

The Northampton buildings are immediately to the east of St Peter's church, under which excavations have revealed a building with stone foundations much like those of the other stone structure's extensions. Recognition of mortar mixers has shown that the buildings had mortared superstructures, even though they were on unbonded footings. Unquestionably they were of high status, but the precise nature of that status is elusive. It is a reasonable assumption that Northampton's emergence in the tenth century as the centre of its shire indicates that it was already an administrative centre, and that it was a royal estate is indicated by names like Kingsthorpe nearby. Furthermore, 'minster' churches like St Peter's which in the eleventh century had 'many churches' subsidiary to it, can very often be demonstrated to have been built in proximity to a royal estate centre. Consequently the timber and stone buildings have been deemed to be the 'halls' of a palace complex. Yet there is no clear indication in the archaeological record of their use. Both may have been ecclesiastical, not secular, or their use may have changed if a king gave his existing palace to the Church. Furthermore, only a hundred metres from and almost due east of St Peter's is St Gregory's, not mentioned in a document before the twelfth century, but where graves with eighth-ninth-century radiocarbon dates have been found. It is just possible that the whole formed a single, vast ecclesiastical complex that is unmentioned in any documents – unless this is the elusive *Clofesho* where synods are recorded as being held.

Another candidate for *Clofesho* is Brixworth, a church about ten miles north of Northampton which is generally agreed to be a mid Saxon structure, yet which despite its scale is not recorded by name in any document of the period. Unlike the stone buildings in Northampton, there can be no doubt of its primary function because of its apsidal crypt, and the internal divisions of its side aisles also suggest a church; its precise date, however, is not known, and parallels drawn with it can place it anywhere from the later seventh to the early ninth century, depending on whether it is considered to be most similar to seventh-century Kentish and Swiss or to ninth-century Carolingian buildings. The latter seemed to be supported by a radiocarbon date obtained from the vestiges of a scaffold pole found within a 'put-log' hole in the clerestorey, but again the problems of radiocarbon are illustrated, as this date has been recalibrated and now seems to indicate a phase of restructuring at the end of the ninth century or later. No doubt it will change again one day. More revealing has been close analysis of the mortar, brick and stone used, including reused Roman material which may have come from Leicester, the nearest Roman city. Since most of the newly quarried stone also comes from Leicestershire, the reliability of a twelfth-century record that Brixworth was founded as an offshoot of Peterborough is in question, since any connection with that area would probably have meant Barnack stone, from Northamptonshire, being brought to build the church.[7]

Excavations in Brixworth have shown that a ditch about a hundred metres from the church may have surrounded it, enclosing it within a bank and ditch to separate it from the outside world. Burials have been found and lumps of iron slag which could be associated with the building of the church, or could derive from more regular craft activity. There were pottery sherds, bone needles and loom-weight fragments which suggest domestic (not necessarily secular) occupation, as well as mortar and window glass which were certainly associated with the church building. It is a great pity that this range of finds cannot be directly compared to that from the Northampton complex, but at the latter disturbance from later use of the site meant that many fewer artefacts survived to be recovered. What will eventually be comparable are the burials: there are only eleven at Brixworth, but nine of those were recognisably male. Is this to be taken as proof that Brixworth was a male monastery, or was it a cemetery for high-status laymen who chose to be buried at an important church, regardless of their family ties and traditions?

Despite the importance which archaeology demonstrates them to have had, neither Northampton nor Brixworth is directly documented in the eighth century. This is a contrast to some of the great Northumbrian monasteries such as Wearmouth and Jarrow, but is by no means unusual. Just as nothing is known archaeologically of such documented churches as Wimborne, Dorset, a 'double-house' for monks and nuns founded by King Ine of Wessex for his sister – a good example of royal involvement and of the importance of high-born ladies in the Church – so the converse can apply: a large cemetery and accompanying timber buildings at Nazeingbury, Essex, is most probably the site of a nunnery, since eighty-six of the 118 skeletons whose sex could be identified were women, and twenty-nine were aged over forty-five. Although disease had affected some of their bones, they did not show the sort of pathological traits that usually result from heavy manual labour; only one appeared to have had a child. Some of the burials were of children and adolescents, but fewer than would be expected in a cemetery of that size, and almost none were infants, so the skeletons may be those of young people too weak to survive the nuns' schooling. That many of the nuns were elderly indicates a protected environment and careful nursing. Most of those who had suffered most, from fatigue fractures and so on, had been buried inside the buildings, not in the open air, as though their cares and troubles had caused them to be specially selected to rest within the church.[8] The ability of the society and economy of the eighth century to support and protect such sheltered communities indicates that there were considerable production surpluses to be diverted to the Church. Nazeingbury suggests that numbers of women could be removed from the community at large without grossly distorting the population balance. The effect on family and kin structures may have been partly to reduce subdivision of property by the need to provide for a range of dependents.

The importance of burial and burial-place is shown by a major church which stills stands at Repton, Derbyshire. The *Anglo-Saxon Chronicle* records that King Ethelbald of Mercia died in 757 and was buried *aet Hrepandune,* and later but reliable accounts state that in 849 Wystan was buried there in the mausoleum of his grandfather King Wiglaf. Recent excavations and surveys in Repton have shown that there were already buildings and a cemetery on the site when the present church was started, and an early eighth-century coin was found in its foundations. This does not prove that the crypt (**3, 1**) was built for Ethelbald, of course; indeed, drains around it may show that it was originally a semi-sunken, single-storey baptistry. It was later raised in height, columns were inserted, openings altered and passages created to give access into a church built to its west. Suitable as it would be to have been a crypt for Wiglaf's mausoleum after these changes, the existence some eighty metres to its west of another stone building, a two-cell east-west structure sunk into an earth mound, in the eastern chamber of which there was probably a burial, shows that to identify any particular structure or phase of its development with any particular recorded event or person is scarcely possible unless more information is given than just a mention of a place-name. Without doubt Repton was an important royal burial-place, but other sacred associations there may have drawn the kings to it, so that its church would have had more than just a mausoleum function. With at least two low buildings, it might be seen as the eighth-century equivalent of Sutton Hoo with its barrows similarly placed overlooking a river.[9]

The early eighth-century coin from the foundations of the crypt at Repton is a small silver penny of a kind usually referred to as a 'sceat' to distinguish it from the thinner but wider pennies that were introduced at the end of the

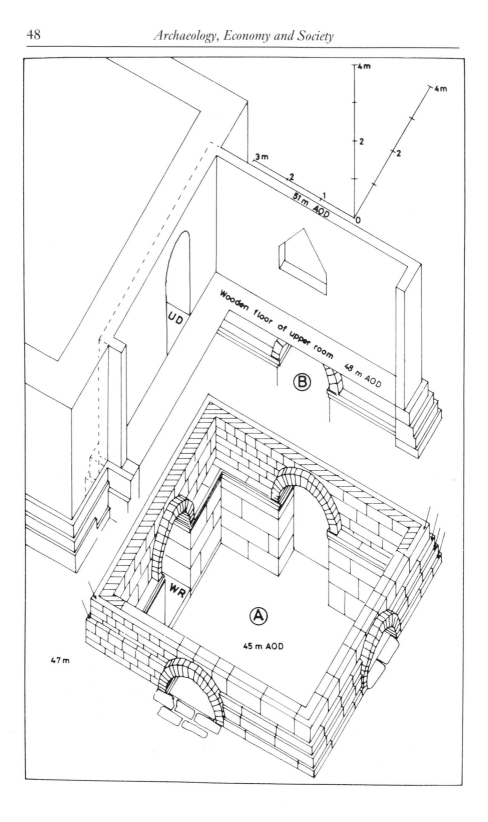

4m

2

51m AOD

3m

.2

1

4m

2

UD

Wooden floor of upper room

48 m AOD

Ⓑ

WR

Ⓐ

45 m AOD

47 m

Opposite: **3, 1a**. Isometric drawings by H. M. Taylor of the crypt, phase A, and the room added above it, phase B, now attached to the east end of the church at Repton, Derbyshire; originally it was a free-standing structure. Both drawings show the external stepped plinth, which would probably have been visible from the outside, and three of the arches would have been open at the top as windows, with internal recesses below - perhaps for relics and altars - while 'WR' in phase A may have been the door. The roof probably started immediately above the arches: a wooden pyramidal structure is suggested. This was removed in phase B, the walls were heightened and a room was created over the crypt, entered by a door at 'UD'. Subsequent changes, not shown, included the insertion of four columns inside the crypt and new access arrangements made when the church to the east was integrated with it.

Above: **3, 1b**. Photograph of the east end of the church at Repton. Excavations around the building have not only clarified the phases of its construction, but have also shown substantial earlier use of the site.

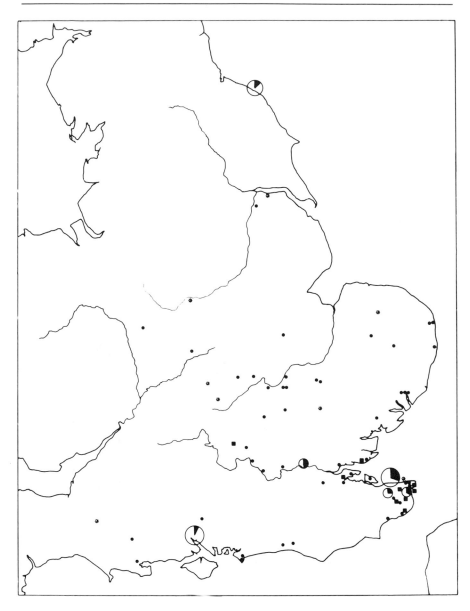

3, 2a. Distribution map prepared in 1984 by D. M. Metcalf of finds of 'sceattas' generally agreed to belong to the 'primary' phase of that coinage (but not including the very earliest examples). The pie-diagrams show sites where quantities of 'sceattas' of all periods have been found and the proportion of them that are 'primary'. Diagonally divided circles mark poor quality, debased specimens of certain types; squares mark hoards or grave-finds.

3, 2b. Dr Metcalf's map of the secondary sceattas, later in the eighth century. Not only are there many more, but they are much more widely found, suggesting that their use was spreading - though not yet to all areas. The (predominantly Kentish) custom of burying some in graves seems to have all but disappeared, an indication perhaps of a change in religious belief about deposition of objects in graves, or that increasing familiarity with the use of coins in everyday transactions meant that they were no longer regarded as sufficiently exceptional to be used in some symbolic rôle.

century. The 'sceattas' were the same size as the seventh-century gold coins, and there may have been no interval between the production of the gold and silver coinages, the 'pale-gold' issue of the later seventh century indicating the decline in availability of the more precious metal as increasing quantities of silver were alloyed into it. By the end of the century, it would seem that the coins were thought of as silver, for analyses show that they had a high silver content – usually over 90 per cent – and negligible gold: copper, tin and zinc are the base metals that occur in them and one of the problems of this coinage is to know the extent to which the alloy composition and weights were control-led, and how far debasement and lighter coins reflect differences of chron-ology or of place of production.[10]

Deciding where the 'sceattas' were produced is mainly a question of study-ing the distribution of the different types produced. Very few carry the names of mints, moneyers or issuing authority, and no archaeological evidence of their minting has been found even though it is said that their 'flans' were cast, like Iron Age coins for which clay moulds have often been found. Presumably the casting was done simply by allowing a melted weight of metal to dry and harden on something flat like a touchstone or a slate, so that surface tension caused it to form a disc. The flan was then struck, though no dies have been found.

Some of the earlier 'sceattas' are inscribed with the same moneyers' names as on some of the 'pale-gold' coins, so there was little interruption in produc-tion, sporadic though it was. These names seem to link the new coins to Kent, with the Essex kingdom perhaps also being involved: distribution goes as far as London, but hardly any further, and too few are known for there to be certainty that they were in everyday use as currency, even around the lower Thames. During the early eighth century, their numbers increased and they are found more widely: Northumbria also began to have coins, as the first royal name of a 'sceat' appears to be that of Ealdfrith, a king who died in 705. That the kingdom which brought masons and glaziers from Gaul to work at Wearmouth and Jarrow, and could support men like Benedict Biscop, Ceolfrith and Wilfrid, all seasoned travellers on the Continent, should have been among the first in England to strike the new coins is no cause for surprise despite its remote position in the north. Because so few 'sceattas' have inscriptions, precise dating is very difficult. Those which are generally agreed to have been issued in the second quarter of the eighth century and later are common enough to suggest wide use of coin in eastern and southern England, and in the south part of Northumbria. The distribution maps are a remarkable demonstration of increased geographical spread through time (3, 2).

As well as geography, site contexts must be considered carefully in any dis-cussion of the extent to which the 'sceattas' were used as 'prestige valuables' or as weighed units of exchange or as currency. Some are found in graves until about the end of the first quarter of the eighth century, which could mean that they were deliberately sought out when required to accompany a

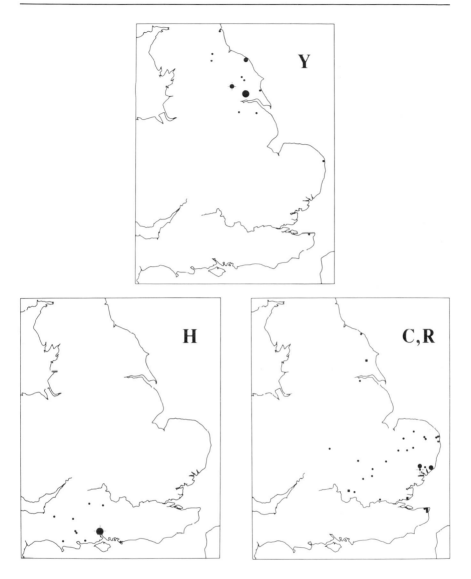

3, 3. Distribution maps by D. M. Metcalf of particular series of the 'sceatta' coins. Series Y is almost exclusive to the kingdom of Northumbria: it must have been minted and used there, but its near-absence from other kingdoms need not mean that there was no trade - other kings may have refused to allow a rival's coins to circulate where they had control. Series H is equally clearly a Wessex coinage: but in this case it is almost exclusive to Southampton, as though it was not circulating very much in the rest of the kingdom. The complicated Series C and R are found in East Anglia, Essex, Kent and Mercia: in this case, frontiers seem not to have been a barrier. This creates problems even of being sure where the coins were minted - Series C may have been Kentish, not East Anglian. (These maps were prepared by Dr. Metcalf in 1984, but he very kindly updated the Series H map for this book in 1988.)

burial, and does not prove that they were circulating and were therefore readily at hand when needed for some special purpose. Rather similarly, one or two early ones are pierced, suggesting that they were worn as ornaments or amulets rather than valued for their use as coins. Nevertheless, the quantity of later 'sceattas' that are found in rubbish-pits, floor-levels or simply as stray finds with no known association at some sites really does indicate that they were being accidentally lost while in everyday use. The designs on them increasingly ceased to imitate contemporary Frankish or earlier Roman coins, but followed trends general in English art, such as contorted but recognisable birds. This suggests that coins were being integrated into the general culture of the period, and were no longer something rather separate and special.

The extent to which these coins were at first only used by merchants and princes can be argued from such evidence as the three large hoards of them; none is reported to have contained any other artefacts, which suggests ownership by merchants rather than an assortment of valuables assembled and hidden by an ordinary citizen or a priest. One hoard was found at Aston Rowant, near Oxford, close to the ridgeway route between East Anglia and the south. Other coins have also been found on or close to road and river routes, suggesting loss in transit. A significant few are from hill-forts, where people may have congregated for fairs. Many are from the trading-stations. But many also are from church sites like Repton, centres to which people who were not necessarily merchants brought their gifts and taxes.

One series of early 'sceattas' (nicknamed 'Porcupines' because on them a diademed imperial head has become more like an animal than any human representation) is very widely found in England, the Low Countries, up the Rhine and north into Denmark, but with only a few in modern France and Belgium. This suggests that they were acceptable in areas controlled by the Frisians and those with whom they traded, but were not acceptable in Francia, a rival territory. If so, they must be seen as a coinage that facilitated international commerce in particular areas. Other 'sceatta' types are much less widespread, however, and their distribution seems almost confined to particular kingdoms: Series Y, for instance, hardly appears outside Northumbria, H outside Wessex (**3, 3**). Since they are not evenly spread across the whole of a known territory, distributions of coins cannot be used to reconstruct a kingdom's frontiers accurately; Series Y is effectively confined to south-eastern Northumbria, H almost to Southampton, but such exclusivity is not usual. A coin type's frequency in one kingdom may indicate its production there, but there may be scatters into other territories, which can show either that they were acceptable there despite being 'foreign', or the precise opposite, that they were not acceptable and that therefore if they happened to reach alien territory they were likely to be discarded as having little value. Series C and R, for instance, have mostly been found in East Anglia, but also in Mercia, Northumbria and Kent. They are virtually absent from Essex, so they make an interesting comparison with the distribution of Ipswich-type pottery, which seems also to have been all but excluded from that kingdom.

But if the 'sceattas' were closely linked to kingdoms, why did they not all carry explicitly political images and inscriptions to proclaim their originator's prestige?

It could be argued that some kings did not wish to upset powerful overlords by too open a display of independence, but in that case, those who were independent would not have hesitated to boast about it. So it is possible that most of the 'sceattas' were not issued by kings for their profit or prestige, but were struck by merchants for their own affairs, perhaps under licence. The Church may have played a rôle; there are coins with the name of Ecghberht, Archbishop of York 734–66, but he was the king's brother, so may have enjoyed special benefits. 'Sceattas' from Northumbria are the earliest known that bear a royal name, but it is tempting to associate a 'London' issue with the Mercian King Aethelbald's takeover of the city in the 730s, though there is no direct evidence. Moneyers' names reappear in East Anglia in the reign of King Beonna, who ruled from 749 to at least 760. He may not have been able to issue his own coins until Mercian overlordship was weakened by Aethelbald's murder in 757, after which there was an interlude before Offa re-established Mercian supremacy. A moneyer named Wilraed who had worked for Beonna is probably the same man as the Wilred who struck pennies for Offa, presumably as the latter asserted his domination by preventing the East Anglian king from putting his own name onto coins.[11] Such political machinations can sometimes be recognised in the coinage, although too much significance can be read into the small corpus that is known.

There are many anomalies in the distribution of the 'sceattas', well illustrated by the two that have been excavated in Northampton, one of them associated with the stone building. Both are irregular versions of Series G, otherwise known only in Sussex. Could there be any connection between the two areas, perhaps a common interest in iron production?[12] The 'sceat' from the crypt at Repton is probably a Mercian coin in its home territory, but another found in the earth mound is one that may have been produced in the territory of the Hwicce to the south-west. Part of their known involvement in trade was salt from Droitwich: was the Repton coin used in some transaction which involved that product? Did people wanting lead have to visit the royal centre at Repton in order to obtain it, because it was from there that the Mercian king controlled its distribution from the Derbyshire mines?

Another eighth-century coin from Repton is an import, a silver 'denier' issued by King Pepin the Short: on it is the mint name VIRDUN for Verdun, later recorded as a slave-trade centre. Were slaves also passing through Repton? The only other recorded Pepin coins in England are from Kent and Dorset, and there are very few finds of Frankish eighth-century coins in England generally, compared to the number of gold coins and other objects in the seventh. This could be because the amount of trade conducted with the Franks had fallen away, reflecting difficulties of access to Mediterranean products; or it could be that an unfavourable balance of trade with Francia meant that any coins brought in by Frankish merchants to purchase slaves,

cloth, hides and other products were all sucked out again in exchange for wine
and other commodities; or, since few English 'sceattas' have been reported in
France, kings prevented the circulation of English coins and vice versa, unlike
the policy pursued in England on the Frisian coins.

That there was an unfavourable balance of trade with what is now France
may be the implication to be drawn from the all but total absence of seventh-
and eighth-century coins from there found at the trading-station at Southampton, where there are several probably Frisian coins, and where they might
be most expected because northern France is Southampton's natural trad-
ing-partner.[13] Quantities of various types of pottery from Normandy, the
Seine and Loire valleys have indeed been found there, but apparently none
from around Bordeaux and the south, disrupted by Arab invasions, so that the
Wessex port had not taken over the trade with that area which Cornwall and
the south-west had enjoyed in the seventh century – a coin from Spain and
another from Toulouse might show some revival in the late eighth and ninth
centuries. Many sherds came from the Rhineland, but proportionally far
fewer than those from north France, where Southampton's equivalent was
Quentovic, the site of which has recently been located on the River Canche.

Many of the pottery imports could have been brought to Southampton by
foreign merchants for their own use, if they were dissatisfied with the quality
of the indigenous cooking and tableware that was available to them; since
relatively few imported vessels are found inland in Wessex, they do not seem
to have been widely redistributed. Although there are not really enough excavated sites of the period for a pattern to be regarded as established, there
is some indication that there are rather more pottery imports at inland sites
north of the Thames, which is a pattern similar to that of the 'sceattas', with
the Series H distribution being very limited outside Southampton. This is
not, however, because those who dwelt at Southampton were predominantly
foreigners, using their own pots and handling coins in a way scarcely understood by the natives in the interior, for there are few other signs of cultural
differences in the town; two burials with weapons are unlike the norm in
England by the second half of the seventh century, so may well be the bodies
of Franks or Frisians, but apart from a couple of shroud hooks, none of the
metalwork from the town is out of place in an English context.[14]

Nevertheless, the assemblages of material from mid Saxon Southampton
show some surprising contrasts. As well as the imported pottery, there are
large quantities of glass beakers and other vessels, and a few fragments of
window glass. Some glass vessels may have been made in the town, since
many of the fragments cannot be paralleled elsewhere, and waste rods show
that bead-making at least was practised.[15] Somewhere there existed a
demand for these very high-quality products, but if they were being distributed from Southampton to the kings and aristocrats of Wessex, they are proving very hard to find. Yet in other respects the town's artefacts are far from
prestigious. Although both gold- and silver-working are known from the discovery of crucibles and the like, no gold objects have been found, although a

few base-metal strap-ends and other small decorative items were being gilded. Only a few things like pins have a significant proportion of silver in them. Yet there are getting on for 150 of the silver 'sceattas', and the frequency of the H series suggests that its types were minted in the town. Their infrequency in the rest of Wessex makes it seem as though Southampton was a coin-using enclave within a non-monetary economy.

Another sign of this difference between the town and the rest of the country is the burials, for men outnumber women by almost two to one. Was Southampton a male-dominated craft-working and trading centre existing outside the normal social and economic structure? It is not yet known if Southampton is typical of all the English trading-stations in this, but preliminary results from Burrow Hill, Butley, Suffolk, indicate a majority of males in a cemetery in which only two of the 200 burials were not adults. This could suggest an exceptional population: the site is on a river, near Sutton Hoo and the recorded East Anglian centre at Rendlesham. With thirteen coins, imported pottery, glass and other objects, it could well have served as the place where goods for the royal service were landed and commercial transactions took place. The absence of children might just be because it was a monastery, however. The objects are not dissimilar to those found at known churches such as Whitby, Northumberland. Indeed, coastally-located churches may very well have been important landing places, developing a trading rôle because of their need for supplies. Equally, another Suffolk site, Brandon, has a church and cemetery that may account for its apparent wealth, such as eight 'sceattas', vessel and window-glass and a gold plaque from an altar cross or similar object. These East Anglian sites certainly seem very different from the fishing village with a side-line in quern-stones that seems indicated at Medmerry, Sussex, which had the more restricted range of pottery and other goods that might be expected at small coastal sites.[16]

Although substantial enough, as the sizes of their post-holes indicate, the buildings in mid Saxon Southampton that have so far been located were all of timber, and nothing comparable to the stone structure and its timber predecessor at Northampton has been found. The food remains also suggest a substantial but not flamboyant lifestyle, with no part of the town significantly richer than any other. The animal bones show that cattle provided most of the meat; almost half of these were elderly, no longer useful for hauling ploughs and carts, and getting too old for calf-bearing. There was a higher proportion of younger sheep, but many animals were eaten only after they had outlived their usefulness as providers of fleeces: at Portchester, the sheep seem to have been raised increasingly for their wool, as they were at Ramsbury, an interesting contrast to the earlier assemblages at West Stow, and one which suggests a significant economic trend to production to meet demand for textiles. Pork was also usually from mature rather than young and tender stock. The animals were being culled and driven in for slaughter from some distance away, for there are fewer young animals in the bone assemblages than there would be if breeding herds were represented. Some pigs may have been reared close to or even in the town, but no cattle and sheep, which must have come from well-established herds tended in well-farmed meadows. Wild animals such as deer made hardly any impact on the diet, and even the remains of shell-fish and fish from the local rivers and the sea suggest that they were eaten rather less frequently than might be expected in view of their ready availability. Fragments of querns, mostly made from stone imported from the Rhineland, and cereal grains show that bread formed, with meat stews, the basic foodstuffs. The cereal grains found in the pits had already been winnowed and dried before being lost, and nearly all were therefore brought into the town ready-processed, just needing to be ground into flour.[17]

The effect that this market for produce had on the hinterland of Southampton cannot at present be fully assessed, as too few sites have been investigated. It may be, however, that the rapid development of large centres like Southampton, Ipswich, Canterbury, London, perhaps York and others contributed to that rearrangement of much of the rural settlement pattern that led to the abandonment of sites like Chalton, so that production of an agricultural surplus could be more vigorously pursued, and new land brought into cultivation. Some of the English-made pottery in Southampton was made ten to fifteen miles away, suggesting that somewhere locally potters were stimulated to produce wares to sell in the new market. The Church was also creating new consumption centres, with monasteries like Wearmouth and Jarrow at times numbering their inmates in hundreds: these were exceptional, but even a 'minster' with a dozen priests – later records would justify that sort of figure – would have had at least an equivalent number of servants who would also have required feeding and clothing.

One site which may have been deliberately founded in this period in order to service a church institution is North Elmham, Norfolk, probably though not certainly the centre of the East Anglian bishopric. Excavations south of the present church have produced parallel ditches thought to delimit unmetalled streets, along which were various, generally small, two-roomed buildings with wells, one timber-lined from which dendrochronology has produced a date of *c.* 794; two 'sceattas' help to confirm eighth-century occupation.[18] Unfortunately there were not many other artefacts: remarkably little pottery seems to have been in use, with Ipswich ware conspicuous by its virtual absence in the eighth-century features. There were, however, a few imported sherds, apparently from both northern France and the Rhineland. Three silver objects, a decorative strip, a strap-end and a pair of tweezers are better in quality than anything from Southampton. The bones had slightly fewer mature cattle than at Southampton, though up to three-quarters of the sheep were fully grown: there were more pigs, and a few roe deer. Coins, pottery and silver, but not the bones, point to rubbish discarded by a somewhat richer community, and the excavations may have revealed the occupation area of the cathedral's priests and their servants rather than of an ordinary rural site. The Burrow Hill site makes an interesting comparison: possibly the difference is merely that eastern England was wealthier than the south.

The animal bones and other finds from the iron-working site at Ramsbury make a more direct contrast with those from contemporary Southampton, as the sites are only thirty-five miles apart; at the former, there was proportionally much more deer, both red and roe, as well as beaver, fox and badger. A few large dogs were kept, probably for hunting. Local wildlife was a significant, but at less than one-fifth not the predominant, part of the diet, and provided furs – at least one of the beavers had been skinned. There were also rather more pigs, which suggests that they could be fattened up in local woods. Their age-range is closer to what would be expected from a breeding herd than that at Southampton, unlike the sheep which were mostly mature and suggest that they were being brought in from a distance rather than locally reared. If these bones really represent what the iron-workers were eating, they show people who had closer contact with the countryside than townsmen, but who were specialised to the degree that breeding livestock was not their major activity.

The bone assemblages in mid Saxon sites are probably not affected only by demand, but also to some extent by crop specialisation. There was a greater proportion of cattle than of sheep-bone fragments at Southampton, whereas at North Elmham sheep out-numbered cattle, perhaps because the town required greater quantities of meat and this bulk demand could be more economically met by cattle carcases which have a far higher meat ratio than sheep. Alternatively, North Elmham may have been in the midst of an area where rearing of sheep was more important than of cattle. A site at Maxey, Northamptonshire, on the edge of the Fens is like neither Southampton nor North Elmham as it had roughly similar proportions of cattle and sheep bones, the cattle perhaps fattening in summer on the nearby marshes. The animals there are much more typical of breeding herds, with many more dying – not necessarily being killed – when young.[19]

All these sites yield horse bones in varying ratios, from as high as 14 per cent in one phase at Ramsbury down to as little as 0.1 per cent at Southampton, even though the port might have been expected to have had to stable a quantity of pack animals. At Ramsbury, the horses could be a status indication, as indeed could the deer bones. More likely, however, is that they were used to collect ores from areas difficult to reach by ox cart. It is not known if they would have been required for the distribution of finished products. Transport of metals was clearly not dependent on water, however, as is also shown by an iron-working site of a rather different sort at Millbrook in the Ashdown Forest, Sussex, far from any navigable river. Here a single bowl-furnace for smelting, with associated hearths probably for forges, seems to have been an isolated operation, not directly attached to an estate centre.[20]

Other changes that seem to become apparent at these mid Saxon sites include the virtual disuse of sunken-featured buildings; North Elmham, Maxey, Portchester and Southampton all have a range of building types which seem representative, but all are ground-level structures. Sunken-featured buildings still occurred in Northampton, however, as contemporaries of both the timber and the stone buildings, and it is not yet established whether they can be seen as forerunners of cellared buildings in later towns. Another change is in pottery, as the crudest and simplest (though quite effective) chaff-tempered wares all but disappear, and with them the likelihood that many households were making their own pots solely for their own use. Coarse and hand-made though most of it is, eighth-century English pottery seems to have had sufficient care in its making, and has enough possibility of regional classification in its identification, as to suggest that specialist, albeit perhaps usually still part-time, potters were by now virtually the norm wherever pottery was in use. Both these changes could reflect the passing of the less stable social conditions with which the sunken-featured buildings and the chaff-tempered pottery were most associated.

Greater stability can be seen both socially and politically. The seventh century had witnessed an élite expressing its newly-acquired dominance through its burial mounds and it treasure: in the eighth, it is as though this dominance was accepted. Kings and princes might bolster themselves with earthworks, mausolea and other obvious symbols which both proclaimed their leadership of their people and parity with rival kings, but the aristocracy who are shown by charter witness-lists to have ruled under them had achieved a social position which did not demand so much personal display. Their status might be indicated in death by burial at a distance from their social inferiors, at a major church, as perhaps at Brixworth, rather than in a mound on their own estates. If so, their families must have felt that there was no longer any need to proclaim their rights to ancestral lands by such highly visible tokens.

Sculptured stones may have marked some aristocratic burials, as at Wirksworth and Ramsbury, but since most are from northern monastic sites many may have been for monks rather than the laity. Crosses may sometimes have been memorials – fragments of one found at Repton might even be the earliest representation of an English king[21] – but they also had functions as churchyard foci for processions. The aristocracy did not routinely mark themselves out ostentatiously in death, therefore, and in life too they may have had much less use for personal display than their forebears. Without grave-goods, it is difficult to know what jewellery was circulating, and there may have been more than is now witnessed by stray-find discoveries. Most dating has to depend upon parallels with manuscript art, although an occasional object of obvious quality is found in context, like a cast copper-alloy mount recently excavated with two 'sceattas' in Canterbury.[22] That, however, was not certainly for personal wear, and a good many of the best pieces, like the Ormside bowl, have symbolism which make ecclesiastical use as likely as secular. A few of the objects in hoards coin-dated to the ninth century may have been made in the eighth, and thus were old when buried. There are certainly a few high-calibre individual pieces which may be of the eighth century, such as a gold sword pommel from the River Thames at Windsor, some gold finger-rings in twisted wire filigree, and a set of silver-gilt pins from the River Witham in Lincolnshire. But they are only a few, and their paucity cannot be because silver was not available, as the many coins that have been found show. It may be that the difficulty of getting gold, and the cessation of the supply of garnets and amethysts, meant that it was very hard to obtain materials that were really prestigious, and silver was too common to be a significant status demonstration. That would account for the attempts to disguise it by gilding, a process for which at least some gold, as well as imported mercury, was needed. But if ostentation had been considered desirable, it could have been achieved: indeed, it would seem that an aristocracy reasonably confident of its lands and its social position, and despite the personal upsets that political involvement might bring, did not need the sort of status display that the seventh century had known. Nevertheless the burial in a plank-lined pit at Coppergate, York, of a spear and helmet inscribed with the name Oshere and a Christian prayer suggests practices about which there is all too little evidence.[23]

If precious objects are difficult to date, then base-metal trivia are even more intransigent, as they do not have the level of detail which allows styles to be defined. The heart-beat may not quicken at the thought of pin-heads, but pins with large, flat discs bearing tortuous ornament are almost the only distinctively eighth-century personal ornament, and even they may have been made well into the ninth century. So far as the evidence goes, however, it does seem that there are no obvious regional styles: there is nothing characteristically 'Mercian' or 'Northumbrian'. Despite political divisions, there was cultural uniformity within eighth-century England, with no distinctively 'Kentish' style as there had been in the seventh.

Greater stability made possible the great intellectual achievements of Bede and other writers, particularly in northern England; the manuscripts from Lindisfarne, Wearmouth/Jarrow and perhaps other houses, the stone crosses at Bewcastle and Ruthwell, and the churches at Hexham, Ripon and Escombe are a fine tribute to the power and inspiration of Christianity during the second half of the seventh and the first half of the eighth centuries. At the same time, there seems to have been an expansion of settlement. Wharram Percy, high in the Yorkshire wolds, seems first to have become recognisable at this time as a nucleated centre, drawing to itself some of the dispersed sites in the area that pottery shows to have existed earlier. Imported pottery may indicate an aristocratic presence there, and there was a smithy.[24] No such status seems likely to have been attached to the isolated, high moorland sites like Simy Folds in Upper Teesdale, where drystone-footed structures and evidence of iron-smelting have been found. At the same time, pollen diagrams indicate a phase of forest clearance in the area.[25]

Although the great works of Northumbrian art seem to have been produced before about the middle of the eighth century, the kingdom's buoyancy continued at least at commercial level, since it was able to keep its coinage going even when others may have had interludes in their production. Analyses suggest that Northumbrian issues had a higher silver content than most of their contemporaries, which could mean that the kingdom was maintaining a favourable balance of trade at a time when those further south were finding difficulty in obtaining enough precious metal to keep their currencies viable.[26]

It may have been a commercial revival, or merely a desire to imitate continental kings, that led to the production of a new silver coin modelled on the reformed coinage introduced overseas by King Pepin in 755. Although still nominally a penny, the new coin was struck onto a wider flan than the 'sceattas' and was cut from a flat sheet of metal, a process which probably made it easier to achieve precise alloys and weights than did casting. Wilraed was striking something transitional between the 'sceattas' and the new pennies for King Beonna of East Anglia, so the changes cannot be attributed solely to the ambitions of King Offa. The 'sceatta' currencies may have petered out during the 750s generally, but certainly continued in Northumbria as the king's names show, and perhaps in Wessex, where so few of the new pennies have been found that they may have been kept out by still-circulating 'sceattas'.

Offa's pennies are distinctive for their very high standard of production: well-cut dies gave a clear image, and the designs were well thought-out. They also generally had a very high silver content of up to 96 per cent, and at over twenty grains were heavier than the 'sceattas'. The actual number of the new pennies that is known is not great, however, for it is not only in Wessex that they are scarce. It may be, therefore, that the new pennies were less successful as currency than the 'sceattas' had been, perhaps because such pure silver weight units were too valuable for most people to afford and use. Certainly a political motive seems evident: Offa invariably added *Rex* to his name, though he did not claim to be more than King of Mercia, despite his overlordship of other kingdoms. His is not the only name on the coins, for the archbishops of Canterbury were also issuing them, and some moneyers' names are on both the royal and the ecclesiastical pennies. Offa's quarrels with the archbishops may have led him to license the bishop of London to strike coins too, as there is one issue with the name Eadberht on it, which could be that of the bishop in the 780s. None, however, is certainly from Lichfield, where Offa sought to set up an archbishopric, nor are there any from Tamworth or his other Mercian power-bases. His use of Canterbury, Rochester and London as mint centres could show that he was not concerned to achieve a general circulation of coins in his kingdom. Certainly not intended for circulation were the gold coins that were very occasionally struck for ceremonial use or for alms distribution: one with Offa's name on it has a stylised imitation of an Arabic dirham on the reverse. This is one of the few pieces of evidence that shows that all contact with more distant worlds had not been lost: another is that the only known coin with a woman's name, that of Offa's wife Queen Cynethrith, can be explained as following a contemporary Byzantine practice.[27]

A regular coinage is an essential part of a monetary economy, but it is fairly clear from the limited circulation of even Offa's pennies that this could only have existed in parts of England at the end of the eighth century. Important though they were in asserting political authority, the coins cannot yet have done much to alter the basic structure of the economic system. Tributes and taxes must still have been paid mostly in kind, not cash, and the argument that Offa's supervision of his coins was to ensure that they were used by those subject to him when they were paying him their dues could only be valid if they were as frequently found in the Mercian heartland as in the south-east. Coinage use is certainly one way by which societies can be changed, permitting dealings in a medium acceptable between strangers. Consequently kinship and other social ties can be less necessary for the acquisition of resources, and the rôle of the authority that issues the coinage is enhanced as its regulation is increasingly needed to ensure that transactions are fairly conducted. Authority's protection is also needed to reduce the risk of theft, which cash attracts because of the difficulty of recognising and reclaiming it and the ease with which it can be passed on. In turn, the authority can increase its power by insisting that transactions are done at a place where they can be supervised, and a toll-charge levied upon them. It is this that leads to licensed markets, such as can be inferred at the trading-stations. Inland sites are more difficult to recognize, for nowhere has produced unequivocal evidence that commerce was the main motivating force. Places like Ramsbury and Northampton have shown that considerable activity was taking place in them, and some were later to become towns: but to what extent was this activity directly related to the foundation of churches? Oxford's causeway may have been to create a road, but was it for the benefit of St Frideswide's, its probable contemporary? Bedford is another Midlands place, later a shire centre, which may perhaps have had a single street line established at this time, but there is no archaeological evidence, any more than there is for the view that such places should be seen as proto-towns with single streets through a defended perimeter and an extra-mural market. If any of the latter existed, it would be difficult to trace them, but they are certainly not substantiated by coin finds, even though these are at least sufficiently common for the idea of fairs at hill-forts to have been mooted.[28]

The eighth century was nevertheless one in which new developments can be seen, with a particular emphasis upon Church and estate centres, trading-stations, and innovations in the coinage. Eighth-century kings were beginning to flex their economic muscle, although they were not yet exploiting it to the full. If Offa did indeed build his dyke, it was probably because he was a traditionalist at heart.

Chapter Four

THE NINTH AND EARLY TENTH CENTURIES

Holding Out Against the Heathens

When, in 793, 'the ravages of heathen men miserably destroyed God's church on Lindisfarne, with plunder and slaughter', many contemporaries saw the Viking raids as a sign of God's direct intervention in human affairs and a punishment for their own failures to walk in paths of righteousness. There are no records that either state the Vikings' own motives for their raids – whether lack of land or lack of silver – or give a realistic assessment of the impact that they had on western Europe. The drama of the narrative of ravaging, fighting and atrocities has tended to obscure other tensions that also affected development of the period.

Despite the chronicler's vivid description, Lindisfarne was not totally destroyed, for there still remain from it the wooden coffin and other relics of St Cuthbert, which would certainly have been lost if devastation had been absolute.[1] An evocative reminder of the raid may be a tombstone from the site that seems to show a war-band; if it is correct to interpret that scene as a Viking ship's crew, the stone would be archaeological evidence of at least continued use of the area for burial purposes after 793. There is, in fact, no reason to doubt the twelfth-century record that the monks 'continued for a long time' to live at the abbey, only leaving the island for safer territory later in the ninth century. Physical evidence, limited as it is, gives no direct evidence of the effect of the 790s raids and their immediate successors on the northern churches, or of their abandonment at that time. Some decline in spiritual life may be shown in Jarrow by the change of use of what had been a high-status building into a metal-working craft-shop. Similarly at Whitby, where the coins and other artefacts show that occupation of the abbey site continued long into the ninth century, a late building overlies the edge of the Anglo-Saxon burial-ground, perhaps indicating that the cemetery's sanctity no longer commanded the respect that it should have enjoyed.[2] Such signs of physical and spiritual decline are consistent with the decline in output of major works of art and literature from these monasteries after the middle of the eighth century. Pre-eminence in the north had perhaps passed to the archiepiscopal centre at York, and falling standards at the older, more isolated houses are not necessarily to be associated with the initial impact of Viking raids.

Since archaeology does not suggest that the Norse plundering parties had much immediate effect upon the monasteries which were their most obvious target in England, few signs of their effect in other spheres might be expected, particularly away from the vulnerable north-east coast. Although the charters suggest that bridge and fortress-building were increasingly added to the services owed to their king by land-holders,[3] the evidence of the causeways at Mersea and Oxford and the ditched enclosures at Hereford and Tamworth show that such impositions were well established before the Viking raids, at least in central England, and were probably an extension of what must have been much older duties to engage in earthwork construction, shown not only by Offa's dyke, but also by the many earlier dyke systems. The charters' in-structions are the expression of the increasing formality of royal authority. Whether any constructions were actually undertaken to protect the coast from Viking raids, as Charlemagne was doing on the other side of the Channel, is not known: no fort-building or restoration of walled Roman sites can be ascribed to the first half of the ninth century. According to the *Anglo-Saxon Chronicle*, it was not until the 830s that the Vikings became a threat to the whole fabric of English society, leading in the 870s to the collapse of kingdoms. These, mainly Danish, raiders were prepared to fight at sea or on land near their ships, storming in quick succession Canterbury, London, Rochester and Southampton, nowhere on or near the coast being safe. There were major churches at most of the places important enough to merit naming in the sources, but they were also for the most part known as trading-stations. The degree of physical damage done to the ports cannot be assessed – nothing at Southampton suggests wholesale burning, for instance, in contrast to evidence left by the much later French raid in 1338. What Southampton does show, however, is a considerable decline in trading activity, witnessed by the diminishing number of coins found. This is not an ideal standard by which to measure change, for even in the early years of the ninth century, when there is no other reason to doubt the port's prosperity, there were fewer coins lost, perhaps because the new broad-flan pennies were easier to handle than the 'sceattas'. Nevertheless, such pennies as there are at Southampton date mostly from the early part of the ninth century, tailing off to almost none at its end.[4] This is consistent with the other artefacts, none of which seem necessarily to post-date *c.* 850. The mid Saxon port was effectively abandoned. Other English trading-stations may have declined similarly, though the evidence is much less clear-cut, their sites having had greater sub-sequent use. The limited information from the Strand area of London does not contradict claims for its ninth-century disuse, however. Most signifi-cantly, the waterfront installations at the great continental harbour at Dorestat were not being repaired after *c.* 830; even though activity there did not cease altogether, the coin record tells a similar story of trade decline.[5]

The effect that the Vikings could have on economic systems had already been seen in Northumbria in the 790s, where their raids seem to be the best explanation for the abrupt end of the kingdom's 'sceatta' coinage, which

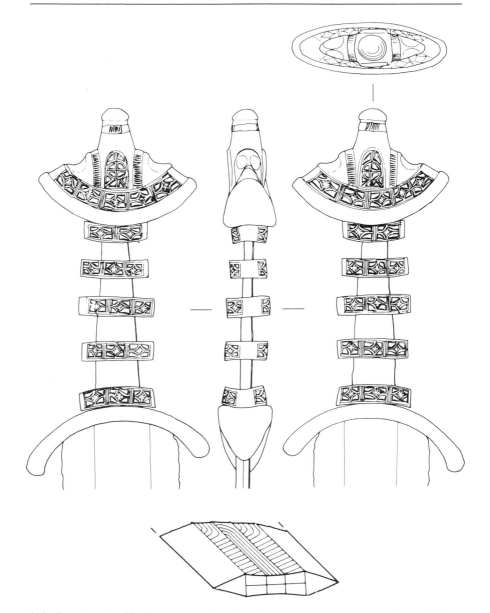

4, 1. Drawings by H. Humphries of a ninth-/early tenth-century sword from Gilling West, North Yorkshire, found in a stream in 1976 - finds of swords in rivers suggest deliberate 'sacrifice', but this one was perhaps just an accidental loss. The hilt has silver bands, wider than the iron as they would have been set over a wooden or bone handgrip. The schematic animal heads on the ends of the pommel may be a reference to the creatures that would feed on the sword's victims. The blade was pattern-welded, i.e. composed of iron rods, alternately twisted and left straight, then welded together, and etched after grinding and polishing to show up the pattern. The edges were also separate strips, with a higher carbon content for extra hardness. The pattern welding reduced brittleness, making the blade less likely to shatter. (Width of pommel : 838 mm).

could not be maintained if silver stocks had been depleted.[6] The trading-stations suggest similar disruption, the raids creating a crisis of confidence – and physically destroying or removing any ships drawn up on their beaches. Coins did not cease to be minted, however, even if minting was episodic. Although fewer in terms of stray-loss finds than the 'sceattas', pennies in many ninth-century hoards (themselves a token of particular crises of confidence in the 850s and 870s) show that considerable numbers existed. The silver in these pennies became increasingly debased until the 870s, probably because the kings were manipulating the coinage to increase their revenue.[7] If scarcity of silver bullion had been a serious long-term problem, there would not only be fewer coins, but there would not be such a large number of silver brooches, strap-ends and other ornaments found with the coin-hoards, which provide dating evidence for the many objects – more than for the eighth century – that have been found without associated coins, notably swords with a range of finely decorated hilts (**4, 1**). Nor was silver the only precious metal: gold was used for rings and some sword-hilts, and a few gold coins were imported, such as the *munus divinum 'solidi'* of Louis the Pious and imitations of them. All this ninth-century metal had to come from the Continent, and its quality does not suggest that trade was brought to a virtual standstill for more than very short periods, if that; there is a sprinkling of silver coins of Charles the Bald and other ninth-century Carolingian monarchs, especially in southern England. Only Northumbria stands apart from this general picture, and even there coinage was re-introduced after an interlude, although the new 'stycas' which were unique to that kingdom never had more than a 40 per cent silver content, and were increasingly debased to as low as 2 per cent.

Despite the decline of the international trading-stations, the coins and objects show that commerce and exchange must have continued, although there are no sites that can be said to have been primarily market centres. Royal residences and other estate centres may have retained their economic rôle, with food renders still brought to them by subjects – hence the Vikings' concentration upon gaining possession of them, the construction of the mill at Tamworth in the 850s despite the raids and the merchant Othere's visit to King Alfred's court. The continued importance of such places is shown by the excavations at Cheddar, Somerset, where a long timber hall, perhaps two-storeyed, is a record of ninth-century expenditure at what was at any rate in the next few decades a royal palace.[8] Its economic rôle is shown particularly by the metal-working debris found there, although it was not on the scale of the iron production at Ramsbury, which seems to have come to an end during the first half of the ninth century. Goltho, Lincolnshire, is a complex that came into use probably some time later where a spread of smithing slag and a stone hearth interpreted as 'industrial' suggest craft activity of some kind. The buildings associated with it are of a size to suggest no more than farmsteads, but their replacement by a ditched enclosure containing a twenty-four metre long 'hall' and ancillary buildings could imply that the site was for high-status use from the first. The quantity of objects associated with weaving around one of the smaller buildings has led to its designation as a 'weaving shed', suggesting production on a greater than domestic scale.[9]

It is difficult to assess the effect of the ninth century upon rural settlements generally. Dating of excavated sites is usually imprecise because coins are rarely found and the different types of pottery have a very wide time range – if pottery exists at all, since some areas of England, particularly in the west except Cornwall, seem still to have been aceramic. Consequently, few developments in settlement patterns tend to be attributed to the ninth century specifically, although in East Anglia, Ipswich and the new Thetford wares are valuable indicators. Field-walking in parts of East Anglia has produced quantities of Thetford ware in areas around churches, suggesting that it was in the later ninth and tenth centuries that these were becoming village centres. This does, however, assume that the earlier Ipswich ware would be found if those areas had been in use during its period of manufacture, and it is not certain that that would be the case, particularly since it was not found in the excavations at Maxey, although it is known in the immediate area.[10] Although there were quite substantial buildings at Maxey, they were not rebuilt and probably did not outlast the ninth century.[11] Nevertheless, occupation seems to have continued within the immediate vicinity. The ninth century has not yet produced evidence of the widespread abandonment of sites that was such a feature of the preceding parts of the Saxon period, and this suggests at least stabilisation of the settlement system, rather than contraction caused by Vikings or other external factors. Only in the 890s does the *Chronicle* record plague and, although contemporaries could not have known it, the end of the century was the beginning of a long-term climatic improvement which gave warmer summers and a longer growing season. Expansion of agriculture on the high ground in the north seems to have continued, for although Simy Folds may have been abandoned, at least for permanent occupation, Gauber High Pasture in West Yorkshire's Ribblehead had a farmstead with a building sufficiently substantial to suggest year-round occupation, and the extraordinarily fortunate find within it of four coins to prove ninth-century use.[12] In friendlier environments, Wharram Percy seems to have prospered, and on the north Cornish coast at Mawgan Porth a courtyard-farm complex was probably founded in the ninth century, or soon afterwards.[13]

These sites all stress the pre-eminent role of agriculture in the economy, and Goltho shows something also of the processing of agricultural products. There is a little information about the importance of metals also, though no new iron-smelting complexes such as the eighth century has produced have been found. The quality of iron-work available is shown by the sword blades, many of which were made of iron rods twisted and welded to achieve some malleability from phosphorus-rich ores, and now with hardened steel edges. Ores for the latter probably had to be imported, and in any individual case it is usually not possible to be sure that the complete blade is not an import, though English smiths must have been responsible for many. At any rate, the swords were now much more effective weapons than they would have been in the fifth and sixth centuries. By varying the twisting of the rods, different patterns could be achieved which, etched to bring out the brightness of the phosphorus, would produce a light-catching, gleaming blade (**4, 1**). The valuable hilts added to many swords show the prestige that they bestowed.[14]

It is not known which iron-ore deposits were being exploited in the ninth century. Other metals that were probably being extracted included tin, less a feature of the ninth-century coinage when the silver alloy was pure, but certainly added very deliberately and in some quantity in the 860s to the Wessex and Mercian pennies. The hoard of silver at Trewhiddle, Cornwall, with a range of coins that show that it was deposited no earlier than 868, may well be an indication of the importance of Cornish tin. Earlier debased pennies contained much more zinc than tin, and zinc was also a major component of the Northumbrian 'stycas'. The ores may well have been extracted from deposits around Alston, in Cumberland: were supplies from there not available to southern England in the 860s because of Viking activity?[15]

Coinage debasement is one measure of the economic difficulties of the middle part of the ninth century, and other disruption can also be seen, particularly in the Church. Although they survived the 790s, the great monasteries of the north did eventually disintegrate; apart from Norham, used by the migrant Lindisfarne community, none was still in existence by the end of the ninth century. The centre and south of England also had their losses, as King Alfred lamented. The nunnery at Nazeingbury probably survived well into the ninth century, but radiocarbon dates end at 870 at the latest. At North Elmham, on the other hand, there were considerable changes, with mid-Saxon ditches and wells being filled in and reorganisation taking place from at least the end of the century, but not with any obvious interlude or change in the site's function or the status of its occupants.[16] The size of the church at Brixworth and the quality and range of sculpture at Breedon-on-the-Hill show something of the physical scale and breadth of contacts of ecclesiastical establishments in the eighth and early ninth centuries: neither of those churches was to regain its prestige and wealth after the ninth century. The position is graphically shown at Canterbury, where the number of literate scribes at Christchurch can be seen from surviving manuscripts to have declined sharply in the 850s, until by 873 only one elderly writer was left, his work now pathetically inept. The Viking raid of 851 seems to have made its mark. The middle years of the ninth century at Canterbury were a great contrast to the early years, when Christchurch had been rebuilt, estates purchased and the archbishop's moneyers very active.[17]

Other evidence of the raids are graves recognisable as those of Vikings. A male found just outside Reading, Berkshire, had with him a horse and a sword which no Christian would have been supplied with. The sword's hilt was ornamented in a purely Scandinavian manner, now known as the 'Gripping Beast' style. The grave was in an area called the 'Vastern', an English word for stronghold, between the Thames and Kennet rivers, a likely position for the rampart recorded by Asser as constructed at Reading by the army which seized the adjacent royal residence in 870–71. If the buried man was a Viking who died during that episode, he had with him a sword on which the hilt was already three-quarters of a century old when buried, for 'Gripping Beast' is an eighth-century style. The hilt is fairly well worn, and could have been of some age when it went into the ground, though it does give grounds for caution in too readily associating recorded raids with particular archaeological discoveries. This can be done with greater certainty when coins are found with burials: another grave at Reading had a coffin for which a small collection of coins provides a date in the early 870s. That grave was in the churchyard of St Mary within the town, which was probably close to the site of the royal palace.[18]

Many Viking-style burials and objects have been found in churchyards, implying that the aliens' wish to identify themselves in death with a place of religious significance overrode any distaste for lying alongside the forebears of their vanquished, although in some cases the Viking may have come first and the churchyard developed around him because of his remembered importance. Some important burials were in mounds that appear to have been and to have remained isolated.[19] One dramatic instance of Viking use of a Christian site is Repton, where a gold ring was found close to the eighth-century crypt and whatever enlargements it had by then accrued in a burial which also had five pennies in it dated to 873-76. Furthermore, the sunken masonry structure to the west, by then apparently in a state of disrepair with stucco falling off the walls, contained a mass of bones from at least 249 individuals, an axe, knives, animal bones and five more pennies, of 872-74. These cannot but be a testimony of the presence of the Viking army recorded as being in Repton in 873–75. That army probably dug the ditch which has been found leading towards the River Trent, perhaps to create a defensive enclosure incorporating the church as a tower. A seventeenth-century record suggests that the other masonry structure had had a central burial, probably that of a Viking leader.[20]

The Repton-based Vikings had presumably gone there because it was a known centre, and their use of the Mercian royal family's burial-place for their own leaders may have been a deliberate claim to have inherited governmental authority, since it was at that time that they 'drove King Burgred across the sea'. The 870s saw Viking armies 'sharing out the land . . . to plough and to support themselves' in Northumbria, East Anglia and parts of Mercia. The change of government in the north can be seen by the cessation of minting of 'stycas', which had continued in the 860s and perhaps into the 870s, showing that some sort of central authority survived in Northumbria until then. Existing dynasties and land-ownership patterns were disrupted throughout what became known as the Danelaw, though the extent to which the territory was actually peopled by Danes or other Scandinavians is not easy to judge from archaeological evidence. Sites like Goltho and North Elmham are in the Danelaw, but do not reflect anything markedly Scandinavian in their culture sequences: the claim as negroid for the skeleton of a woman whose presence would at least have shown long-distance slave-trading such as the Vikings were famous for must, rather sadly, be discounted, as a similar person in Norwich has been shown to have had merely a protruding jaw![21] At a site lower in the social hierarchy, 'stycas' demonstrate that Gauber is quite likely to predate Healfdene's army's settlement, and cannot be used to support the old argument that there was such an influx of new arrivals that widespread colonisation of new land was forced upon them.

The arrival of new landlords in parts of northern England towards the end of the ninth century was once thought to be witnessed by burial markers such as the ring-headed cross at Middleton, North Yorkshire, carved with a contorted beast on one side of the shaft and a helmeted male surrounded by weapons on the other. The beast is a crude rendering of the 'Jellinge' style, one which is derived from the sort of creatures found also in southern England: the male is un-precedented in the English world, however, and it was argued that a Viking who had recently taken over an estate at Middleton ordered a local craftsman to make for him a Christian monument which nevertheless would represent him as though buried in the old style with his weapons. This theory received a jolt when excavations in York produced fragments of Jellinge sculptures in contexts firmly dated to the first half of the tenth century. Monuments like that at Middleton cannot therefore be used as evidence of the aspirations and the tastes of the founding fathers of a Viking aristocracy.[22] What the sculptures do show is that concepts about commemoration of people and representation of ideas in northern England during the tenth and eleventh centuries were very different from those further south. It is not, however, a difference that the dis-tinguished the whole of the Danelaw from 'English' England. East Anglia has no such sculpture, the aristocracy there choosing to do without stone grave-markers and crosses. This is not just because of the difficulty of getting stone, since it could have been acquired from Barnack and other limestone quarries if demand had been sufficient; it could, however, be a sign of different practices, perhaps of quicker assimilation. Different parts of the Danelaw were quite likely to have had, or rapidly to have developed, differ-ences of this sort. Nor are there other signs of a Danish culture in the rural Danelaw; stray finds of metalwork are infrequent and as likely to be found in English as in Danelaw England, ball-headed pins being an example.[23] There were no differences in the type of agriculture practised in Denmark which can be recognised by new techniques introduced into England. Both countries seem already to have been in the process of introducing the wheeled mould-board plough, fields divided into strips and nucleated settlements. Similarities of buildings at sites like Gauber to Norse structures may simply be a common response to similar terrains.[24] Place-names rather than ar-chaeology suggest Scandinavian rural settlement, and they leave unresolved the problem of the extent to which they result either from the impositions of a new aristocracy whose words came to be used by English peasants or from the influx of migrants on a large scale; the latter is perhaps indicated by the use of Scandinavian words even for everyday things like field names, not just for the names of estate units. Scandinavian personal names such as those of moneyers on coins issued at Danelaw mints could also result from the influence of an élite, unrepresentative of the peasantry. In York, indeed, Scandinavian names did not even predominate on coins until the eleventh century.[25]

York was used as a centre by Danish, and in the early tenth century by Norse, kings. Recent excavations there have produced some objects that are certainly imports from Scandinavia, or the Scandinavian-settled Shetlands, such as soapstone vessels; amber, used for beads, could have come from the Baltic. A few objects show a markedly more Scandinavian taste, wherever made, such as a strap-end with Borre-style interlace ornament. Scandinavian trade contacts are indicated by fragments of silk, a cowrie shell from the Red Sea or the Gulf of Aden, and a forgery of an Islamic coin, all probably brought to York from the eastern Mediterranean and beyond, first overland to the Baltic, and then across the North Sea via such places as Hedeby at the base of the Jutland peninsula. To the later ninth century are ascribed the first signs of regular activity at Coppergate (5, 3), a site outside the Roman fort area, but burials in places that were neither then nor later churchyards indicate both some instability of property use and alien customs. There is evidence for a range of crafts, including glass-working, and also of the availability of a new type of pottery, known as 'York ware' although its actual place of manufacture is not yet known. Broad-flan pennies were minted in York from the middle of the 890s onwards. The probability is of considerable changes and expansion at York and in its trade, with a Scandinavian presence larger than that just of kings and jarls. But there are many types of Scandinavian object as yet undiscovered in York, which would be expected if a new cultural tradition had arrived *en bloc*.[26]

Other places in the Danelaw were also developing in the late ninth and early tenth centuries. Norwich seems to have expanded from a complex of scattered sites along the River Wensum (4, 2). A bank and ditch on the north bank perhaps created a small enclosure, and recent excavations have found much evidence of eighth-century activity there.[27] The new developments took place mainly on the south bank, however, as though new initiatives were taking place. Thetford presents a rather similar picture, a little Ipswich ware and a 'styca' showing use of the north bank of the River Thet early in the ninth century, but with the major expansion being the in the tenth on the south side.[28] Concentric ditches at Stamford indicate a small enclosure on the river there, dated to the ninth century by a coin of King Alfred, whereas most of the town developed from the tenth.[29] At Colchester, however, where there is a certain amount of eighth-century evidence, there is no sign of ninth- or early tenth-century resurgence although it was clearly a Viking centre in 917 when captured by the English.[30] It would have been the logical place for Guthrum to use as a mint for the pennies which he issued in the 880s, but he seems to have preferred London even though it was on the border of his territory. At Lincoln, coins were being minted from the 890s, and a penny of that decade

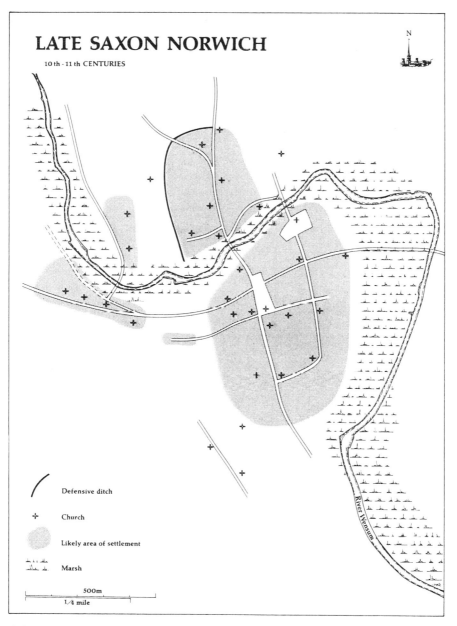

LATE SAXON NORWICH

10 th - 11 th CENTURIES

N

Defensive ditch

Church

Likely area of settlement

Marsh

500m

1/4 mile

River Wensum

4, 2. Plan of Norwich, Norfolk, in the tenth to eleventh centuries, prepared by B. S. Ayers. On the north side of the River Wensum, at least part of the occupation area was enclosed by a ditch and bank. Some of the earliest, eighth-century, material has come from this area, near the river. On the south side, the open area in the north-east marks its later importance as a waterfront market zone beside a major road crossing (whether by bridge or by ford). The large number of small churches emphasises the rather scattered spread of settlement (cf. **6,3**).

at the Flaxengate site helps to date the limestone-cobbled road and buildings of the first phase of intensive post-Roman use.[31] Actual Scandinavian activity is less recognisable at these places than at York, although Thetford, Norwich and Lincoln have produced fragments of soapstone vessels, those in Lincoln all being in the earliest levels and interpreted as treasured possessions of the first settlers. At Lincoln also can be recognised a taste for amber and jet, shared with York, and there are many hones from Norway, which now became a standard trade item throughout the Middle Ages. Reflecting political rather than social trends, early tenth-century coins minted in Lincoln bore Scandinavian designs, unlike those of the late ninth century which had copied King Alfred's pennies. Silks and sherds of Islamic and even Chinese pottery show long-distance contacts. But querns and pottery show commerce with the Rhineland also, a trade that need owe nothing to Scandinavian influence. Nor was all this development in the eastern Danelaw, for in the north-west a cellared building at Chester shows activity between the Roman fort and the River Dee: Chester was another place where a mint started to operate in the 890s.[32]

These developments were not confined to the Danelaw, however. It seems to have been in the 870s that occupation within the City of London reappeared, probably replacing the Strand area which thereafter became known as 'old *wic*' – hence Aldwych; the Roman walled area has produced two 870s coins and a coin-weight of 870-80, evidence that fits well enough with the *Chronicle*'s statement that King Alfred took possession of London in 886. Refurbishment of at least part of the Thames waterfront was taking place from the late ninth century, with logs and planks forming a 'hard' onto which boats could be hauled, and rows of pointed stakes which may both have prevented erosion and offered defensive protection. These timbers have yielded radiocarbon and dendrochronological dates congruent with charter grants made by King Alfred, and perhaps also with the new grid system of streets that appears along the Thames frontage, where further north in the City the street lines could be earlier, associated with the churches and the enclosures referred to as *hagas* in charters.[33] 'Dark-earth' layers or organic build-up cease to occur, as they do in other former Roman walled towns such as Gloucester, where the late ninth-century mint provides a context for the excavation evidence of renewed occupation, much of it the residues of manure from stables: a large quantity of iron tools may have been a farrier's kit-bag.[34] Regeneration in the ninth century is not easy to distinguish from tenth-century developments, except for the establishment of mints, and even those can be uncertain. No Oxford-minted coin of Alfred's reign is known, but that a mint did exist there seems to be indicated by coins inscribed 'Ohsnaforda', a name probably copied from genuine Oxford contemporaries and slightly blundered. Minting in Northampton is also possible but unproven, since no fewer than nine St Edmund Memorial coins of the turn of the century have been found in the town. There is no other evidence of moneying there until much later in the tenth century.

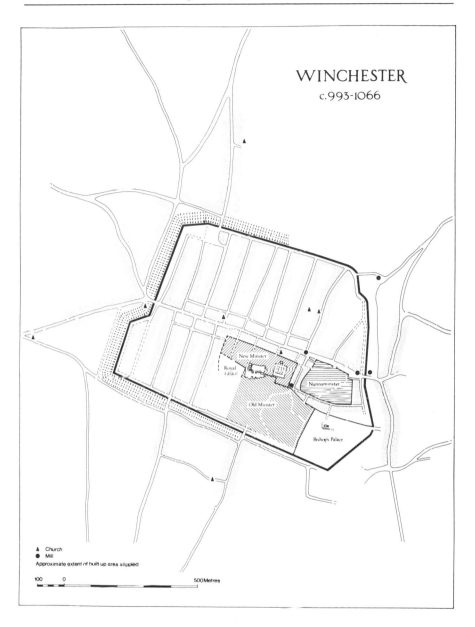

WINCHESTER
c.993-1066

New Minster

Royal
Palace

Nunnaminster

Old Minster

Bishops Palace

▲ Church
● Mill
Approximate extent of built up area stippled

100   0   500 Metres

4, 3. Plan of Winchester, Hampshire, in the tenth to eleventh centuries, prepared by M. Biddle. Here the Roman walls confined occupation more tightly than in Norwich (**4,3**), with suburbs developing along the major route-ways. Over a quarter of the town was already taken up by ecclesiastical and royal enclaves. Streams were directed through these to provide a water supply, and they also turned the mills which are recorded in Winchester's excellent documentary sources. The same factor was to cause the cloth-working and tanning industries to cluster in the north-east segment of the city.

In Wessex there were also new developments in the second half of the ninth century. Excavation in Winchester, another place which first certainly became a mint then, has shown that a new street pattern was established, the regularity of its grid layout and its conformity to a four-pole system of measurement, and the similarities to each other of the earliest street surfaces combining to suggest that it was a planned development of a single period (4, 3). Chichester has hand-made pottery attributed to the ninth century, a date supported by at least one coin find; large numbers of pits and traces of building show its more intensive use. At Exeter and Bath, however, pottery is cautiously dated to the tenth rather than to the later ninth century. In Kent, there is some evidence at Canterbury of ninth-century pottery, but it does not suggest as much activity as·previously: extra-mural areas went out of use towards the end of the century, suggesting that there was no quick recovery from the Viking problems.[35]

If places like these do not have mints or clear evidence of streets it is difficult to classify them as towns in the ninth century, even if they were to become towns thereafter. Portchester (2, 4) has produced as much evidence of ninth-century pottery and artefacts as Chichester, for instance, yet it is never considered to have been urban.[36] Portchester is one of the names that occur in the *Burghal Hidage*, a document prepared either in the reign of King Alfred or of his son, which gave a list of defended places in Wessex and the number of hides attributable to each which were to provide men for its maintenance and defence. There are different texts of the *Burghal Hidage*, and attendant problems of identification, but its unique interest is that it shows a planned defensive system, and names sites that were all meant to be available for use at a single time – though for how long, if ever, it was operational is unknown.[37] The defences at these places were not all constructed at the same time. Some, like Chisbury in Wiltshire, were hill-forts where it is not known how much if any work was done on the Iron Age ramparts to re-create a usable camp. Others, like Portchester, were walled Roman sites which probably required little attention; excavations here have shown both earlier and later occupation within the fort, and a phase in the area excavated when all structures were removed from it, perhaps to clear it for action. Some defences were neither prehistoric nor Roman, like those at Wareham where, however, the bank and ditches need not have been dug at the time that the *Burghal Hidage* was drawn up; the place is described by Asser in terms that suggest that it was an existing *castellum* when taken by a Viking army in 877; there was certainly an important church there. The walls at Winchester had received attention before the ninth century, the Roman gate on the south side having been blocked. It is not possible to recognise any refurbishment of the stonework that can be associated with the ninth century but the two parallel ditches outside the west wall certainly seem to have been dug then, for their upcast has been found and pottery in layers overlying it dates from the end of that century.

Places outside Wessex were also receiving defences, or having their existing works refurbished. The best-explored sequence is at Hereford (**4, 4**) where a gravel rampart overlying buildings on the west side was replaced by a turf-and-clay, timber-faced bank which seems likely to have been built to make a circuit round the river crossing: a mortared stone wall on top of their bank seems to be of the late tenth or eleventh century but there is no clear dating for the earlier phases because of the lack of associated pottery. They could be ninth-century, but there is no certainty[38] More often it is ditches rather than banks that have been found, and it is their in-filling not their original excavation that can be dated. In a number of cases, the only physical evidence of early defensive circuits is streets that are claimed to be aligned on them, as in Northampton where no ditch or bank of the period has actually been seen. It cannot of course be assumed that every bank and every ditch is an English construction; the Repton ditch seems to confirm documentary records such as Asser's about Reading that the Vikings used earthwork defences too. The small enclosure found at Stamford has led to the suggestion that it could be Viking also, as could those at the other Danelaw centres. The King's Gate area at York could have had something of the same sort around it, an inner core within the larger defended area; it is not known when the existing Roman fort walls on the south and east sides were demolished, and an extension taken out to the rivers.

The actual construction of bank-and-ditch enclosures like that at Wareham would have been neither difficult nor particularly time-consuming. At Wallingford, now in Oxfordshire (**4, 5**), the partly visible ditch which ran round three sides of the approximately 6,250 foot-long defence (the fourth side is the River Thames, apart perhaps from a small bridge-head on the opposite bank) has been shown by excavation to be about twenty-five feet deep and eight feet wide. There is no trace of a second ditch.[39] Wallingford had 2,400 hides attributed to it, a figure equalled only by Winchester. If each hide had to send one man to work there for forty days, the army-service period recorded in Alfred's reign, each would have had to dig an average daily depth of about a foot from an area of about 130 square feet, hardly a crippling stint! The upcast had to be used to build the bank, of course, and there would have been timber to cut and collect. But a large team of men could easily achieve such a task in a single season; the difficult part would be to assemble them and to keep them supplied, and it is that which is a better indication of administrative ability than the mere size of the defences. Those responsible were no mean organizers and can validly be assumed to have had considerable powers of coercion – exactly as would be expected from the charters.[40]

The extent to which this authoritarian structure may also be seen in the street layout in some of these centres is more difficult to judge. Even if it is accepted that deliberate planning lay behind Winchester's new roads, the applicability of that model elsewhere is uncertain, for other places do not have dating evidence. The four-pole unit of measurement can be applied to various towns, but perhaps because it remained a standard unit for some centuries [41] Even in Wessex, other towns do not have plans quite like Winches-

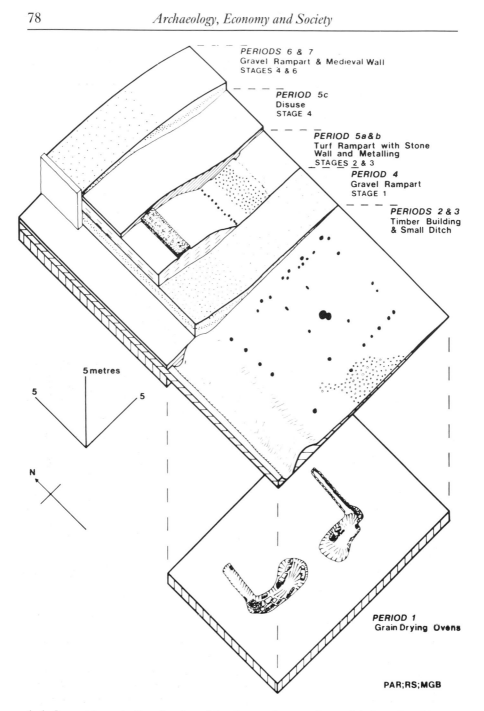

PERIODS 6 & 7
Gravel Rampart & Medieval Wall
STAGES 4 & 6

PERIOD 5c
Disuse
STAGE 4

PERIOD 5a & b
Turf Rampart with Stone
Wall and Metalling
STAGES 2 & 3

PERIOD 4
Gravel Rampart
STAGE 1

PERIODS 2 & 3
Timber Building
& Small Ditch

5 metres

5   5

N

PERIOD 1
Grain Drying Ovens

PAR; RS; MGB

4, 4. Isometric projection drawing of the phases of occupation and defence found in excavation by R. Shoesmith and P. Rahtz on the western side of Hereford. Grain-driers, reusing some Roman stones, suggest large-scale agricultural processing, succeeded by a timber building, which in turn was overlain by a sequence of ramparts.

ter's, with back streets close and parallel to the High Street on both sides (**4, 3**); nor are roads inside the perimeter of the walls invariable. The street grids are more regular than those in, for instance, the Coppergate area of York, but the extent to which contour lines and streams played a part determining topography needs to be taken into account. There does, however, seem to have been some concept in the south of what a town should look like, and a structure was imposed upon it. Direct physical imposition is shown at Hereford, where the new bank was laid out over the site of timber buildings (**4, 4**); whether this was done regardless of someone's property rights is unknown. The grid at Winchester probably respected the boundaries of the *haga* associated with the stone structure on the cemetery site at Lower Brook Street; at any rate the building itself survived to become a church. It is likely enough that agreements were reached, even if pressure to reach them was

4, 5. Wallingford, Oxfordshire (Berkshire until 1974). The trees mark the outer perimeter line of the area defended by an earth bank and ditch, the River Thames being the fourth side. Unlike Winchester (**4, 3**), Wallingford has no Roman antecedents, but in the *Burghal Hidage* it rated the same size of garrison. In the north-east quarter, the Norman castle was extended across the town walls in the thirteenth century, blocking the north gate and causing the road to be diverted to the west. Much of the open area in the north-west was occupied by a medieval priory, but that in the south-west was never built over, an indication of lack of pressure on internal space despite considerable prosperity, particularly in the twelfth century.

applied; Edward the Elder paid money for the properties which he needed to provide space for Winchester's New Minster, so such procedures existed then just as charters show that they had done earlier in London and Canterbury. Similar processes may sometimes have been needed to produce nucleated villages and new field systems in the countryside.

As in the previous two centuries, so in the later ninth century it is difficult to establish the degree of involvement in these places of royal, rather than Church, control and interest. Nearly all can be shown to have developed from a nucleus, if not within the town, then very near by. The ownership of the Northampton 'palace' is not known, and might have been a property of the church of St Peter adjacent to it. Gloucester's revival could owe as much to the interest of its St Peter's church as to its extra-mural palace, Oxford to its St Frideswide's rather than to the royal palace of Headington outside its defences. Towns that were the centres of bishops' sees were particularly likely to be a focus of Church interest. The charter given to the bishop of Worcester by the governors of Mercia, allowing him rights that included a market, shows clearly the interest of at least one churchman in the trading possibilities of his

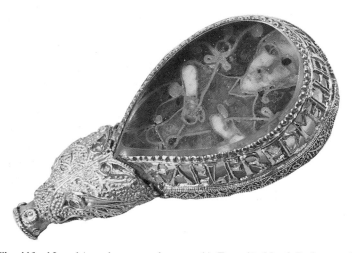

4, 6. The Alfred Jewel (see also cover photograph). Found in North Petherton, Somerset, in 1693, this gold, rock crystal and enamel object has been associated since its discovery with King Alfred the Great of Wessex (871-99) because of its inscription *Aelfred mec heht gewyrcan* - 'Alfred ordered me to be made' - although the royal title is not used. Various suggestions have been made about the identification of the enamelled figure: Christ personifying wisdom is one attractive possibility. The beast's head at the end holds a short nozzle, in which a gold rivet possibly held in place a wooden or ivory rod for pointing at words in a manuscript. Recent work has shown that the crystal was not new and is probably a reused Roman mount - a precious object which would have been an appropriate gift to someone of the highest status. The shape of the crystal would thus have dictated the shape of the jewel as a whole. (Photograph actual size.)

property. At present, there is very little evidence from excavations in Worcester to clarify the late Saxon period there. At Hereford, the changes to the west of the cathedral may have affected the bishop's rather than the king's property. Winchester's new street pattern may have been the bishop's plan: certainly Bishop Swithun was later credited with the construction in the 850s or 860s of a stone bridge over the River Itchen to take the principal axis road out of the town.[42]

The stress laid upon kingship can certainly be seen in the coinage, for the broad-flan pennies invariably carry a royal name, apart from the few minted at Canterbury for the archbishop. Similar emphasis is hinted at by royal names on objects such as a gold finger-ring from Laverstock, Wiltshire, with *'Aethelwulf Rex'* inscribed on it, and probably the Alfred Jewel, although it does not have a title in its inscription (**4, 6**).[43] Such things were in the gift-giving tradition of the past, but they carried an explicit message and also meant that the king was not weakening his patrimony by giving away grants of land. The defences at the *burhs* are another manifestation of authority, but it should be remembered that not all those sites were in royal ownership in the ninth century: Portchester certainly belonged to the bishop of Winchester. The Church's sense of authority and organisation is typified by the earliest example of an English seal-die, made for Ethilwald, bishop of East Anglia from 845 to 870.[44] The rôle of the written word in administration was growing.

The ninth century can be described as one of disruption and new impetus. The extent to which the Vikings were responsible for all the many changes can be exaggerated, but equally they should not be underwritten. York's growth as a commercial centre does seem to have been more rapid than that achieved by London or Winchester, and trade contacts that stretched as far as China put northern and eastern England into a global network. Furthermore, the disintegration of the great churches, particularly in the Danelaw, led to changes in the landowning structure which gave the laity renewed ability to accrue wealth and power. The new towns would also have provided opportunities for the ambitious amongst their tenants' children who could not see their way to obtaining land of their own. The peopling of these places suggests mobility, and already some surplus population to be absorbed; there is no evidence that Viking raids had an adverse effect upon overall levels, whatever they did to particular targets. Without documentary evidence, much of the disruption that they caused would be recognised, but not their political impact. Only Wessex survived intact as an English kingdom, but English culture mostly survived elsewhere as well, and the trends toward a political system of royal authority over a manorially-based rural economy, eventually supported by market centres, were maintained.

Chapter Five

THE TENTH CENTURY

Towns and Trade

Insofar as a century can be characterised by its archaeology, the tenth is notable for an increasing quantity of physical evidence of various sorts, not least pottery. Inorganic-(chaff-)tempered wares (though not the distinctive grass-marked Cornish vessels) were finally supplanted by fabrics which survive better in the ground, even though they may not be more serviceable in use. Not all the known pottery-producing centres were new in the tenth century, nor are the locations of more than a few of them known anyway. Nevertheless, despite the limited data-base, distribution maps of kilns, and of the pottery dispatched from them, often show differences between different areas which may be informative about other economic and social differences.

Most is known about production centres in East Anglia, where several have been found either within or immediately outside the enclosed areas of places which other evidence, such as streets and houses, shows can be termed towns in the tenth century. Whether production at Ipswich, where potters had been using 'slow' wheels since the seventh century, continued without interruption is not yet clear, but if so, there was not much of a hiatus, since in the Cox Lane area there was production both of the earlier 'Ipswich ware' and the later, fast-wheel made 'Thetford-type Ipswich ware'. This cumbersome terminology is used because pottery made in Ipswich was very similar to the products of kilns that have been excavated in Thetford, Norfolk (**5, 1**). Where the new technology was first introduced is not known, but it was rapidly adopted, as the thrown pots show that the potters made little attempt to retain the earlier Ipswich-ware forms. Furthermore, the two products are not often found in the same contexts, suggesting that if ever they were in contemporaneous use, it was not for long.[1]

The fast wheel may have been brought to England by migrant potters, not by English potters who had seen its use abroad, or who had been told about it. Certainly a migrant potter is most likely to have been responsible for the light-coloured, red-painted and glazed pottery being produced at Stamford. These vessels are of high quality, much thinner and seemingly more attractive than the unglazed, thicker, Ipswich/Thetford wares. Red painting, using an iron solution, was practised in Germany, but the decoration at Stamford is most like that produced in northern France at Beauvais, and a potter may well

5, 1. A pottery kiln at Thetford, Norfolk, excavated in the 1950s. The ranging-rod spans the flue through which flames from the stoke-pit were drawn into the kiln; behind the ranging-rod can be seen the floor on which the pots were stacked during the firing. The floor was pierced with vent-holes to let the hot air through. The sides and top of the kiln are missing.

have come to Stamford from there.[2] The kiln complex is in the area of Stamford in which there is the possibility of a ninth-century ditched enclosure, perhaps the original focal point of the town. If so, the location of pottery-making within it around the turn of the ninth and tenth centuries is a remarkable example of a craft manufactory attaching itself to a market centre as it began to evolve from what may originally have been a Viking army base. At any rate, Stamford made rapid progress during the tenth century, as did pottery production within it, for although the red-painted wares soon ceased to be made, other kilns were turning out quantities of lead-glazed wares for the next 300 years.[3]

The Stamford pottery industry's history is very different from that of other centres. Red-painting was not adopted anywhere else, and glazing only spasmodically. Ipswich, Thetford and other kiln centres produced only unglazed wares, though with much the same range of bowls, spouted pitchers, cooking-pots, storage vessels and other household equipment. This cannot have been through ignorance of glazing's existence, as Stamford wares have been found at Thetford and other known kiln sites, as well as at many places where potting is suspected but not proven: and imported Islamic sherds found at Lincoln show that knowledge of glazing was available from other sources.[4] Indeed, there is evidence of lead glaze on some locally-made sherds at Lincoln which suggests that potters were experimenting in its production. Yet even in the eleventh century, glazing was only practised at a few places, and most of those a long way from Stamford. It is as though Stamford established itself quickly – although its earliest products do not seem to have reached Thetford – and its quality kept out competition within the area over which it could be transported without unacceptable risk of breakage, perhaps fifty miles overland, as far as Oxford or Worcester, and further by river and coast (**6, 4**). A high-quality clay may have helped: the use of Stamford-ware crucibles and lamps even in Thetford suggests that the clays may have had particular refractory, heat-resisting qualities. Nor should the cost involved in glazing be underestimated, for it has been reckoned that a kiln load of 200 pots would have required forty-four pounds of lead. Tinkers' scraps would not have been enough to supply this sort of quantity on a regular basis, and lead must have been brought to Stamford in bulk, presumably from Derby-shire – it is unlikely to be coincidence that considerable amounts of Stamford ware have been found in Derby. It is not easy to envisage some form of gift-exchange servicing the Stamford kilns: if the archbishop of Canterbury managed to retain possession of the Wirksworth mines purchased in 835, no reciprocal gift to him from the potters would account for the regular consign-ments they needed. There must have been commercial arrangements of some complexity, perhaps arranged by a kiln-owner employing potters, rather than by the producers themselves.

The list of other known kiln sites of the tenth century where wheel-thrown, mostly sandy wares were being made is almost a litany of the towns of the northern and central Midlands: Nottingham, Thetford, Norwich, Ipswich, Northampton, Lincoln, Torksey. Wasters of limestone-tempered and hand-made pottery and fired daub as though from a kiln dome have been found at Gloucester, and there are wasters from Stafford. Otherwise, production in or very close to York and others is suspected but not proven. None of the pro-ducts of these kilns had such a wide distribution as Stamford ware, though many are found thirty miles from their production centres, and Stafford types have been found as far apart as Chester and Hereford. Large Thetford-ware storage jars are found over a wider area than their Stamford equivalents, perhaps because they were used to transport East Anglian grain or flour.

The conclusion to be drawn from all this seems to be that pottery produc-tion can be expected to be a concomitant of places developing as markets, where at least small numbers of permanent inhabitants were not engaged full-time in agriculture, but were involved in trades such as pot-making and selling. Because of the investment that was necessary, there might already have been small-scale employers of labour. Further south in England, however, the evidence is generally different: in particular there is no trace of pot-making within the walls of London, where in the tenth century a rather thick but wheel-thrown shelly ware was almost exclusively being used.[5] There is limestone or chalk in this pottery, so it could not have been made any closer to London than Greenwich. Probably it came from as far away as the Oxford area, presumably using the Thames as the main carrier.[6] Surprisingly, tenth-century London seems not to have received pottery from Ipswich or the other east coast ports, nor from the Continent. Although the city's trade in pottery cannot be assumed to mirror its trade in any other product, both the distance that vessels were brought, and the direction from which they were coming, is exceptional.

There is a possibility of ceramic production in Canterbury, but the types of tenth-century pottery found in the town are not very different from those of the ninth.[7] Wasters and daub have been found in a pit in Chichester, but clamp kilns nearby are dated by archaeomagnetic techniques to the mid-eleventh century. The pottery was wheel-made. These fairly recent finds may disprove earlier suggestions that both wheel-thrown and hand-formed pottery were being produced in the town in the tenth century.[8] No other southern towns have yet produced tenth-century evidence of production within them or very close by, but glazed pottery was available in Winchester by about the middle of the century, and the absence of it in any quantity elsewhere in Hampshire suggests that it was being made near the town.[9] Otherwise, there are some types of pottery that were probably being made at various different places, such as the shelly 'St Neots' types widely found north of the Thames in the south Midlands which can be attributed neither to a single manufactory, nor to manufactories specifically associated with, for instance, Oxford or Bedford. There is another type of pottery for which a fifty-mile wide distribution may be claimed, probably based somewhere in Wiltshire and serving that county and east Somerset.[10] In broad terms, however, it seems that the pot-producing centres from about Suffolk southwards were not located in towns, and that most places, despite the London evidence, were obtaining a variety of different types of pot of indifferent quality made by people whose use of the wheel was intermittent and of glaze non-existent, apart from what was available in Winchester. They are more likely than their urban counterparts to have been part-time and self-employed. If this pattern is valid, there are at least two interconnected explanations of it. One is that the southern part of England had been less disrupted by Viking raids and settlements, and its traditions of pot-production were able to continue much the same as they had before, merely increasing volume of output to meet any increased demand. Further north, either there were fewer producers – Essex, for instance, seems to have used little in the way of pottery – or any existing networks were broken up: the absence of Ipswich vessels from tenth-century London may be evidence of this. Changes would have facilitated the

5, 2. The boat found in the marshes near Graveney, Kent, before lifting and removal to the National Maritime Museum. Most of the keel and lower planks survived: the clinker (overlapping plank) construction is clearly shown. Dendrochronology gives a felling date in the 880s for the timbers.

emergence of new systems of production and supply to integrate with the places which were acquiring enough inhabitants to create a market focus. Unencumbered by traditional modes, pot production could be sited in the new markets, close to the main point of sale.

Distinctive in southern England are Cornish flat-bottomed pots which have handles inside raised lugs on their rims, as though they were meant to hang over a hearth from cords, which the lugs would protect from burning.[11] Similar 'bar-lug' vessels are found in the Low Countries north of the Rhine: were Frisian traders visiting Cornwall for its tin? Lead is another English metal which may have been exploited. Metal travelling in the opposite direction included copper, for recent analysis of some from a Hampshire site, Netherton, has shown the presence in it of antimony, characteristic of the Harz Mountains in central Germany, also a likely source of silver.[12] A hoard of English coins found in the Pass of Roncesvalles could indicate that gold from the Muslim world was coming from Spain,[13] as perhaps was steel for the edges of sword blades and the like.

These things cannot have been carried in very large consignments because of the need to cross the English Channel in boats which could not carry heavy loads. The carrying capacity of any ship depends on how low in the water her sailors are prepared to risk her. Consequently cargo-weight estimates cannot be precise, and would depend also upon the size of the crew, but six or seven tons seems the likely viable maximum for an almost complete boat of the period found in the marshes at Graveney, Kent (5, 2). Dendrochronology on her timbers shows that they were cut in the 880s, and she was probably abandoned after some eighty-five years of use, to judge from the date of the stake to which she was tied. Although best suited for shallow waters such as southern English estuaries, her duties could have included short cross-Channel journeys carrying such things as quern-stones from Mayen, some of which were found with her, as were hops and a single northern French pottery sherd. Cargoes of medium-value goods may be indicated, but it is doubtful if she could have carried more than 300 quern-stones at a time. She had been drawn up onto an artificial timber 'hard' but there was no other evidence of a harbour or of shore facilities.[14] Such landing-places are not easy to locate, and are a reminder that many cargoes of agricultural produce and coastally-produced salt would have been loaded onto boats without going through institutionalised ports.

Nevertheless, many of the places which can be recognised through their archaeology as developing in the tenth century had a port function. At York, the waterfront on the south bank of the River Ouse was laid out with property boundaries, and the number of finds increases, as it does also on the north side of the river in the area between the Ouse, the Fosse and the old Roman fort.[15] The excavations in Coppergate have shown how the area which was beginning to be used in the ninth century was in the early tenth formed into long, narrow tenement strips divided by fence-lines and with buildings at the street frontage (5, 3). A busy community of craft workers became established,

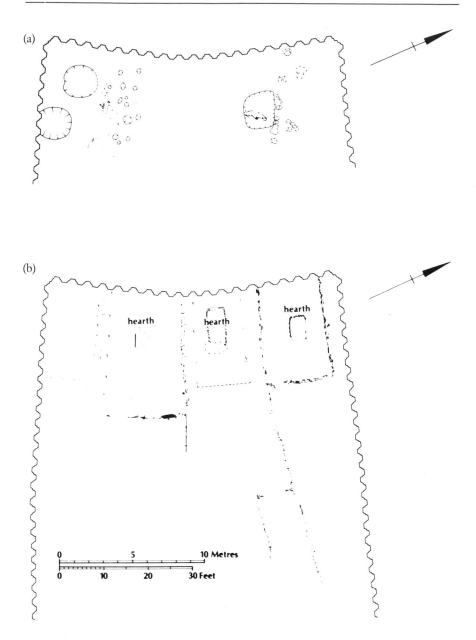

5, 3. Two of the phases at Coppergate, York, excavated by the York Archaeological Trust. In the second half of the ninth century (a), features included a glass-working furnace later abandoned and partly destroyed by a pit in which a male skeleton was found. By about the middle of the tenth century (b), the site had been divided into separate tenements with domestic hearths in each, and post-and-wattle buildings. The boundaries of these tenements were to survive for a thousand years.

as the rubbish from the site's pits indicates. In particular, the discovery of two of the hardened iron dies from which coins were struck, together with six lead 'trial-pieces', from two adjacent tenements has given new insights into the production of coinage; actual minting may not have taken place at Coppergate, which may have been where dies were cut, not necessarily just for use in York. One of the lead trial-pieces is stamped with a Chester moneyer's name. It is possible that the trial-pieces were kept as a record of what dies had been approved and issued.[16]

One of the two York dies is associated with the currency known from the inscriptions on it as the St Peter's coinage. Some Lincoln coins have 'St Martin' with '*Lincolla Civitat*'. These ecclesiastical dedications may imply Church involvement in coin-production, symptomatic of good relations between the ecclesiastical and Norse authorities, which would have helped trade to continue despite political problems. An example is a York-minted coin of the 940s found in Lincoln, even though at that time York was temporarily again under a Norse, not an English, ruler. Not quite so well dated, but more remarkable, have been pieces of silk in both York and Lincoln which can be recognised from a weaving fault in them to have come from the same bale, probably an import from the eastern Mediterranean or the Near East.[17] The merchant dealing in that material was able to trade in both towns.

The man responsible for the Coppergate die-production workshop was probably Ragnald, a moneyer named on many contemporary coins, who worked both for York's Norse kings and then, after 927, for the English king, Athelstan. As he was at times the only known York moneyer, it is likely that he would have been responsible for cutting the dies as well as striking the coins. He probably did not live on the Coppergate site, however, for the wicker-walled buildings and the noisome industrial and other refuse of the tenements would seem inappropriate surroundings for the residence of a man of his status. Was he ultimately responsible for the other crafts being practised at Coppergate, for there is evidence of a range of metal-working, including crucibles, moulds and an unfinished piece of lead jewellery? The raw materials for these would have been expensive and quite probably as much beyond the means of an ordinary craftsman as was the silver used in coins. Textile-working would be another industry likely to come under a financier's control when wool was brought into a town rather than spun and woven in a farmer's household from the fleeces of his own sheep, and dyes for the cloth also had to be acquired – some, such as clubmoss, were imported. Craftsmen in such industries were, like the Stamford potters, likely to be producing a better-quality product and to have more expertise, but as full-time specialists they were dependent upon others for their supply of raw materials and increasingly therefore were also losing control of the sale of their own output, and thus of its profits. Other petty craftsmen, such as the wood-turners and those making bone tools, and perhaps the stone-masons making the sculptures, could retain their independence longer.

Coinage was different from other crafts because of its centralised control, and the moneyers had to be particularly wealthy because of the bullion that they had to stock. Furthermore, theirs was the only craft that was required by law to be practised in particular places. Not only is this apparent from the mint names on many coins – though not all until the 970s – but it is also explicit in such laws as Athelstan's Grateley Decrees, which are probably based on an earlier set of instructions.[18] To some extent, the volume of production and the number of licensed moneyers are likely to be a measure of a place's economic and commercial activity, with output responding to demand; but a mint may also have been a catalyst, bringing people there to acquire coins, and was not necessarily set up to meet an already existing demand. London, for instance, was far and away the largest coin-producer, but archaeology is uncertain about its speed of development as a town in the tenth century.[19] Cellared buildings found at various sites cannot be very precisely dated, and the dendrochronology of a timber and clay embankment with stakes for wooden jetties at Billingsgate gives a construction date in the next century, *c.* 1039–40.

Although trial-pieces have been found in London, evidence about coin production like that from York is known nowhere else. General evidence of urban activity during the first half of the tenth century has come from a number of places, however. At Flaxengate, Lincoln, between the Roman fort and the river, the first road and associated buildings may have been laid out before the end of the ninth century: thereafter the road was maintained, although occasionally encroached upon, and loam layers were periodically spread across the occupation area when new buildings were required. Soon after the middle of the tenth century, if not before, the street frontage became fully occupied, with all but one of the buildings aligned gable-end to the street, where earlier alignments had been parallel to it: more houses were being packed into the space. Loam spreads continued to be dumped across the whole site, implying a single owner renting out the tenements and able to reorganise them as he wished.[20] In Stamford, east of the later castle, the High Street was laid out over an area where residues show that iron-working had been taking place. Although the precise dates of each episode are not clear, the iron-working was on quite a large scale, using a fairly simple technology of roasting hearths to separate ore and slag. There was some glass-making, and pottery-making expanded, with new kiln complexes replacing that in the castle area: the new locations suggest that the potters were being kept at the margins of the town. This seems also to be the case in Thetford, where the known kilns are close to the ditch that surrounds the occupied area south of the river. Within the enclosure, there are metalled roads, buildings and pits with enough in them to indicate considerable activity in the early years of the tenth century. In Norwich also potting is only known on the fringe of the developed areas: here too there is evidence of much-increased activity from early in the tenth century, both on the south side of the River Wensum and within the enclosed area on the north which has yielded eighth-century material.[21] The only kiln in Northampton is difficult to relate to a peripheral area, since it is not yet established where the periphery actually was – early defensive ditches are suggested by street lines rather than proven by discovery. It may be that Northampton had a layout that did not become formalised as early as at York or Lincoln: the buildings seem to be grouped in complexes rather than aligned on street frontages in narrow tenements.[22]

Within the old kingdom of Wessex, Winchester is the only town where urban growth in the first half of the tenth century can be archaeologically demonstrated: the development of extra-mural suburbs is evidence of pressure for space within the walls. The western suburb in particular has produced ninth- and tenth-century pottery and other evidence. Nevertheless, it was not until the end of the tenth century that the Brook Street site within the walls had a built-up street frontage, and there were still open spaces in which the bishop could build himself a palace in the 970s.[23] It may be that the pace of the second half of the ninth century slackened off for a time in the tenth. In Chichester many pits have been excavated with pottery attributable to the tenth century and there is evidence of building, but not necessarily from an early part of the century. Canterbury also has pits and cellared buildings of the tenth century, although certainly not everywhere within the walls, and the extra-mural area near the abbey in use in the ninth century was thereafter used for agriculture until the twelfth. Elsewhere in the south, evidence of large-scale development in the tenth century is elusive, even at the larger new 'burhs' like Wareham or Wallingford. Exeter has a little pottery to show for the tenth century. The Itchen-side area at Southampton did not regenerate, and a Test-side replacement seems to have grown only slowly even though there is the evidence there of a ditched enclosure.[24] Wessex was not developing urban centres at the same pace as the eastern side of England, despite the stimulus that might have been derived from minting of coins in many of the places that appeared in the *Burghal Hidage* list.

The western part of what had been Mercia seems to have had a more mixed tenth-century urban history. At Hereford, one site has produced ditches and gullies tentatively ascribed to property boundaries, but other structural evidence is lacking, and well into the tenth century the quantity of pottery found there is small.[25] In the centre of Gloucester the byres and stables of the ninth century were cleared away, and at least one building with a cellar was constructed, possibly associated with replanning of the streets inside the walls. The pottery-making evidence is tenth-century, and two parts of treadle looms have been found, showing that cloth was being woven using more complex technology than that of upright looms (**5, 4**).[26] It may well be, therefore, that Gloucester was developing as a craft-specialist centre quite early in the tenth century, for this type of loom is not readily dismantled, requires permanent housing in a wide space and demands skilled workers for its effective operation. Minting of coins was another Gloucester craft, but is only known from discoveries of the name-stamped coins in places other than the town itself. This evidence coincides with documentary evidence of royal interest in Gloucester. Worcester, however, has not produced any substantial archaeological remains concomitant with the late ninth-century charter that refers to its market, although what little pottery has been recovered comes from a wide range of sources – Stamford, Northampton, Gloucester and the Thames valley.[27] The restricted, river-surrounded location of Shrewsbury has created pressure for useable space within it, causing terracing later in the Middle Ages that may have destroyed early evidence. Stafford has so far produced quantities of pottery, but not much else. None of these places is yet able to match Oxford, where street surfaces have been observed at various sites, with a coin and pottery stratified within their lowest layers which allow an early tenth-century date for their organisation to be suggested.[28]

Discussion of all these places shows that archaeology is beginning to be able to claim that not only did different towns differ in their course of development, but that there is a real difference between one area and another. Relatively rapid growth by and large characterises the eastern side of England, north of London. A political explanation is the obvious one, for this is also the area of the eastern Danelaw. The 'five boroughs', such as Stamford, are usually taken to be the centres from which Viking armies were organised, because that is what the sources imply. There are no such sources for East Anglia, but it is not a long step to associate Norwich, Thetford and others with Viking leaders such as Guthrum. This does not seem entirely adequate, however: a place needs to be more than an army camp or an administrative centre to develop the large-scale, long-term potting facilities that were established, and the tenth-century evidence can be used to argue that these places had some rôle as trading-stations already by the late ninth, particulary since most of them are on navigable rivers. They are, however, mostly well inland, suggesting that overseas commerce was a secondary consideration, and that a wide hinterland to exploit was more important. The speed of growth suggests a mobile population, perhaps forcibly settled from that hinterland, but equally likely indicative of people untrammelled by old ties as Viking disruption brought new landowners temporarily less able or less

---

5, 4. Three different types of loom, drawn by S. E. James. A is based on a vertical loom photographed in use in Norway within the last fifty years; the clay weights are of the sort found on many early medieval settlement sites, often associated with sunken-featured buildings - one possibility is that the weaver stood on planks spanning the 'cellar' and that the weights dangled into the void, making it easier for the weaver to reach the top beam. B is redrawn from a manuscript and shows ladies at a beam-tensioned vertical loom, which would leave little direct archaeological record. (Although painted in Canterbury in the twelfth century, this picture copies one in a ninth-century continental book and therefore cannot be used as evidence that this type of loom could have been seen in the Norman city.) Two of the ladies hold cutting shears, the third seems to have a comb in her right hand, and the fourth holds one end of the skein of wool. C is redrawn from a thirteenth-century manuscript and shows a horizontal-tensioned loom with foot-operated treadles. Longer lengths of cloth could be produced and male weavers had taken over the craft.

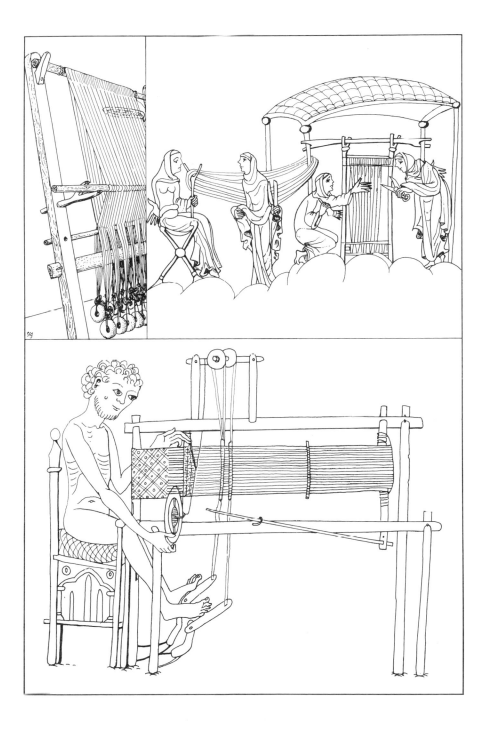

concerned to retain their tenants. So the Thetfords and the Stamfords may be a consequence of political upheaval, but as much an upheaval that caused changes in social patterns as one that led to deliberate colonisation. There is even less evidence in them of a Scandinavian population element than there is in York.

Not every place which was important in the ninth century, perhaps as a religious centre, became a tenth-century town. Repton, for instance, faded into obscurity, despite having had a church, important burials and a defensive enclosure. Nor did all the places such as Witham, Maldon or Towcester mentioned in the *Anglo-Saxon Chronicle* as being fortified centres during the advance of the Wessex-based royal dynasty into the Danelaw in the first half of the tenth century inexorably develop into towns. It is also difficult to link episodes in the *Chronicle* to archaeological phases. At Chester, for instance, there are timber buildings with cellars which may relate to street frontages being developed outside the Roman walls. In the absence even of pottery to provide dating, is it permissible to associate these structures with the year 907, when it is recorded that Chester was 'restored' by the English Aethelflaed? Later on, there is pottery evidence which suggests the abandonment of the same area during the second half of the tenth century – should this be linked to the Viking raids in the 980s which are usually blamed for the decline in activity at Chester's mints at that time? Chester's tenth-century history was heavily influenced by political factors; its proximity to north Wales may have meant that silver paid to English kings as tributes by the Welsh was minted there, creating a mint output which might otherwise be taken to imply a greater level of commercial activity than actually occurred. Four tenth-century coin hoards, one also with several ingots, show that there was no shortage of silver there. Chester was a focal point in the earlier part of the century for interaction between the Vikings in Dublin and York, and the attempts by Norse kings to create an empire.[29]

The politics of empire may well be responsible for the huge hoard of over 7,000 coins and 1,000 silver arm-rings, ingots and broken-up fragments (**5, 5**) deposited at Cuerdale, Lancashire in *c.* 905, which may represent the supply thought necessary to pay an army which was attempting to regain Dublin for the Norse after their temporary expulsion.[30] It was this period which saw Norse settlement in the north, although the evidence of it comes from place-names and words rather than archaeology, apart possibly from sculpture. The 'hog-back' stones, perhaps grave-covers, are grouped predominantly in areas in which Norse place-names are found, and may be a taste developed by people living there in the tenth and eleventh centuries. But they are not a Norse style of monument: not only are they unknown in Norway, but they are also unknown in other areas of Norse settlement, even on the Isle of Man despite its proximity to Cumberland and north Lancashire. Sculpture may also show the effect of the Norse links with Ireland through the use in the north of England of designs that seem to be Irish in origin: the ring-heads on crosses like that at Middleton are best explained in this way.[31]

Whatever their racial origin, the people who came into the new urban centres had to be supplied. Food requirements would have been a major catalyst for market development, with regular bulk consignments having to be available for everyday purchasing in places where little was stored. The Gloucester evidence is of decrease in stabling, and there are few indications of animals being reared within towns: bone evidence from Lincoln shows that a breeding stock was not maintained there, for the animals being eaten were nearly all fully-grown, not young stock periodically culled. Cattle, which probably account for three-quarters of the meat consumed, were mostly cows, so the bulls were being kept at a safe distance from Lincoln! The bones show evidence that the cattle had been used as draught animals, presumably for ploughing and hauling carts, but as they were slaughtered before they had reached a great age, they were probably not kept primarily for dairying. They were slightly smaller on average than those at the earlier Saxon site at South-ampton, but were nevertheless reasonably robust and well developed. Similarly the sheep were mostly at least three years old when killed, but not actually very aged: although still useful for wool or milk, their meat value caused their slaughter in their prime. Pigs were also usually allowed to grow to full size before being turned into pork. Fairly similar results, from evidence spread over a longer time period, have been obtained from Bedford. It is clear that the animals were drawn from well-established herds of reasonable quality,

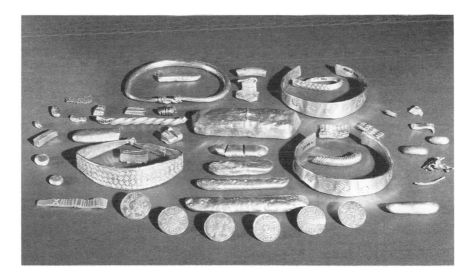

5, 5. Part of the hoard of silver coins, ingots, rings and fragments found at Cuerdale, Lancashire, in 1840. Less than a tenth of the original items now survives. Deposited *c.* 905, it may have been gathered in York and been in transit to pay for a Viking raid on Dublin. The deep gashes across one ingot show that it had been tested to see if it was solid metal, not just a base-metal lump gilded with silver. About half the coins are Anglo Saxon, the rest mostly Frankish and Italian, probably acquired as loot during Viking raids in the 890s.

which argues for a very adequate agricultural hinterland around these places, able to support them without distortion of existing breeding patterns. If there were diseased animals, they were at any rate not getting into the towns. Actual numbers of animals are no more known than the human population, but the Lincoln estimates based on the later Domesday figures are instructive. If the town then had some 4,000 people in it, each consuming an average of twenty-five kilogrammes of meat annually (a figure based on modern consumption levels in non-European societies), 500 cattle, 700 sheep and 400 pigs would have been slaughtered per year. Since to cull 700 sheep requires a flock of some 5,000, and each animal needs between one and two acres to graze, very large acreages become necessary just for the stock, let alone the ploughland.[32]

Unfortunately, there is less archaeological evidence from tenth-century rural sites to set against that increasingly available from towns,[33] and to throw more light on the scale of organisation that was sending them its products. Most pottery dating has to be within very wide time limits, because few sites produce the quantities needed to establish a valid sequence. From evidence obtained at a few places, however, it is at least possible to postulate that considerable changes were being made in the organisation of the countryside, although whether they continued already existing trends is difficult to see. A good example is Walton, where there is sufficient pottery to show substantial occupation, with the strong possibility that the main village street was established, for gullies to mark property divisions were aligned to it. This late Saxon material overlies a mid Saxon site, but there seems to have been an interlude of at least a century between the two phases.[34] What happened in the interim? Had the area generally been abandoned, or just the particular part excavated? Was the renewed occupation part of a complete refoundation, or of a long drawn-out process of expansion from a central core? It is very difficult to answer such questions without excavation of large areas, such as is now taking place in Raunds, which is demonstrating different uses at different times of quite small areas within the present-day settlement.[35] Field-walking is another source of information, but leaves open the question of whether the recovery of late Saxon sherds in increasing quantities is symptomatic of increased populations, or merely of increased availability of pottery.

One major reason for thinking that village sites were being established as nucleated centres is the increase in the number of known rural churches. This is, of course, not an absolute guide, for many churches never had villages round them, but served scattered, isolated farms and hamlets spread over a wide parish. Nevertheless a church could be a focus around which a village might be deliberately planted, or might slowly develop. Many existing churches have demonstrably Anglo-Saxon styles of work surviving within them to show that their origin is at least eleventh-century: these relatively minor churches are often difficult to attribute to a particular hundred-year period. What excavations at many have shown is that below them there may survive the vestiges of an earlier, often timber-built, structure, presumably

the original church building regarded as too small-scale for later requirements. This is not invariable, and sometimes post-holes may relate to
scaffolding erected for the construction of the stone church. But even where
no traces of timber have been found, it need not mean that none existed, for
they are very easily lost to later burials and burial-vaults.

One of the best sequences has been obtained at Raunds. Here, probably by
the end of the ninth century, a small rectangular timber building had been
constructed ouside the existing enclosure: because the next use of this part of
the site was for burials and a building that is clearly a church with nave and
chancel, it is reasonable to interpret the first building as a 'field-chapel', used
for services but not yet licensed for burial. The second building was itself replaced by a slightly larger church after about a hundred years, which also only
lasted about a century and was then destroyed so that the site could be used
by a secular manor house. This last stage was unexpected, for it is usually
assumed that, once established, a church tends to become a fixed point for as
long as there are people wanting to use it. The Raunds sequence means that
even a church cannot be taken as an unchanging node within a village. It also
indicates the association between landowner and church, for the first chapel
was next to what seem to have been high-status buildings, and it was clearly
the manorial owner who was later to build over the site without respecting the
graveyard. Although such an act could have been done with communal agreement, it seems unlikely that local feelings would not have been against it.
There is plenty of documentary evidence for 'proprietary churches', so the
association with a manor house and its curtilage at Raunds is unsurprising,
and indeed is still visible in very many villages and hamlets today. In some
ways more interesting is that it does not appear that the site was used for
burials before a church was built, and that a building that could have been a
chapel pre-dates the cemetery. Since burial was one of the fees charged by
the church, a graveyard was a source of revenue, and it may be that when the
Raunds owner won burial-rights for his church, he was thereafter able to di-
vert part of the fees for the interment of his tenants into his own pocket, reducing the income of the church which had previously had sole burial-rights
in the area. Occasionally records exist to show the original superiority and
greater authority of the earlier church in this kind of situation. The larger size
of many late Saxon churches compared to the 'proprietary' churches is often
a clue to their early status as 'minsters'. It may just be the result of inadequate
investigation, but there seems to be slightly more evidence of ninth- or tenth-
century small cemeteries and churches to the north of the Thames than to the
south, and it certainly seems easier to reconstruct the territories of the
'minsters' in the south. The older, well-established southern churches were
probably able to prevent the loss of income represented by the building of
'proprietary' churches for perhaps a century or so after the changes in land-
ownership further north had made more difficult the resistance of those
ecclesiastical establishments that had survived.[36]

It was not only in the countryside that small parish churches were being built in the tenth century, for they are a feature also of towns, both north and south of the Thames. One of the first to be investigated was in Thetford, where foundation trenches and post-holes indicate a timber-built nave and chancel, the two elements divided from each other by a substantial screen. It was replaced after about a hundred years by a slightly bigger church using stone foundations.[37] The original nave was only seven metres long, an indication of the small size of the congregation that it was to serve. Urban parish churches were often built very close to each other, so they can only have had a limited catchment area. Like their rural counterparts, they can be regarded as speculative ventures by property-owners, since many entries in Domesday Book indicate privately-held urban churches, sometimes divided between two or three owners. One apparent example is St Mary, in the Brooks, Winchester; since its nave reused the ninth-century stone building interpreted as part of an aristocratic enclave, its conversion to a church seems to indicate private ownership.[38] A door in its south wall giving access to an adjoining tenement could have been to give the owner private entry, but that property does not seem to have had high-status domestic use, and the extra door cannot be used as positive evidence of proprietorship. There could be another factor influencing the choice of site, for the church is also adjacent to the small, seventh-century burial-ground whose inhabitants, from their accompanying grave-goods, were certainly high-status. It might therefore be that it was religious associations surviving from that earlier phase of use which led to the establishment of St Mary's, rather than merely expedient reuse by the owner of some of his existing property. Such instances may be unusual, and there seems no reason other than sensible exploitation of a street corner location to account for the position of St Pancras, another Brooks church, founded in the tenth century, only a few yards from St Mary's. Similarly, many churches were built near gates in a town's walls, or were even part of a gate's structure. A very different reason behind the choice of a particular site may be St Helen-on-the-Walls, York, with its mosaic head, perhaps to be associated with a cult of the Emperor Constantine's mother.[39]

Whereas many of the new rural churches won burial-rights for themselves, many of the urban churches did not. The difference may indicate the land-value factor, for a graveyard in a town would represent a space lost for building and renting. But here there is a difference between the north and south, for small churches in towns like Lincoln were more likely to have a graveyard than those in towns in the south, as though the greater churches in the latter were able to hold on to their rights. The same may well be true of baptismal rights, but the existence of a font can be very hard to locate. Whether owners chose to be buried in their own churches, or to be taken to some more ancient and venerable institution more worthy of their status, is another practice that may have varied in different areas. The cross-shafts, tomb-slabs and memorials in many northern churches, even in a small urban church like the recently excavated St Mark's, Lincoln,[40] are an indication that the rich people who could afford such markers elected to be buried amongst their fellow-citizens, perhaps even their tenants. An elaborate stone grave-cover over a burial given a prominent position separated from other adults at Raunds indicates the same thing there.[41]

The Church shows another geographical division in the tenth century, the second half of which saw a major reform movement associated with Benedictine monasticism. This affected many existing churches and led to others being built, but few of the reformed houses were to the north of the central Midlands. Much patronage was extended to the new foundations and patrons, and probably others, sought to be buried at the most prestigious centres. Consequently, elaborate grave-markers have been excavated at the Old Minster at Winchester, and the few such things known elsewhere in the south of England tend to be at major churches – if not great cathedrals and abbeys, then at least older 'minsters'. North of the Wash, landowners did not seek total separation from those of lower status as aristocracies usually tend to do, but were perhaps still using distinctively-marked burials as an assertion of their hold on newly-acquired estates because they did not yet feel secure in their possession of them.

The extent to which the Reform movement led to physical restructuring of the churches at which Benedictinism was introduced is difficult to estimate because so many of the most important have been totally destroyed. Although the ramifications of the Old Minster at Winchester have been revealed by excavation of its ground plan, showing how a complexity of chapelry was added, especially at the west end so that king and bishop could preside in splendour at services, the building could not match in width at least the New Minster, an aisled building established early in the tenth century. Nearby, recent work has shown something of its contemporary, the Nunnaminster, which was less than ten metres wide, but had substantial western apses: it was replaced, perhaps during the Reform period, by a church of much the same width but with thicker walls, implying support for an elaborate superstructure.[42]

Elsewhere, the regular order of Benedictine life may be mirrored by the rectangular or square cloister attributed to Dunstan at Glastonbury, but this is far from being a complete plan. Another very important building has been found, partly still standing, at Gloucester where the core of St Oswald's Priory surely cannot be anything but the late ninth-century foundation of Aethelflaed of Mercia.[43] At the east end of the original church, a separate, square building with a crypt was added early in the tenth century. The later tenth may have been when the chancel was rebuilt and the crypt building joined to the rest of the church (5, 6), but it is not possible to associate this with the Reform. Because so much is known about this movement from documents, it is tempting to ascribe to it buildings and rebuildings which are perhaps really only symptomatic of the constant process of change necessitated as much by need of restoration as by liturgical change. Nevertheless, knowledge of services and prayers helps understanding of church design: the *Regularis Concordia*, which laid down the rules for the Order, shows that altars were needed along the central axis-line of a church, and thus helps to explain

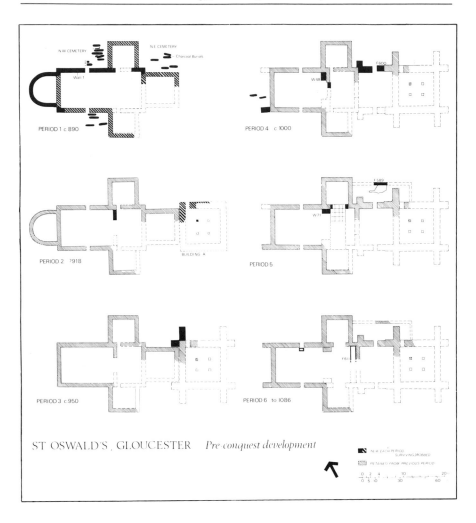

ST OSWALD'S, GLOUCESTER *Pre-conquest development*

structures like Deerhurst, Gloucestershire, with rooms over the west doors
for one of the altars; another would have been at the east end of the nave and
a third in the sanctuary or chancel.[44] Similarly, the Maundy Thursday service
required responses to be sung across the choir or crossing, and provides an
explanation of the side porticuses which Deerhurst and many other churches
have. Bells had to be rung, accounting for a proliferation of bell towers –
Deerhurst had its porch raised, probably for this purpose. Careful excavation
can reveal other features: details of the wear pattern on the floor of St Mary,
Winchester, indicate that the priest took services while standing in the
sanctuary, coming forward to face the congregation across the altar at the east
end of the nave when he raised the Host during the Mass. It has been
suggested that this is one of the ways in which the rôle of a priest can be interpreted as having been more closely integrated with his congregation than later
in the Middle Ages, when the altar was against the east wall in the sanctuary
so that when the Host was raised, the priest had his back to the congregation,
who could see little of what was going on. In such ways the immediacy of contact between priest and people was lost.

The Reform movement introduced Benedictine rules of work to the inmates of its houses, and many of the finest English decorated manuscripts are
a product of their labours. The *Benedictional of St Ethelwold*, for example, is a
book of blessings, written on expensive vellum and painted in gold leaf and
costly colours for Bishop Ethelwold of Winchester, its creation an act of worship to turn God's treasures into God's word, as well as to flatter the bishop's
ego. Although the Reform movement promoted the writing and embellishing
of books, there are decorated manuscripts of the first half of the tenth century
also, so that it is an enhancement of output that is recognisable. The same is
true of other ecclesiastical treasures, some surviving in church treasuries,
others having been recovered during excavation. A purse-reliquary of the
later ninth or early tenth century, found in a rubbish pit outside Winchester
in 1976, and perhaps made in the town, can be compared with continental
styles, and its function demonstrates the importance of cults of relics. It is
made of gilded copper alloy, not pure gold, and this has been used to call in
question whether the numerous contemporary descriptions of precious metal
altars and other treasures in tenth- and eleventh-century English churches
are not an exaggeration of their real worth. Cast copper-alloy cruets and
censers, well made but not intrinsically valuable, are further instances from

---

5, 6. St Oswald's Church, Gloucester. The phase plans by C. M. Heighway show its
structural development from a late ninth-century structure with western apse, north and
south porticuses and square east end. Probably to accommodate the shrine of St Oswald,
a square building was added and later incorporated into the rest of the church. The model,
by R. Bryant, shows how it may have appeared in the second phase: the west apse is on the
right. The stones outlined on the wall survive in the ruins of St Oswald's today.

the tenth century. It is probable that what survives is representative of the norm, not the exceptional, as with most archaeological artefacts, and that the purse-reliquary and other things are what would be found in many, perhaps parish, churches while the greatest treasures of cathedrals and abbeys were the ones that attracted comment. Exceptional in the way that they have survived are the vestments of coloured silks and gold thread embroidered, ccording to their inscriptions, for Frithestan, Bishop of Winchester from 909 to 931, on the orders of a lady named Aelfflaed, probably to be identified as Edward the Elder's queen. After Frithestan's death they seem to have been taken as an offering to the shrine of St Cuthbert by King Athelstan: owned by a bishop, probably donated to him by a queen and thought worthy of royal presentation at England's premier shrine, they must represent the reality of the finest textiles, splendid in quality and costly in material. They suggest that texts do not exaggerate too wildly in their descriptions, and that what is recovered from the ground is normally a lower stratum of craftsmanship and cost.[45]

This is true also of private treasures, and it is always difficult to know the extent to which discoveries of gold and silver rings and brooches, swords and knives, are representative of what existed. The tenth century was not a particularly peaceful one except in its third quarter, but rather fewer hoards were deposited during it than in the ninth: consequently less is available to demonstrate private wealth. Chance finds from random loss of notable objects are many fewer, however, and there does seem to be a real decline in the quantity of highly-decorated personalia that was worn: there are no finger-rings inscribed with a king's name, no swords with silver and gold plates. There are gold and silver arm-rings, referred to in wills, which are probably represented by the twisted rods and wires of various diameters that are known from hoards of both the tenth and the eleventh centuries, so the metals were available. These rings are like bullion stores carried on the person, rather than the filigree and niello-enhanced decorations of earlier centuries. This change suggests that the wealthy found it less important to express their status in display of objects admirable in workmanship and design, redolent of the gift-giving tradition that cemented earlier societies. Social evolution diminished the rôle of such ties.

At the same time, and over the eleventh century as well, there is evidence of increased numbers of base metal brooches. This is partly because of the towns: York, for instance, has produced many copper-alloy rings and brooches, and also some of pewter, indicative perhaps of increased availability of and demand for tin and lead. It is possible to see in these things the growth of a broad-based consumers' market. Another type of object to consider in this context is the strap-end of cast copper alloy, tongue-shaped in the Carolingian fashion, and often of very high quality casting, but not all of these may have been for personal use: some could, for instance, have come from the straps on book-covers in church libraries. Certainly personal, however, are translucent enamel brooches, only recognised recently but clearly available in some number from the later tenth century, suggesting a taste for bright things, although the best of this effect is soon lost because the copper base tarnishes unless gilded, and ceases to reflect the light. Although most have a cross design, some have what seems to be symbol intended to ward off the 'evil eye': if so, they are 'apotropaic' in the same way as much later medieval jewellery.[46]

One explanation of the changing use of precious metals in jewellery could be that it was dictated by their availability, not by fashion or social evolution. The large quantities of English silver coins found in Swedish and Danish hoards of the late tenth and early eleventh centuries show that there was enough bullion coming into England to feed the mints, so that it is unlikely to have been in short supply except for temporary interludes. The degree to which coins circulated, as opposed to being used to pay taxes or to keep in hoards, is difficult to measure as there are not very many stray finds. Nevertheless, the larger urban excavations have produced enough to show that coins were available in towns, even though some have been surprisingly unfruitful: Bedford, for instance, has yielded no pre-thirteenth-century coins at all.[47] Away from the towns, the evidence does not at present seem to suggest any greater usage than in the ninth century. Coins in hoards always come from a number of different mints, which is evidence that coins were acceptable no matter at which English centre they had been minted. Hoards were usually assembled by merchants travelling from place to place: such commercial interaction led to rapid intermingling of coins from different mints, a pattern also reflected by stray losses in towns. Rural losses give a slightly different picture, as coins on rural sites are rather more likely to come from a local mint than from one further away, even if the nearest was not one of the biggest mints. A silver penny found at Mawgan Porth, the north Cornish coastal site, is a good example, for it was struck at Lydford, Devon, between 990 and 995.[48] People went to their nearest mint to collect their new coins and took some of them back to their villages.

Mawgan Porth is one of the relatively few excavated sites which seems to be a rural settlement of no particular consequence in the tenth century. A little more is known of higher-status rural sites, though recognition of their precise role in the hierarchy can be difficult. It is instructive to look at Portchester in this context, for the comparison that can be made between its archaeology and the written statements about it. It was listed in the *Burghal Hidage*, and was bought by King Edward the Elder in 904 from the bishop of Winchester. It was never a mint, however, and was not listed as a 'borough' in Domesday Book; by 1066, all but a small part of the estate of Portchester, probably including the old Roman fort, had passed out of royal ownership. The excavated buildings datable to the tenth century include an aisled struc-ture, indicative of a fairly well-to-do owner, and subsequent development suggests that Portchester was indeed the residence of a substantial lord. Yet the sheer volume of finds, such as the pottery and bones, indicates that there were more people than the lord's immediate household living there, and at least one minor craft, bone-working, was being practised. The evidence is of an estate centre of some complexity and scale, but it is not possible to say from the archaeological evidence when it left royal ownership and became a thegn's property.[49]

The best-studied estate centre that can certainly be assumed to have been a royal one, in the tenth century if not in the ninth, is Cheddar, where the original bow-sided hall was replaced during the middle part of the tenth century by a shorter but much wider rectangular timber building, the posts of which survived for about fifty years before being replaced by another building of similar size. Other structures included a rectangular one built on unmortared stone foundations, recognisable as a chapel mainly because it underlay what were certainly chapels in later periods: there were, for instance, no burials in it, and nothing that can be seen as a font-base. Debris from around it suggest that its superstructure was stone with timber reinforcements, stuccoed and painted to look like freestone masonry: some stones from it were drilled, probably to hold pliable rods to be used in a basket framework for creating round-headed, or even circular, windows from stucco and plaster. Also probably in use at this time was a curious structure interpreted as a fowl-house, and other ancillary buildings.[50] The whole complex suggests a substantial hall in which the king could entertain, a private chapel for his devotions, and an associated complex in which farm stock was kept. There is also continued evidence of various craft activities from the rubbish pits and other contexts. Bits of bowl furnaces and iron ores attest smelting, and unfinished tools being worked up by smiths. There are crucible fragments and residues from gold, silver, enamel and copper-alloy working, moulds, and a cast blank apparently waiting to be turned into a strap-end. Much of this came from near the chapel, so there was a focal area for metal crafts there.

Another site with known ownership is North Elmham, centre of a bishop's see until its transfer, first to Thetford and then to Norwich, after the Norman Conquest. The area of what may have been the bishop's palace, in the late ninth and tenth centuries, which overlies mid Saxon buildings and wells, contained a timber structure large enough at eighteen by seven metres to be regarded as a 'hall', with other buildings including latrines grouped irregularly around a courtyard. There is no evidence from this site of craft-working.[51]

Some residential sites with halls have not been investigated on a large enough scale for all their functions to be clear. Waltham, the estate in Hampshire which King Edward exchanged for Portchester, has for instance produced a building perhaps to be identified as a hall of the early eleventh century, but there is no indication of any production activity linked to it. Goltho, however, whose pre-Conquest owners are unknown, still probably had weaving sheds (6, 1). Another Hampshire site of this kind, Netherton, had a complex of timber buildings probably at one time owned by a rich lady named Wynflaed whose will survives. Associated with it is evidence of metalworking in gold, silver and copper alloy that implies regular if intermittent production. Itinerant jewellers might be responsible, but if so it is difficult to

coins recorded in the rest of the county, as in the Goltho excavations. In the town itself, the coins are not just from the Lincoln mint, but from York, Hereford, Stamford, Hertford and, after the Conquest, London, Thetford, Wallingford and Exeter. There are also two Scandinavian coins.[31] This is much more eclectic than York, in which eleventh-century coins only of York itself and of London and Exeter are recorded before the Conquest, with only Derby and Huntingdon added to the list in William's reign.[32]

The Lincoln and York coins are not inconsistent in that they show the former looking less towards the north of England and increasingly to the south for its trading contacts, although still to Denmark and the Baltic for its overseas trade. York was becoming more isolated: any rôle as overland entrepôt between Ireland and Scandinavia was reduced not only by the English kings' conquests in the tenth century, but by the Irish kings' bottling-up of the Viking enclaves in Dublin and the other 'longphorts', although the number of ringed pins of eleventh- and twelfth-century Irish type shows that connections were far from broken off. Craft industries continued, but there are signs that the town was not producing, or attracting, quite the same range or quality of goods. Certainly the only silk found is tenth-century material, as may be the better-decorated objects. More drastically, the Coppergate street frontage went out of use despite its earlier thriving building line. Whether this was before or after the Conquest is not clear – indeed, its only direct evidence seems to be a dump of soil probably brought in to counter the threat of flooding caused by the diversions to the River Foss associated with construction of one of the castles.[33] Although there are three, perhaps five, coin hoards deposited *c.* 1069–70, which surely here attest Swein's invasion, the English revolt and William's harrying of the north, other substantial evidence is lacking, and there is some reason therefore to think that York was already in decline by the middle of the eleventh century, its international function lost, and that it was starting to take on the more limited rôle of northern capital and regional centre which it had through the rest of the Middle Ages, with a trading potential limited by its fringe position in relation to most of the main European commercial developments.

Lincoln's adaptation to changing circumstances as seen in its coins is also notable in the pottery from Stamford, with less going north to York and Lincoln, and more going south to places like Oxford, Bedford and London (6,4).[34] This search for new markets is seen also in other pottery reaching London, which in the eleventh century was being supplied from several more production centres than before. London's trade contacts with Stamford may not have been confined to pots: at least one of the many different types of cloth of which fragments have been recovered is of a weave that may be typical of Stamford. It is one of a number of high-quality fabrics available to the citizens, including silk, and the range of dyes recognisable from chemical analysis shows that madder, indigotin probably obtained from woad, and lichen were used to produce a wide range of reds, yellows and purples – the Bayeux Tapestry provides the best surviving example of the colours available in English wooliens. The London textiles also demonstrate the major change in production techniques from the warp-weighted vertical to the beam-tensioned horizontal loom already foreshadowed at Gloucester (5,4): the London fabrics show a marked change in the eleventh century from a four-shed to a three-shed twill, some of very high-quality cloth, and this twill type was the norm for the rest of the Middle Ages. Its introduction also coincides with the virtual disappearance by the end of the eleventh century of clay loom-weights of the sort used by weavers working on a vertical loom.[35] A tensioned

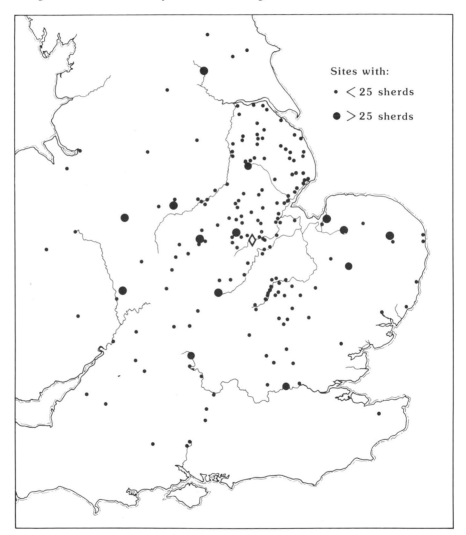

6, 4. Distribution map of Stamford ware by S. E. James, based on the work of K. Kilmurry: the larger circles are sites at which more than twenty-five sherds have been found. Stamford's location on a river would have helped its potters to spread their wares, but overland routes would have been used to get to the upper Thames and Severn Valleys.

lower beam can be used with a vertical loom, and this may have been used in the tenth century at Goltho, where there were weaving tools but not loom-weights.[36] This type of loom seems unlikely to have been used after the eleventh century, for the bone weaving-tools such as 'pin-beaters' used with it also disappear from the archaeological record. The horizontal loom requires more specialised workers, but its products virtually supplanted domestically-made cloth. Weaving is another example of the increasing rôle of urban craft industries.

The development of urban textile industries was occurring also in other parts of north Europe, particularly in the Low Countries. England may have begun to suffer from competition, with its own towns held back by heavy taxation in much of the eleventh century.[37] Archaeological substantiation of this is limited, since even the east coast towns, apart perhaps from York, do not seem to have had their tenth-century growth truncated in the eleventh. It could perhaps be argued that the new initiations of the tenth were not matched and that investment in what might be termed the infrastructure of streets, guildhalls and substantial housing was not pursued – but the churches tell against that argument. Few new towns were established in the eastern part of England in the eleventh century, whereas the south had a relatively larger number of towns, many with no clearly urban tenth-century use, and usually also much smaller in size. This could be a sign of restriction particularly affecting the eastern side of the country. It could also, however, be a result of many other different factors: more navigable inland waterways in the east would have caused towns to be more widely spaced apart and to be individually larger; grain, wool and cloth can be transported greater distances than live animals and need to be moved only at certain times of the year, and so stimulate more distant and more seasonal markets than trade in cattle and dairy products; tenurial arrangements were different.

The more easterly towns also stood to lose from declining trade contacts with Scandinavia.[38] The silk found in tenth-century York and Lincoln may have come to England via the Baltic and the overland, trans-Russia routes from the East. The tenth-century London silks are as likely to have been brought through France, via Italy and the Mediterranean. The decline of Scandinavian trade would especially have affected the north, and only Durham developed as a new town in the century before the Conquest, with timber buildings from the second half of the tenth century. Its range of craft activities, artefacts and buildings does not suggest overseas trade, but growth that was internally stimulated.[39]

Mediterranean trade, and particularly English interest in the market at Pavia, is well documented, and King Cnut wrote home enthusiastically from Rome about the trade arrangements he had negotiated. It seems very likely that Cnut's interest was because of his understanding of the complexities of contemporary weight systems: at any rate, it was during his reign that a low-weight penny was minted which seems to have conformed to a unit of the Byzantine ounce, presumably to facilitate trade as well as to benefit the king.[40]

The association in people's minds between weight units and coins is suggested by the increasing number of lead weights that are being found which have been stamped with coin dies, from Alfred's reign onwards. Cnut's ability to maintain his new country's coinage is comparable to William's fifty years later; neither made major changes to the system by bringing in new moneyers, though both adjusted the weight of silver in their pennies, probably to extract higher tax returns. The underlying stability of the English coinage is impressive.

The hoards found in Sweden and Denmark that contain many thousands of English coins, some at least representing Danegeld payments, are the best source of information on the numismatic patterns of the late tenth and early eleventh centuries, but even thereafter relatively larger numbers of coins are known – nearly 9,000 from Edward the Confessor's reign, for example.[41] The quantities strongly suggest money firmly entrenched in the economy, probably stimulated by demand for taxation payments to be made in coin, and with an increasing number of people living by craft and trade who required coin as the medium through which they could acquire both their food supplies and their raw materials. That transactions involving coin were at a relatively low level is shown by the numbers of cut pennies that are found – literally half-pennies (and even four-things), though these were no longer minted as coins in their own right, perhaps because the moneyers found difficulty in controlling the size and weight of such small coins, rather than because there was no demand for them.

Another indication of the extent to which coinage was carefully controlled is shown by the continued exclusion of eleventh-century foreign coins. Lincoln has the two from Scandinavia, but York has none at all. There are rather more in the south: a Spanish dirham from Cerne, Dorset; a Utrecht coin from Old Sarum; single French deniers from Netherton, Winchester, Alfriston and a hoard from Southampton; and a Hungarian denier from Exeter. The numbers are few, but their generally coastal locations may indicate that they were lost before being reminted into English coin, or shipped back to the Continent. The French deniers suggest the sort of pre-Conquest trade links indicated by Exeter's pottery. Other types of contact, such as diplomatic missions, could account for the arrival of some: the Hungarian denier could result from a pilgrimage, as Hungary was on one route to Jerusalem. There were royal family links too. In general, of course, the very existence of a silver coinage in England testifies to trade, since the bullion for nearly all of it had to be imported – there is no indication of high levels of activity at English mints such as Bath, Lydford or Derby, near to where silver-bearing ores can be found, and there would not have been sufficient 'reserves' in the form of plate that could be melted down to maintain the quantities of coins that were in circulation.[42]

Despite the coin evidence, the Domesday Book reference that some estates in Derbyshire paid £40 tax 'in pure silver' each year suggests that some extraction was taking place in the Peak District, presumably in association with lead mining. Whether the technology for separating the two minerals existed, or output depended on the discovery of naturally pure ores, is not known. Another aspect of metallurgy on which more information would be useful is iron-smelting: the Stamford data do not suggest technological development or increase in furnace size, although demand for iron must have been increasing if the population was growing, and the range of specialised crafts was calling for specialised equipment. Excavations suggest that large quantities of tools were in demand, as well as items of domestic and kitchen equipment. Both smelting and smithing slags are being found at an increasing number of town sites – Bedford, Colchester, Norwich, Northampton, Thetford. Yet Gloucester has not produced much evidence, despite its proximity to the Forest of Dean with its high-quality ores and readily available charcoal. Domesday records the town's obligation to supply the king, but the collection of tools and other items found at the castle site included what seems to be part of a Roman shield boss, as though someone was anxious to collect scrap for reworking rather than relying upon freshly smelted ores. Some difficulty in obtaining adequate supplies of raw material is also suggested by what seems to have been a metalworker's hoard found at Nazeing, Essex. Axes, spears, a ploughshare, knives, and a fish-spear were among the finds. Although some of these objects were made in the eleventh century and show that that was when the hoard was deposited, others were up to 400 years old, and there was even a Roman axe-head. Although this does not prove an actual dearth of newly-smelted iron, it at least shows that scrap metal was worth collecting and recycling.[43]

One major change in iron-working in the period was in the production of sword-blades. Pattern-welding gave way to the simpler technique of forging from a single homogeneous bar. This was made possible by the use of low-phosphorus irons from purer ores: the names Ulfberht and Ingelrii (or mis-renderings of them) are often inscribed into these blades. Presumably these were famous sword-smiths, and the distribution of weapons purporting to have been made by them shows that they were internationally renowned. Many of those found in England would have been imports: others perhaps were made from imported ores.[44]

Although the new swords were more effective than the old ones, and could be decorated with wire inlays, they did not quite have the panache of the pattern-welded blades, and they demanded less skill in their making. Even so, it is reckoned that a sword would take some 200 hours to produce, and a mail 'hauberk' 140.[45] Considerable expenditure was therefore involved, and the sword would have remained a weapon for the fighting élite. At the same time, that élite was learning new techniques of warfare. Iron was not only needed for swords, axes and other long-used weapons: completely new equipment was required as stirrups, spurs, horse-shoes and more elaborate horse-bits became increasingly common. Stirrups were of various forms, but the most usual English ones are like a rounded A with a rectangular loop at the top, and wide plates at the bottom of the arms. They are often decorated with copper-alloy wires, forming running scrolls and leaf patterns, some of high quality (**6,5**).[46] This decoration shows that they were not everyday items, but owned by those who could afford to be lavish; appropriately they were associated with horses, increasingly the expensive adjunct of the mounted aristocrat. Whether any Anglo-Saxon actually fought on horseback before William's victory at Hastings is unknown, but they certainly had the necessary equipment – the stirrup gives the charging rider sufficient purchase on the saddle to meet the shock of impact, the spur pushes a reluctant horse forward. If the Bayeux Tapestry is to be believed, the Anglo-Saxons also had the cavalryman's shield, a long 'heater' shape which protects the lower leg on one side

6, 5. Two stirrups, both decorated with overlaid brass wire. Although not a matching pair, these were found together on the bank of the River Cherwell in Oxford - and could have been lost in the Viking raid on the town in 1009. Use of stirrups may have been promoted by the renewed Viking attacks, but there is no reason to assume that they were exclusive to the Scandinavians.

of the horse, rather than the more wieldy round shield of the foot-soldier. All these equipment costs put further pressure on the aristocracy, extending their need to extract what they could from their estates. At the same time, it set those who could afford the equipment even further apart socially from those who were not required to have it.

Another aspect of social control to be considered is the increasing intervention of governmental administration. The ability of kings to control and manipulate the coinage to their advantage is one aspect of this: closely allied to it is the evidence of increasing use of seals to authenticate written instructions. A token, such as a ring, could be used as a guarantee of the validity of a statement delivered by a messenger, since it would be recognisable as something entrusted to him by the sender: such use would not be apparent in the archaeological record. What do begin to appear are seal dies: initially used by churchmen such as Bishop Ethilwald of Dunwich in the ninth century, they came increasingly into the affairs of the laity; dies in copper alloy, walrus ivory and bone have all been found.[47] Best-known is an ivory example from Wallingford, with one side inscribed in Latin which translates as 'The seal of Godwin the thegn', the other, probably secondarily, 'The seal of Godgyðe, a nun given to God'. Their identities are unknown, but they were clearly people of high status, Godgyðe possibly being Godwin's widow, for high-born ladies who outlived their husbands often went into religious retreat. Use of seals in administrative and business routines emphasizes the way in which the written word was replacing folk memory as a legal record. A similar development in the eleventh century is the increasing use of the 'writ', literally a written order of instruction, instead of the 'charter' which recorded a decision but did not itself initiate any action.

Since the designs and the lettering of the seals seem to be imitative of the coinage, the same die-cutters may have been making them. Many of the handles of the seals are very finely crafted, showing skills usually associated with ecclesiastical work such as book covers and reliquaries. Godwin's seal has a handle on which are carved figures representing a scene from one of the psalms, which suggests a producer with access to iconographic models, either working for church as well as lay patrons, or possibly even working in a church which sold or gave artefacts made there to outsiders. Church interest is also shown by a die recently found in Lincoln, cut for a '*Legatio*'. The scene on this shows a cleric standing at an altar: his vestments and the objects shown with him are appropriate to a sub-deacon – so it was carefully designed by someone who knew the ecclesiastical niceties. The likelihood is that it was for a papal legate, the sub-deacon Hubert, who was in England in 1072 and 1080; his business in Lincoln may have been concerned with the transfer of the bishopric.[48]

It is highly symbolic that Hubert's seal should have been found, for renewed papal intervention in the English Church was one of the consequences of the Conquest, revitalising links that had been weakened by Archbishop Stigand, and bringing the influence of Hildebrandine reforms. One major difference between Cnut's conquest and William's was that the former had little direct impact upon the Church. The effect of the new men introduced after the Conquest was considerable, often a rude shock to the English communities. Most tangible is the rebuilding of so many of the great churches; it was not so much their scale that was new, for Edward the Confessor's Westminster Abbey was as big as any that followed it, and it was also a fully 'Romanesque' building.[49] Elsewhere, most Anglo-Saxon builders had respected the work of their predecessors by incorporating earlier structures within their own work, thus reconstructing rather than totally rebuilding. Above ground there survive parts of the churches of only two major houses: Sherborne, Dorset, has parts of a north porticus and of its west end, but its plan is not known in detail; Bradford-on-Avon, Wiltshire, has the 'chapel' probably built by the nuns of Shaftesbury as a refuge to which they could retreat with the relics of St Edward the Martyr if Viking raids threatened Dorset. Bradford was not therefore meant for congregational use, and cannot have been typical in its scale, although the surviving sculptures, two flying angels placed high above the chancel arch where they would have flanked a Crucifixion, show the calibre of its execution. From excavations at other major churches have come such things as polychrome relief tiles, showing the extent to which colour was important, as is also demonstrated by wall-painting and window-glass fragments.[50]

Few of the post-1066 Church leaders regarded its buildings as relics to be preserved,[51] although at least some respect was shown to earlier graves by the builders of York Minster. The stout oak beams used in the foundations at York are just one example of the vast costs involved in the new abbeys and cathedrals: revenues were squeezed, superfluities weeded out. It is in these buildings rather than the castles that Norman investment, sense of grandeur, self-confidence and down-right arrogance are best seen. Consequently eleventh-century pre-Conquest building survives mainly in 'lesser' ministers and parish churches. A few of the former, like Breamore, Hampshire, or St Mary-in-Castro, Dover, Kent, seem to preserve most of their original features, and characteristically are cruciform churches with a central crossing surmounted by a tower (or spire, though none survive): their side chapels are still '*porticuses*' not quite as wide as the nave, and entered through narrow openings. A Romanesque building has 'transepts' as wide as the nave and with arches that form a square with a chancel and crossing arches, so that the church seems an integrated unit rather than a series of discrete cells. That this was not an introduction entirely dependent upon the Norman Conquest is shown by the crossing arches at Stow, Lincolnshire, which are not quite the entire width of the building – and which have undergone reconstruction – but which foreshadow what was to be developed in fully Romanesque buildings.

A great deal of investment went into many of the churches of the 'minsters' in southern and central England, but at the same time lesser parish churches were also being built (e.g. St Martin's, Wareham: front cover). It is often very difficult to be at all precise about their dates, for constructional features

characteristic of Anglo-Saxon masonry, such as double-splay windows, continued to be used for at least the whole of the eleventh century, although there
were additions to the masons' repertoire such as more complex mouldings.
From details like these, it is becoming possible to recognise the work of teams
of masons working in particular areas. Systematic work is also shown by the
increasing recognition that exact measurement and proportion were important: at Bradford, for instance, the external height and length of the chancel
form a square and the chancel's length is the same as the nave's width, while
at Breamore the chancel is twenty-seven feet long (8.22 metres) long, the
tower twenty-seven feet square, commensurate with the old English rod of
sixteen and a half modern feet (5.03 metres), twenty-seven feet being within
inches one and two-thirds of a rod.[52]

Distribution of known churches depends to a very large extent on proximity
to quarries, since only a single timber church survives, at Greenstead, Essex,
and it is therefore difficult to assert that the preponderance of examples in
certain areas is in any direct way indicative of a greater degree of manorialisation. In some cases, stone was transported over considerable distances;
products of Barnack, Northamptonshire, had the advantage of being close to
navigable rivers, but overland carriage was also undertaken, for there is Bath
stone in Breamore. The frequently found fragments of Rhenish quern-
stones are another type of quarry product widely distributed. Stamford pottery shows that lead, despite its weight, was taken overland from the Peak
District, and documentary evidence reveals something of salt distribution. It
seems likely, from both the bone evidence and Domesday Book, that sheep
were being bred for wool, and fleeces may already have been regularly transported not only within England, but overseas as well. Recorded improve-
ments to river navigations, such as on the Thames at Abingdon, show the
need to ensure safe carriage of goods.

Excavations of churches do not only produce evidence about fabrics, plans
and decorative features, for the graveyards that accompany those that had
burial rights yield information about contemporary populations. The dating
of the skeletons is usually within fairly broad parameters, and it is scarcely
possible to relate observed changes to particular episodes or decades. In general, data from both town and country sites are in line with the animal-bone
data from the former, that the population was adequately fed. The giants of
the early period had died out: very few adult men seem to have grown to over
six foot, but 5ft 3ins was the shortest at both Norwich and North Elmham, the
two largest tenth-eleventh-century groups for which figures are available.
The average at the former was 5ft 7 ins, virtually the same as at St Helen's,
York, from a longer time-span; it is only since the First World War that average male height has increased from this. Women average 5ft 3 ins and 5ft
2ins respectively. At North Elmham and at York it is suggested that the
female norm was relatively lower than the male, suggesting that women had
less good food than men, or at least that the men had access to better diet.
More evidence on whether anything but a very great difference would show

in the bones would be welcome. It is more certain that women had a higher death-rate in the seven to twenty-five year age bracket, presumably because of risks in child bearing, and those that survived had problems resulting from it, such as tooth loss. The balance in the urban cemeteries between males and females is approximately what would be expected: there is not the heavy bias to males seen earlier at Southampton, which shows that the towns now had a balanced population, unlike what is so far known from the earlier trading-station evidence. Life-expectancy for those who lived beyond twenty-five becomes increasingly difficult to assess closely, but the Raunds figures suggest that those who survived to the age of twelve had an average age at death of thirty-three. In York, fewer than 10 per cent reached the age of sixty. Death by violence is not in evidence, at least by blows that shatter bones and skulls, though there were some breaks and strains from everyday life, and one North Elmham man who had been slashed lay buried under the cemetery wall, suggesting that he was an outcast (there were small 'execution cemeteries' of this period for criminals, often recognisable from their crossed wrists where they were bound, who were not buried in a churchyard at all – a sign of tougher royal justice?) and one Portchester male may have died from a sword blow. Disease problems are very difficult to assess, because so few can be proven to affect bone structures. Arthritis was certainly prevalent, and at Portchester facets that develop from prolonged squatting are claimed in almost all the adults, although at North Elmham twice as many women were affected as men.[53]

Although most of the skeletons of mature adults show that the population was reasonably tall, and the bones are in general quite robust, dietary problems were not absent. Norwich has a case of rickets, caused by vitamin D deficiency, and other examples are possible. Worn teeth suggest the need to chew coarse food, although pottery suggests increased cooking of stews which would have broken down fibrous materials and therefore perhaps have made a wider range of meat, pulses and vegetable matter available for consumption. By the twelfth century, the sagging-based cook-pot which could simmer quietly in the ashes of an open fire was used throughout the country.[54] But the bone evidence does not suggest a concomitant increase in the number of very old, as opposed to mature, animals being slaughtered, so tougher meat was not being consumed, and whether cook-pots made an actual difference to the diet is an open question. The extent to which flour was finely ground, and to which bits of the millstones came off in the grinding, is hard to assess. Use of teeth as tools must be considered, for instance to cut threads while sewing: women at North Elmham were more prone to arthritis of the jaw than men, so they could have suffered a coarser diet and greater demand on their teeth in domestic life. Again, more evidence would be welcome.

There are at present rather more analyses of burial sites available than of the bodies buried. Differences between different churchyards may be a reflection of local idioms and not have any deep cultural significance. In some, it is possible to recognise graves picked out for special distinction: at St

Mark's, Lincoln, outside the west end of the stone church, a grave carefully lined and covered with mortared slabs was respected and left undisturbed by the later builders of a west tower; at Raunds, there is the isolated male grave under a decorated slab. Whether these were burials of high-status members of the laity, or of priests, is not known. Few grave-markers or slabs are found in their original position, but one at Raunds had a child below it, so special treatment was not reserved for clerics. None, however, seems to have been reported above a woman's grave, and at Raunds there is a slight tendency for females to be kept at the periphery of the cemetery in later phases, which could indicate a status lowering. In York, very young infants seem to have been excluded from burial with the rest of the community, unless buried with their mothers. There is a comparable dearth of the very young at Barnstaple. Other status markers may be 'special' treatment, such as provision of wooden coffins: at Barton-on-Humber, a water-logged site, one of those which was completely intact had been made without any use of iron fittings, the planks being held together by wooden pegs.[55] Such a coffin would not therefore be recognisable in normal excavation conditions, unless it had stained the surrounding soil. In some cases, a coffin's existence can be deduced from the way that the contents' bones have moved while decomposing in the void inside the coffin before it collapsed: but even this would not apply if the body had been provided with a shroud first. Whether it was 'better' to be in a coffin or in a stone-lined grave is unknown. Many had stones under their heads, two at Hereford having these within coffins. Practices varied widely, and no regional differences seem recognisable: none of the North Elmham graves had stone cists or pillows, yet in nearby Norwich flint pillows were common, especially for children.

One curious and unexplained burial custom involved the use of charcoal. This is found in a few pagan graves,[56] yet was also widely used in later Christian cemeteries.[57] Because charcoal is almost pure carbon, it is material that can be radiocarbon-dated with more confidence than most (and, since charcoal is normally produced from immature green timber, the date that it gives is more likely to be close to the date of use than can be guaranteed from other timber, which may have been already old when reused in, for instance, a coffin). There are seventh- and eighth-century dates from Worcester and Hereford, and there are examples in friaries which must be thirteenth century, but the practice seems to 'peak' in the eleventh, generally disappearing after *c.* 1100. It was at first thought that the charcoal was a preservative, used to pack round a body which had to be moved to a church at some distance from the place of death: certainly it would help to absorb body liquids and prevent some of the worst smells. This has been questioned because in many cases the charcoal is a thick 'bed' on the floor of the grave or even round the sides of a coffin, as at Lincoln, so that the body is not in direct contact with the carbon. Also, the rite is not only found at major churches, to which important people might be taken from a distance, but also at lesser churches, the members of whose congregation would have been less likely to die away from home. It could be that charcoal was first used for practical purposes, and that its use transformed into a ritual. If this ritual was an English but not a French custom, it would not have been used by the aristocracy after 1066 (if Normans were transported for burial, they were packed in salt and sewn up in hides),[58] and so it would rapidly have gone out of fashion among all classes.

Some Normans were transported for burial because they died on campaign and wanted their bodies to rest in churches which they had founded or patronised. They did not indulge in ostentatious tombs; it is as though entire buildings were their memorials. Their churches marked their status and their family's endowment: through them, these 'new men' were proclaiming their dominant position, just as their seventh-century predecessors had used earthen mounds and hoards of treasure. Arrogant though they may have been, the Normans too needed symbols to bolster their hard-won social eminence. Although the nature of their memorials was different, the underlying motives for them were essentially the same.

Chapter Seven

THE TWELFTH AND THIRTEENTH CENTURIES

Community and Constraint

Archaeology is concerned with interpretation, and excavation is a process for recovering information from which hypotheses can be constructed. Nevertheless, even the most hardened excavator may still admit to pleasure at finding 'things', whatever their potential for elucidating the society that produced them may be. So it is difficult not to feel envious of the digger who discovered thirty finely-carved gaming-pieces, with parts of the board on which they were used, in a late eleventh-century rubbish-pit on the site of the early Norman castle at Gloucester (7,1). Their full character was only revealed, of course, after careful conservation, which established that there are fifteen antler and fifteen bone pieces, a complete set for use in Tables, a game of luck and skill similar to backgammon. The pieces are carved with a variety of astrological signs, animals, and biblical and other scenes such as were widely used in Romanesque sculpture. On bone strips which would have been nailed onto a wooden board to make the playing surface, there is interlace and animal ornament, some of it in the Scandinavian 'Urnes' style current in the second half of the eleventh and first half of the twelfth centuries.[1] 'Urnes' was the last significant northern contribution to European art in the Middle Ages, and seems to have been expressing very different values from the Romanesque. To have the two in combination is to have a rare cultural antithesis.

The Gloucester Tables set is particularly interesting because of its discovery within a castle, the milieu of kings and barons. Gaming-counters in pagan burials are associated with people to whom high status can be attributed, but the discovery at York and elsewhere of many discs and cones used in board games suggests that such pastimes became more widespread. Tables, however, seems to have been unknown in England before the eleventh century: it is different from simple games like Fox and Geese or Nine Men's Morris in that it requires rather more skill, and since it lends itself to gambling, it can be a game for the rich. Another introduction of the same period was chess, subtly adapted from its oriental version to reflect European feudal courts, with queens replacing viziers, castles chariots (but retaining the Arabic name *rukh*) and bishops, unflatteringly, elephants. Chess is a game of skill, time-consuming to learn and to play, so that only those with leisure could indulge

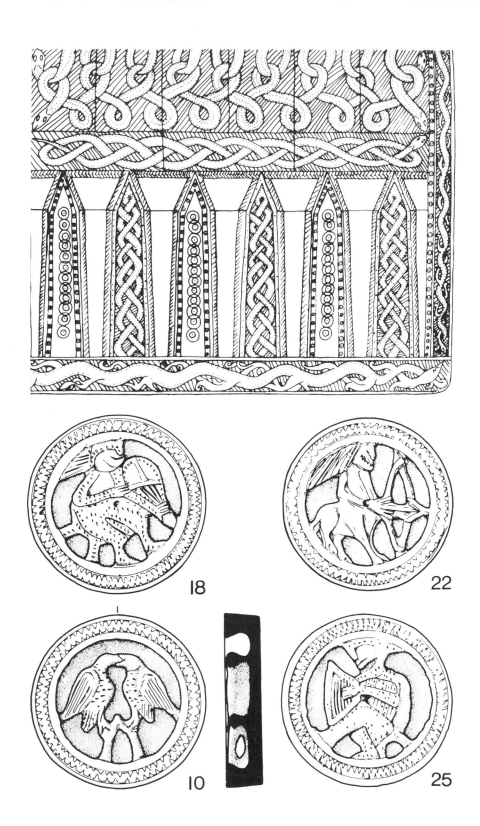

18

22

10

25

Opposite: **7, 1a.** The Gloucester Tables set. The drawing by J. Knappe shows a reconstruction (at about one-third actual size of the board). The selection of playing counters, drawn (actual size) by P. Moss, indicates the contrast between their Romanesque style and the Anglo-Scandinavian ornament of the board.

Above: **7, 1b.** The Gloucester Tables set during excavation.

in it: its need for intelligence and subtlety flatters the self-esteem of the good player, gambling is possible, and it can be played between men and women. Consequently it is ideal as a courtly pursuit, and several chess pieces have indeed been found in appropriate contexts such as the castles at Northampton and Old Sarum.[2]

Chess pieces are not only known from castles – one was recently found in the middle of Dorchester, Dorset, for instance[3] – and any type of artefact is unlikely to be found only in very exclusive contexts. Nevertheless the artefacts found at twelfth-century aristocractic sites and those from other types of site indicate the nature of the luxury goods that feudal magnates required for their status. Musical instruments, for instance, even simple bone flutes, represent another leisure activity. Surprisingly frequent are gilt copper-alloy strips, presumably for nailing onto wooden or leather caskets, indicating superior decoration on functional items. Castle Acre has yielded both a crystal gemstone and a fragment of a glass drinking vessel.[4] A different type of consumption is indicated by the large numbers of horseshoes and nails that are usually found, as well as the rather fewer fragments of armour, which emphasize the high cost of equipping and maintaining mounted cavalry. The castles do not seem to have been production sites, except for black-smiths' work: they were essentially centres of consumption, without the mixture of functions recognisable in some earlier aristocratic enclosures.

Some twelfth-century castle 'finds' do not differ materially from those from other sites: in particular, the range of pottery at them does not show any marked use of higher-quality ceramics, such as glazed wares and imports. Pottery was presumably for the kitchens, and was not something that reflected a lord's status. What was actually cooked in the kitchens certainly shows status differences, however: deer bones, which indicate venison; younger animals, more tender meat; a different selection of bones, steaks and chops rather than stews.[5] Young pigs, the only 'entire' carcases traceable at Portchester Castle, were probably spit-roasted.[6] Swan, wild goose and duck, partridge and hare suggest lords' near-monopoly of the country's non-domestic resources, just as occasional hawk bones indicate one of the ways in which the delicacies were obtained. Nor do such things come only from rural castles where they could easily be acquired locally, for urban castles such as Baile Hill, York, also show much higher numbers of different species relative to the numbers of bones than the surrounding town rubbish pits produced.[7] By the end of the century, rabbit was beginning to appear, and fallow deer were replacing red deer in most areas. There is such a high proportion of deer bones at Barnard Castle, Co. Durham, that there may have been slaughter there for sale of meat on the open market,[8] though records of distributions of fish from the royal or episcopal ponds show that such products were not usually sold, but taken to the owner's other properties for his own consumption or distributed as gifts to those whom it was wished to favour.[9] Fishponds, dovecotes, deer parks and artificial rabbit warrens provide a good measure of the increased attention that was given to careful husbandry and management of a variety of different creatures, all of which gave the wealthy a greater choice and flexibility in their food, and upon which very considerable human effort was expended.

There are perhaps slightly more coin finds at castles than at other sites, but they are not frequent – Hen Domen has yielded nothing earlier than a halfpenny of King John, for instance.[10] In general, the quantity of finds suggests places where there were occasional losses by people rich enough to have coin in their purses, but who were not regularly opening them to make payments. There were few wage earners receiving cash if household work and garrison duty were done by those who owed service, and consequently servants and soldiers had little money to lose. One form of involvement that castles had in the use of coin is suggested by the tumbrel, a balance used for checking the weights of pennies, found at Castle Acre:[11] its use was illegal except at mints, and it suggests illicit checking by a careful steward of the rent and tax payments being brought there.

The conspicuous expenditure of the great lords is also of course shown by the physical structure of their castles, as well as by what can be found in their rubbish pits. A castle was a 'symbol of lordship',[12] its size and scale adjusted as much to its owner's status as to any practical need of defence. Earth and timber castles remained effective until the middle of the twelfth century, many being hastily constructed and as quickly abandoned in Stephen and Matilda's wars, but there is a long list of sites to which keeps, bailey walls, gatehouses and wall-towers were added, all in stone. Although timber buildings remained even in royal palaces like Cheddar, it was stone and dominance that mattered. Particularly in the second half of the twelfth century, as it became increasingly necessary to keep miners and siege engines at a distance, the curtilages of castles were enlarged and providing stone defences on a yet bigger scale was a huge expense, to be afforded only by the king or a principal baron. Whereas at the start of the century a serviceable motte-and-bailey was within the range of almost every knight, he could later beggar himself by trying to keep up with the Warennes. As the scale of building increased, so did social disparities.

The trend towards bigger and more elaborate castles is exemplified at Gloucester, where the Tables set was found on the site of an early Norman earthwork motte-and-bailey. This castle was additional to the extra-mural royal palace at Kingsholm, which seems to have continued in use for state occasions, probably because it was less restricted in size. The early Norman castle, like some others such as Canterbury's, was actually abandoned during the twelfth century; excavations have shown that its bailey ditch was deliberately back-filled, although the site was not built over despite being within the growing town. Probably this was to keep a clear space in front of the new castle which was built on an immediately adjacent piece of land acquired by King Henry I between 1110 and 1120. This area backed onto the River Severn, and the reason for the new building may have been to improve control over the waterway.[13] Certainly it was in the twelfth century that Gloucester's quayside was developed: whatever remained of the Roman wall was demolished, and pottery has been recovered which shows increased activity, with evidence for both tanning and dyeing. New bridges are recorded, with the consequent effect on water flow in the river channels being partly responsible for the growth of the new occupation zone because the changes affected ships' access.[14]

St. Peter's Abbey at Gloucester is a typical Norman refoundation, the work of an energetic abbot who lived to see his great church completed in 1100 after eleven years' work, with a community of a hundred monks.[15] It attracted substantial donations, perhaps because the king was a frequent visitor to Gloucester, and completely overshadowed the Anglo-Saxon establishment of St Oswald's Priory, which followed a course typical of many of the pre-Conquest secular priests' houses by being converted in the twelfth century into an Augustinian priory. Its church was not neglected; a north aisle was built, with an arcade cut through the existing Anglo-Saxon nave wall, and a western extension was added in the following century. But it never again had the prestige or commanded the income which it must have enjoyed as the mausoleum of Aethelflaed and St Oswald.[16]

The stimulus to Gloucester's commerce provided by castle and major abbey in bringing people and goods to the town is presumably one explanation for the increased activity around its waterfront. The importance of riverside land in such towns had already been demonstrated in London, where the shore-line was being embanked in the eleventh century. Twelfth-century work of that sort has not been identified, although several towns are like Norwich where a shift of site of the main waterfront activity is suggested by the abandonment of the 'hard' near the cathedral.[17] These topographical changes in the later eleventh and twelfth centuries seem to be caused by new works like bridges and castles, and not yet by the demands of new types of sailing vessel with deeper draughts. Although recovery of Baltic and Scandinavian wrecks shows that carrying capacities were increasing, it is only possible to demonstrate the same in other parts of Europe by inference. England can, however, claim the earliest representation of a ship with a stern rudder, a feature significant in allowing the development of bigger ships and new sailing techniques, which is clearly carved on the late twelfth-century font at Winchester.[18]

Growth of commerce was the main reason for the creation of many new towns in the century after the Norman Conquest, the biggest of which were ports. At Lynn, Norfolk, irregular ground around St Margaret's church may result from great mounds of sand discarded from the salt-extraction process which probably marked the first activity at this river mouth site on the Wash.[19] By 1096 there was a market and fair, so Lynn flourished though without the benefit of the trade brought by a castle or major church. Boston, also on the Wash but further north, developed at the same time. To the south, Yarmouth had probably begun a little earlier, for excavations there have produced a coin of Edward the Confessor, and eleventh-century pottery.[20] East coast trade was obviously buoyant again, even though the Flemish cloth industry may have continued to restrict English competition. Existing towns like Lincoln and Stamford prospered as cloth producers, but it does not seem that demand was sufficient to create new centres. Nor did all towns flourish: Thetford went into rapid decline, with its main urban area falling into disuse. There is little twelfth-century pottery from it, and no post-1100 coins. Some of the activity may have shifted north of the river, where the castle was constructed, but in effect Thetford had ceased to be a major town by the middle of the twelfth century. This change in fortune might be attributed to navigational problems on the river and competition from Lynn, but there is no similar decline at Norwich or Lincoln, threatened by Yarmouth and Boston respectively. The loss of the bishop's seat is hardly a likely factor, since it was at Thetford only from 1071 to 1095. It is just possible that vigorous competition from Bury St Edmunds was responsible, but there is as yet no full explanation for the way that Thetford runs counter to the general urban trend.[21]

Lynn, Boston and Yarmouth are three of the most successful of the towns added into the growing economic system. Most of the others were considerably smaller, providing marketplaces and minor services for their surrounding areas: most are better known from documentary and topographical than from excavated evidence. Sizes and numbers of towns varied widely according to region: local wealth was obviously a major factor, but so was the nature of the local economy and transport system. The contrasts between areas concentrating upon meat and dairy products and those where wool, cloth and grain predominated are usually apparent from the greater distances between the latter's markets, and towns like Lynn have large marketplaces which reflect the scale of the bulk goods that were being handled in them. Many towns are on or close to geological and environmental boundaries, where, for instance, a cereal district could exchange products with one that had a pastoral bias.[22]

Wool and cloth rather than grain are usually reckoned to have been the staples of England's medieval economy, although there may be a bias in the records causing them to be a little over-emphasized so far as East Anglia is concerned. The wool trade leaves virtually no direct physical trace: the cloth industry can be seen most clearly in the residues of the dyeing and fulling processes because, like tanning and flax-retting, they required large quantities of water; diversion of streams through streets and tenements can be shown in low-lying locations in towns like Winchester, where timber-lined channels and pits can be attributed to this sort of activity.[23] Not all the myriad of small trades attested in the documentary evidence can be directly observed in the archaeological record: ale brewers, cooks and tailors do not make an obvious physical impact. Their production was for the immediate market: such traders did not have the same potential for capital growth that manufacturing industries could have. On the other hand, they may have been prepared to pay higher rents for direct access to their points of sale, so that commerce may to some extent have driven out production as markets grew. At any rate, this could be a reason for one trend of the eleventh and twelfth centuries, the almost total abandonment of urban pottery kilns.

Because Thetford itself virtually disappeared, so would its pottery industry have done, whatever general trends might have been. But even before the end of the eleventh century, rural kilns were producing wares similar to Thetford's, for they have been found at Grimston, Langhale, and Bircham in Norfolk, the first of which was to be a major production site for the ensuing centuries. In Norwich, pot making had died out by about the middle of the twelfth century, and it seems also to have left Ipswich.[24] Of the late Saxon urban-based centres in eastern England, only the Stamford and perhaps Lincoln industries survived into the thirteenth century, nor did production begin in Lynn, which was supplied by Grimston, in Boston or in Yarmouth.[25] The pattern is not substantially different elsewhere: in Gloucester, some production on a limited scale may have continued, but the major supplier was outside the town, quite probably at Haresfield, some five miles away, where Domesday Book records that there were potters. The only other places where potters are mentioned, Westbury in Wiltshire and Bladon in Oxfordshire, were also rural. All three indicate that several potters were at work, and that the trade had a more substantial value than a mere cottage industry would have yielded.[26] Nothing is known of the organisation of these documented potters; their kilns have not been found, probably because they mostly used simple bonfire-hearths which did not require any disturbance of the ground, unlike the up-draught East Anglian kilns. But it is in East Anglia, at Blackborough End, Norfolk, that a clamp-kiln has actually been located, producing only cooking-pots, presumably for very local distribution, and not competing with Grimston for other markets.

Potters may not have worked at any one place for very long, and many may have been operating, singly or corporately, on an almost transient basis over a wide area, often of woodland: 'Malvernian ware' is an example of pottery known from sherds found in Hereford, Gloucester and north to Worcester which are geologically distinctive of the Forest of Malvern area but of which the precise manufacturing sites have not been recognised.[27] Access to fuel, clay and water combined with lower rents to make potting a rural craft, despite the advantages to be derived from reducing transport costs of bulky, easily-shattered pots by being sited close to the point of sale in a market town. Another explanation is that concentration on a single market centre was avoided by a rural kiln, able to distribute to several more or less equidistant centres, particularly as more markets were created. Another is that the potters were not able to afford to meet competition for the best locations within those markets, and a peripheral position was worse than one right outside the town altogether. Unlike some other crafts, pottery had no high-status market to serve, as the castle deposits show. This restricted the likelihood that the industry could develop beyond low-level, broadly-based production, since there was no demand for long-distance transport of high-quality pots. Consequently potters could not achieve a high return on their costs, could not afford urban rents and certainly could not accumulate substantial capital for reinvestment. In leaving the towns, pot-making was to some extent anticipating what was to happen to much of the cloth industry in the following century. It is noticeable that a lot of the twelfth-century pottery is coarse and hand-made, with little decoration (7,2). As the urban industries dispersed, so specialist skills were lost and the highest-quality products disappeared. The small scale of most pottery production in the period was typical of peasant industries, in which investment is effectively limited to time and labour rather than to plant, materials and equipment.

There are exceptions to this pattern, such as the continued production at Stamford; the recently-discovered kiln just inside the walls of Canterbury may have been a short-lived attempt by an enterprising Frenchman to produce glazed and other decorated types of vessel not otherwise being made in England.[28] Clearly there was no absolute ban on pot production in towns because of fire risk. Doncaster also had a kiln in the town centre for a short while, as well as in a suburb, and Colchester had a suburban kiln in the second half of the twelfth century. Most towns had some available open space even within their walls, such as was utilised by iron-smelters in Norwich.[29] Nevertheless, iron-working is another industry which did not establish itself in towns to the extent that might be anticipated. No doubt Gloucester benefited from the iron-working activity in the Forest of Dean by supplying the workers' everyday needs, but there is no evidence that the proximity of ores led to Gloucester developing as a specialised centre for particular skills and products, although smithing slag has been found in some quantity. Nor did this happen elsewhere: in Stamford, smelting continued, for ore-roasting hearths and slag debris have been found, but it was probably on a smaller scale in the twelfth than in the eleventh century, and no forging by blacksmiths of specialised products has been found.[30] Similarly, smelting in Norwich seems to have been a small-scale affair, and there is little evidence from other towns. Also generally lacking in the twelfth century is evidence for other forms of metal-working: crucibles, for instance, are frequently found in the eleventh century but not in the twelfth, although there are exceptions as at Exeter.[31] Metal-working was still practised, as copper-alloy buckles, seal-dies and book- and box-fittings show, but direct evidence that these were made in towns is elusive, although Gloucester has yielded a tuyère. Many fewer small, everyday objects are found that date to the twelfth rather than to the thirteenth century, and, it seems, proportionally if not actually fewer than to the eleventh, if the population had grown. The loss by most towns of the right to mint coins would have removed that very important and skilled metal-working craft, perhaps affecting their production ability generally. By the end of Henry II's reign in 1189, only nine towns were still mints.

One urban industry which has been investigated archaeologically is salt production at Nantwich, Cheshire. Here brine springs were channelled to 'wich houses', two of which have been excavated (7,3). In them, the brine was stored in long, narrow clay-lined troughs before being boiled on large hearths in lead pans, the evidence for which was quantities of lead scraps. Relining of the troughs and the stratification show that the houses were maintained in regular use, part of a well-organised industry. There are records of several other 'wich houses'.[32] It seems likely that Nantwich is almost unique in being a place that became urban because of its industrial complexes.

Salt can only be obtained inland at a very few places, but for so long as its production centres could compete with coastal salterns and imported salt, they were in the unusual position of having a product for which there was a high demand at all social levels, and which could not be obtained from a myriad of small-scale suppliers. Nantwich and the other 'wich' towns were potentially places where intensive activity could have led to the sort of profits that engender capital growth. The only other medieval industry with that potential was cloth-making, which by the end of the eleventh century had become almost entirely urban-based. Archaeologically this can be shown by the evidence of the horizontal loom (**5,4**). The vertical loom did not remain in use in rural areas, for neither loom-weights nor 'pin-beaters' are found at village sites in the twelfth century; nor are sunken-featured or other non-agricultural buildings.[33] Excavated buildings do not seem to have been large enough to have housed horizontal looms, which would have had to be kept permanently in place. Country people were not therefore making their own

7, 2. Glazed tripod pitcher (left) and unglazed cooking-pot (right) both from Oxford: they are typical of twelfth-century pottery - heavy, much hand-worked even if wheel-turned,

cloth, and would have had to be involved in marketing transactions in order to buy it, even if they were making their own clothes. Nor were they able – or they did not need – to augment their incomes by part-time weaving.

Spindle-whorls have been found at many rural sites, so spinning was taking place, although whether to a commercially significant extent is unknown. There seem to be no reports of metal-working, iron-smelting,[34] bone-working or other craft activities from twelfth-century rural sites likely to be of 'peasant' status. Without locating kilns, it is not possible to see whether the potters were integrated with the communities that worked the fields on those estates where they are recorded in Domesday, or whether they were virtually full-time specialists, perhaps paid or bond servants of the lord of the manor, taking little part in agriculture. It would seem that most villagers did not have much involvement in anything but farming and basic crop processing, and therefore neither had supplementary support in times of dearth nor freedom of choice in their activities to give them a measure of independence.

Nearly everthing that villagers required apart from home-grown foodstuffs had to be brought in, either by the villagers going to the markets themselves, or by itinerant pedlars. Either way, barter cannot have sufficed for all the necessary transactions, since dealings with outsiders would surely have been possible only with cash. That the villagers had the wherewithal to acquire

and with little decoration. Practical and utilitarian, they seem to express what a peasant could expect from life. (Heights: pitcher 315 mm; cooking-pot 225 mm).

goods externally is shown in the archaeological record by their pottery, their tools, their whetstones and other items. Most of their buildings seem to have been fairly cheap to build, using techniques such as wooden posts reinforcing earth-material walls, but some longer timbers may have been required for roofs, and these too would often have had to be bought.[35] Tax and rent demands would also have forced the countryman into increasing dependence on the market. Documents show that many villages came to have licences for markets of their own: village greens and churchyards could have been used at least informally for limited buying and selling.

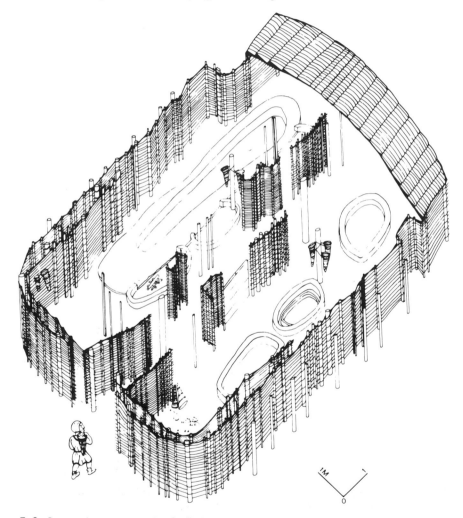

7, 3. Isometric reconstruction by R. McNeil of one of the twelfth-century 'wich' houses excavated at Nantwich, Cheshire. It has a variety of vats for storing the brine, which was then boiled to extract the salt. This was stored and carried in the conical wicker baskets, known as 'barrows'. Wooden salt-rakes are shown in one corner.

Theoretically, agricultural producers were being squeezed harder and harder by landlords who themselves had to meet growing social pressure to build bigger, to ride better-mounted, to fight with more equipment and to consume more lavishly. The archaeological evidence is not yet really sufficient to see if there are any signs of increased stress on rural dwellers, or whether they could meet the demands placed upon them without undue effect upon their living standards. Such things as village replanning, the closing of churches as at Raunds or their opening on new sites as at Broadfield, Hertfordshire, where a new church displaced existing crofts in the early thirteenth century, may show landlords' ability to manipulate whole communities, but may sometimes have been as much in villagers' interests as in lords'. At Wharram Percy, crofts coming into use in the twelfth century may represent in-filling rather than total replanning, but the regularity of their widths suggests more than just piecemeal adjustment. The majority of excavated sites with late eleventh- or twelfth-century use show new areas coming into occupation, but those which, like Goltho, have evidence of formality of layout, have nothing by which to gauge the underlying motivation. The most general conclusion is of expansion of settlement numbers and sizes, indicative of population increase, and of new land development for agriculture, as new sites and dykes in the Fens exemplify.[36]

Some villagers were forcibly evicted from places where the new Cistercian monks wanted privacy, but apart from those well-known examples of landlord manipulation, there are few signs of abandonment or desertion to counter the general picture of growth. The abandoned church at Raunds is probably exceptional, even though there are doubtless others to be located. In general, though, churches were increasing in number and in size, as the Wharram Percy excavation exemplifies. Such growth cannot be a precise index of the growth of a particular community, however, since new building may result from the patronage of a landlord or the benefactions of those who had left the area and done well enough to be able to pay for commemoration at the church where they were baptised.[37]

The need of a growing number of primary producers to acquire goods is a major factor in the development of the market system that could supply them, and it is probably local demand rather than the needs of long-distance trading that caused the establishment of most of the new towns other than ports after the end of the eleventh century. International trade aimed at the king and aristocracy could indeed by-pass inland towns altogether, with the use of seasonal fairs. Merchants need storehouses, however, and increasingly it is possible to see their investment in substantial headquarters, both in the form of partly or wholly below-ground stone cellars in towns like Oxford and London, and in the two-storey stone houses, with warehouse/shop on the ground floor, and living accommodation above – often with sumptuous fireplaces, chimneys and decorated windows – such as can be seen in Southampton and Lincoln. At the latter, the stone buildings have been attributed to Jewish owners: this cannot always be proven, but certainly they would have had particular need of security because they were dealing in large sums of money.[38] The twelfth century saw fairly sophisticated credit arrangements being made, and those involved, whatever their race, would have been rich enough to be very distinct from the rest of the urban community, a distinction physically expressed in the quality of their housing. It may be significant that the two-storey stone houses are almost mirrors of chamber blocks that can be found in castles such as Christchurch, Dorset, and manor complexes such as Boothby Pagnell, Lincolnshire.[39] Two inferences might be that the richest merchants saw themselves as on an equal footing socially with rural gentry even though they were not fully integrated into a social system that stressed military service; and that they were creating their equivalent to a landowner's '*caput*' in the places which they wished to have regarded as their particular territory, the towns. Mercantile enclaves could express their sense of community in this way, as they did in other ways with the attainment of legal privileges; the use of borough seals expressed their new rights.[40]

That there were Jewish communities within many English towns is known from documents, but it would be difficult to recognise their presence from normal archaeological evidence, any more than the 'Frenchmen' recorded in Domesday Book can be recognised as disparate elements in the towns in which they had settled. Cultural divisions were sharply brought home in York, however, when a cemetery was recognised as Jewish from its north–south burials.[41] Particular burial customs can sometimes identify different ethnic groups even if other archaeological remains do not reveal distinctions that may have been maintained in everyday life. There are occasional Jewish objects, such as the 'Bodleian bowl' (7,4), quite possibly once owned by a Jew in Colchester, a town where two thirteenth-century coin hoards are from properties that may have been Jewish-owned.[42] One of these was the largest post-Conquest hoard found in England, with over 10,000 pennies in it, indicative of the very large sums that financiers handled, and of the problems presented by the physical scale of such quantities of coins.

Hoards like those from Colchester make an uneasy contrast to the numbers of coins found as accidental losses on excavation sites; St Peter's Street, Northampton, yielded two twelfth-century pennies but only a single thirteenth-century halfpenny; the same town's Marefair site had one twelfth-century farthing and one thirteenth-century penny; all the 1960s work in Winchester produced but six twelfth-century and twenty-two thirteenth-century coins, excluding those deliberately hidden in small hoards; York has seven twelfth- and about thirty thirteenth-century coins, nineteen of the latter being of Edward I's reign when the king was using the city as the base for his Scots-Hammering expeditions.[43] The Colchester hoards indicate that the stray losses represent only a tiny proportion of what was circulating, which is borne out towards the end of the thirteenth century by surviving mint records which show that millions of coins were issued.

That financiers flourished is scarcely surprising when the amount of late eleventh- and twelfth-century building is considered: St Peter's, Gloucester, is only one example of many Norman projects, and there were new ecclesiastical orders such as the Cistercians to be accommodated. The increasing cost of castles has already been mentioned. Building stone was brought from quarries such as Caen despite the distance and costs of transport involved. Blue slate from Devon found in south-east England is a good example of the importance of water transport.[44] Documentation is not as full as it is for later

7, 4. The Bodleian bowl. This handsome cast copper-alloy tripod vessel has a Jewish inscription round it which states that it was 'The gift of Joseph, son of the holy Rabbi Yehiel'. He was a Talmudic scholar in thirteenth-century Paris, where the bowl may have been made. His sons had associations with Colchester.

centuries, but it seems likely that then as subsequently there was little hesitation in borrowing money for repayment from anticipated incomes. Although usury was forbidden to Christians because the Church would not countenance lending for profit by interest, since humans should not gain wealth through manipulation of God-created time,[45] a merchant could 'lend' money by paying in advance for next year's crop – a motive, perhaps, for the trend to demesne farming rather than leasing which characterised the practice of Church and other landowners in the later twelfth and thirteenth centuries, and which could account for some of the reorganisation of villages and fields that took place.

The rôle of the Church in forming the social pattern of medieval England – by insisting upon monogamy, for instance – is only very indirectly recognisable in physical evidence of this sort. Rural crofts certainly seem best suited to a linear family pattern: the equally-spaced units at Wharram Percy indicate little deviation from a standard unit of accommodation that seems designed for a small number of occupants such as parents and children. The plot which contained them was physically separated from its neighbours, implying little extra-family interaction at a close physical level. The ditches that have been found at a number of sites dividing thirteenth-century villagers from their neighbours may be more satisfactorily explained by such cultural factors than by seeing them as a response to wetter weather, as is sometimes suggested. There is a little evidence that winter rainfall was increasing from about the middle of the twelfth century, but it was compensated for by dry summers until the end of the thirteenth. It does not seem likely that damper conditions would have been clearly enough perceived for drainage ditches or other physical developments such as raised tofts and stone foundations for buildings to have been an inevitable response.[46]

There are excavated rural sites where the neat ladder-like arrangement of Wharram Percy was not emulated. Thirteenth-century Hound Tor, for instance, has groups of stone buildings which suggest at least three farming units (**7,5**); its more informal arrangement may result from the less rigid manorial control likely to have been exercised in more peripheral areas.[47] The largest house has an enclosed garden space attached to it, within which are two smaller buildings, perhaps barns. But both had hearths, and one had a

---

Opposite: **7, 5**. The thirteenth-/early fourteenth-century stone buildings at Houndtor, Devon. The plan has been redrawn by S. E. James from the original by G. Beresford so as to be oriented with the aerial photograph taken by F. M. Griffith on March 17, 1985, when there was a light covering of snow on the ground. The settlement had four longhouses, all with down-slope byre ends. Smaller buildings were also used as houses, at least intermittently. Grain-driers were built into three of them. Garden plots and small fields can also be distinguished. Ridge and furrow behind the buildings is probably not a vestige of medieval ploughing, but rather from an early nineteenth-century phase of intensive land use.

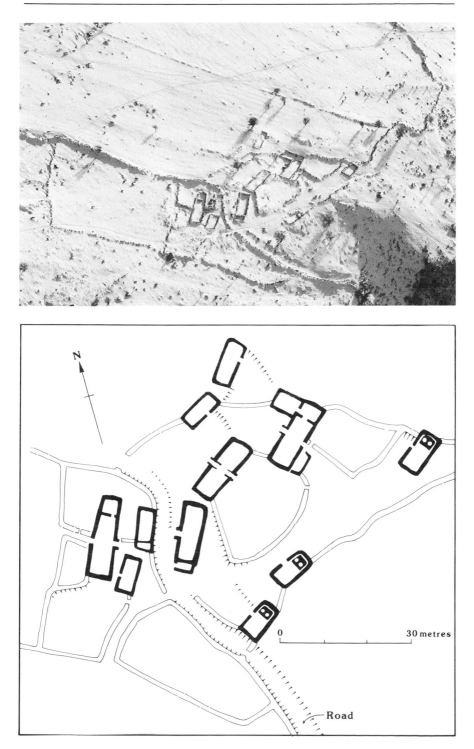

cooking-pit, and it is suggested that for a time each was lived in by someone who was a dependent of the main house, a servant, a grandparent or a son. Upton, Gloucestershire, has produced another possible example. But in these cases the sub-division seems to have been only temporary. Permanent reduction of property sizes might be expected in areas where partible inheritance was regularly practised, and where manorialisation was less rigid. It would be useful to have excavation results from areas such as Kent and Suffolk where partibility is recorded, to see whether it made any real difference, but it could never be easy to ascribe differences between sites to such causes, rather than to differences in farming regimes, local availability of particular commodities and regional wealth levels.

It is more possible to discuss such possibilities for the thirteenth than for the twelfth century, not least because of the adoption almost everywhere of the use of low stone walls or at least pad-stones upon which to construct timber or earth-material houses, as these leave more distinct traces in the ground (7,6). They do not necessarily indicate more investment in building, as most areas have readily available stone which may not be suitable for masonry building, although perfectly adequate for unmortared foundations: but the change would have made such investment worthwhile, as raised timbers were much less prone to rot and so made the construction of permanent housing more viable. Putting up a properly framed timber construction could be a considerable expense, not only because lengths of wood were needed greater than could be foraged from the local hedgerow, but also because cutting the joints and erecting the frame was skilled work for which a carpenter would have had to be employed. Farmhouses and similar structures begin to survive from the later thirteenth century, becoming relatively common in the fourteenth: it may well be that they were already being widely built by those fairly low in the social hierarchy in the early part of the thirteenth as well, enabling them to present a better face to the world.[48]

The late twelfth and thirteenth centuries were years when other material consumption by agriculturalists seems to have increased, with a wider range of goods reaching them. Most rural sites have yielded a scatter of decorated items, not spectacular, but enough to suggest a spending power beyond the barest necessities. The range of finds from Goltho, Lincolnshire, is typical: horse harness pendants, belt fittings, a finger-ring and other copper-alloy trivia. Seacourt, near Oxford, has a very similar range, except for a fragment of gilded glass from the Mediterranean, an exotic piece which may have been brought back by a returning crusader or pilgrim from the Holy Land.[49] Did it reach Seacourt already broken, but still an object of wonder, like the porcelain fragments that are found in the slaves' quarters of the American Plantations many centuries later?[50] The objects show that peasants were not restricted in their daily lives to what they could make themselves, and it does seem that some at least were able to indulge in small luxuries. Documentary evidence shows that there was a very wide range of income and of amounts of land held, but the different internal social levels that must have existed in most villages are scarcely traceable in the archaeological record. This is partly because rubbish was not generally buried in pits but was carted away to be spread as manure. Consequently differences in standards of living cannot be fully explored through analysis of what was discarded on different crofts, although they were so carefully separated by hedges, fences and ditches. It does seem contradictory, however, that there should be such similarity in the sizes

7, 6. A fourteenth-century building at Popham, Hampshire, excavated by P. J. Fasham before its destruction by a motorway. Carefully constructed of flints, the walls were the footings for a timber-framed - or possibly earth-walled - superstructure. In the bottom right hand corner are the remains of an earlier building, on a different alignment from its successor.

of the crofts and of the buildings that they contained, if peasants varied so much in their potential purchasing power. It is as though social and economic status was not expressed in material terms. There is also a very limited range of tools found on excavation sites,[51] an indication that 'division of labour' was limited by there being little specialist craftwork: tools and the people using them were multi-purpose.

Despite the general absence of pits, there are enough deposits to reveal such things as sea-fish bones at Wharram Percy, which show that food was not entirely restricted to what was locally available. Coastal midden sites such as Braunton Burrows in Devon suggest collection and processing of mussels, oysters and shell-fish on a very large scale,[52] and mollusc shells in towns as far from the sea as Oxford show what was available. Peasants' gardens would also have given them some variation from total reliance upon what the common fields and their limited rights to forage yielded.

It is just possible that the thirteenth century did see at least a few villages becoming directly involved in activities other than agricultural production. Pottery-making, for instance, has not yet been found as an integral part of any twelfth-century agricultural settlement, nor do wasters suggest that it will be. Thirteenth-century Lyveden, Northamptonshire, on the other hand, had kilns scattered amongst the the crofts, as did other places in that county and in neighbouring Bedfordshire and Buckinghamshire.[53] It is as though a peripatetic, woodland craft was becoming permanently based at particular centres. Such sedentarism would partly have been the result of assarting (the clearance of scrub and woodland for fields) and the amount of woodland available. It would also have fostered the use of more permanent plant such as below-ground kilns instead of bonfires, if the market demand from a larger population was big enough to justify production of larger numbers of vessels in a single batch. Greater control of the firing would produce a more uniform vessel. By the end of the twelfth century, the most distinctive regional varia-tions in pottery, such as the Cornish grass-marked wares or the Thetford-type wares of eastern England, had already gone, but there was still a wide local variety in jug and cooking-pot shapes which was much less noticeable by the end of the thirteenth. The social position of the potters was not uniform, however. Isolated kilns such as at Mill Green in Essex or Nash Hill in Wilt-shire perhaps suggest potters – and, at the latter also for a time floor-tile makers – less integrated with the communities around them than those at Lyveden and elsewhere.[54]

Although rural cloth-making is a recorded thirteenth-century develop-ment, most excavations have provided thirteenth-century evidence only of agricultural buildings and activities. It seems at present that rural industries generally are more likely to have soaked up surplus wage-labour resulting from population growth than to have provided a supplementary source of income for ambitious small-holders. At Lyveden, however, pot-making tene-ments reverted to agricultural use and vice versa, as though there potting was an occupation pursued only intermittently by any particular family, and on one croft bone-working may have been a cottage industry. Despite documentary evidence, evidence of brewing is everywhere infrequent.[55]

That there was surplus labour in the countryside seems likely not just from the continued growth of towns, which normally are too unhealthy to sustain their populations but have to be supplemented from outside if they are even to remain stable, but also by places which came into use in the late twelfth and thirteenth centuries. Some were expansions of existing sites, like the house recently excavated at Foxcotte, Hampshire; others were single farms probably resulting from assarting, as at Hartfield in Sussex, typical of Wealden expansion.[56] It is impossible to quantify, but there may be justification for an argument that growth was more rapid in the thirteenth than in the twelfth century. This would be consistent with documentary evidence from those few places such as Taunton, Somerset, where it exists, even if the details of increase in such records may owe as much to improved manorial accounting as to an actual increase in numbers.

Population growth could in theory have reached a point where a mass market became more significant than one in which king and aristocracy dominated commerce. That this did not happen was partly because of their ability to maintain social control, not least because the limitations of agricultural production tied small-holders to the land. Even in the most fertile and efficiently farmed parts of eastern England, there is little sign of significant social change, although new crops, applications of more fertiliser and use of better-harnessed horses to plough more quickly allowed more to be produced. Other developments speeded processing, such as the use of windmills, recognisable from the cross-timbers laid in the ground at sites like Ocklynge Hill, Sussex, to augment watermills.[57] Windmills required the use of very substantial timbers, and were therefore expensive. Their importance should not be overemphasized, for they did not allow large areas to develop for grain-growing which had previously only been used for grazing. Whether any were built communally is not known, but seems unlikely from the number that are recorded as a landowner's investment. Similarly, watermills seem to have passed back into lords' direct control on estates where in the twelfth century they had been rented out, or even separately owned, and this represented a loss to rural communities of the opportunity for self-improvement that becoming a miller could offer to a peasant. Field evidence of water channels and pools for textile processing found in the north-west can similarly be associated with landlords' rather than peasants' initiatives.[58]

A lord's profit from milling came partly from saving on labour in the grinding of his own grain, if this was a cost to him, but probably more from his tenants if he could insist that they brought their grain to his mill, upon which he could levy a toll. Establishment of this by 'social control' exercised ultimately through legal control of conditions of land tenure was one cause of tension between peasant and lord, forcing the former to surrender more of his product to the latter. The extent to which it was often a real burden, as opposed to a visibly symbolic one because of the mill's constant presence, may be wondered. Similarly, prohibitions on hand querns may have been as much for symbolic as for real economic reasons, since they are sufficiently common finds on rural sites for it to be clear that the bans were not rigidly enforced – although it would be interesting to know if their incidence is less in the thirteenth than in the twelfth century. Mills provide a good example, however, of a landlord's coercive powers and economic interest in tenants' farming and other activities. It could have been lords' reluctance to see their peasantry becoming involved in non-agricultural activities, from which there were less well-established ways of extracting a substantial proportion of their output, that meant that relatively few villages can be seen to have taken advantage of the possibilities that pot-making and so on provided.

Without gears and pulleys, the actual power output of mills was not great – not enough to heat a modern electric kettle, apparently![59] The vertical wheels at sites like Bordesley Abbey, Worcestershire, were more powerful than the horizontal wheel at Tamworth had been, and there is evidence there of gearing. At Abbotsbury, Dorset, in the fourteenth century, the mill was terraced into a hillslope and the water was fed by a wooden chute onto the top of the wheel, a technique which makes much more effective use of the power source. Such technology was worth applying to agricultural bulk products, but in the cloth industry, for fulling, its advantages were probably more marginal: the two thirteenth-century fulling tubs recently found at Fountains Abbey, Yorkshire, were less than two metres in diameter, yet are likely to have been as large as any.[60] This does not suggest a huge output achieving significant economies of scale, especially when labour to perform the same operation by foot-trampling was cheap. Thirteenth-century fulling-mills were a factor drawing cloth-making out of towns and into rural areas, but they were probably less of a factor than the decline in demand for high-quality urban products in the face of Flemish competition. Providing water supplies for such mills often involved creating dams and diverting rivers and streams as at Bordesley; engineering by sheer physical effort was often on a very large scale, just as new river channels and massive sea-walls in marsh-land areas also necessitated big labour forces for construction and maintenance.

That Fountains Abbey should have had a fulling-mill is not necessarily an indication that the monks were involved in selling as well as making cloth: the scale of the operation does not imply that output was other than for the community's exclusive use – to save them, in fact, from buying in and thus actively fostering the open market. In this way, abbeys and other religious organisations could restrict the economy at least as much as they could cause it to develop. Fountains was a Cistercian order, dedicated to isolation, and thus one which would deliberately keep physical contact with commerce at a distance. Other houses, like St Peter's at Gloucester, were probably having more dealings with local suppliers. Nevertheless, the thirteenth-century husbandry manuals and so on emphasised that good management meant self-sufficiency.

Watermill sites are elusive; Bordesley's is the best known, with sluice-controlled leats, wattle-lined and subsequently boxed in with massive oak planks, and oak wheels. Metal-working debris associated with this complex suggests that it was a smithy, wheels being used for the bellows. Whether its products were sold to boost the abbey's income rather than made merely to limit its need to buy-in metal objects is unknown. Apart from monastic sites, however, the only iron-producing evidence is of small-scale operations which need have involved no more than the supply of a manor's own requirements; the only excavated thirteenth-century smelting complex, Alsted in Surrey, was also a smithy, and was within the confines of a manor. Its technology was so simple that its bloomery hearth was below ground level; slag could not be tapped off so the whole furnace had to cool before the 'bloom' could be removed. No water sources provided power to increase production. A similarly low-key operation is suggested by sites located in forested areas in Northamptonshire, where one excavated furnace at Waterley measured only some 400×200 millimetres. Again, there is no suggestion that water power was used, to turn wheels operating hammers to break up the ore before roasting or bellows to intensify heat in the furnaces. Nor is use of water power likely at all the Wealden production sites located by spreads of bloomery slag, although used at Chingley, Sussex, probably for hammering. The blast furnace, although used in Sweden, was not introduced to England until the end of the fifteenth century.[61]

A major factor limiting the development of a large-scale iron industry was the quality of English ores; even the best, like those in the Forest of Dean, required a lot of time and fuel-consuming work to remove phosphorus and other impurities. For hardness they were all right, but the iron was too brittle: much better ores, with more steel-like qualities, were available from abroad, notably Spain as well as Sweden. English ores could be mixed with imports to produce serviceable goods, and analyses of knife-blades have shown that smiths were adept both at 'piling' the ores to produce a homogeneous bar and at welding steel-quality strips onto cheaper iron cores.[62] Since ordinary ores seem to have been about a fifth of the price of the best imports, it was obviously efficient to combine the two in this way. Consequently, English ores were not simply priced out of the market. What mattered more was the size of that market; if monasteries and manors preferred to produce their own iron, using their own labour, the external producer could only look to towns and rural settlements with their limited needs. Nor did royal demand make up for the deficiency: when the king planned an expedition to France in 1242, he demanded 8,000 horseshoes and 20,000 nails from the archbishop of Canterbury, who, because of his estates in the Weald, was best able to supply them. This order would have required perhaps 3,000 lb of iron; a bloomery furnace can produce some thirty lb per firing (an estimate for the Stamford furnaces suggests seventy-five lb). Consequently six furnaces working on a twenty-four hour cycle would have supplied the whole lot in eighteen days. These estimates are very inexact, but they are useful because they show how little the efforts and quantities involved in meeting what was an exceptionally

large order by the standards of its day actually were. Supplying medieval armies might make an individual armourer wealthy, but it would not support a
large-scale armaments industry even when payments were offered, and thus
would not act as a sufficient catalyst to raise an industry to the point where investment in technology was worthwhile.

Another industry which may have established itself in the Weald in the
thirteenth century is glass-making, although the earliest known furnace is
fourteenth century.[63] English glass production was limited by poor-quality
sands, but Near Eastern and Italian imports at Southampton, Boston, Nottingham and Reigate[64] show a demand for vessels as well as for window glass,
and these are not from the high-status sites such as castles and palaces where
they might most be expected to occur. They may be merchants' status symbols, not imported to sell as trade goods, but even so they show considerable
demand for such luxury items.

Something of the same increase in demand for more than the most basic
commodities can be seen in pottery. Most obviously, the proportion of glazed
wares recovered from rubbish pits and other contexts becomes greater. Bulb-
ous tripod pitchers (7,2) were generally supplanted by taller, more slender
jugs, usually wheel-made; colour contrasts were achieved by applying different clays to the surfaces, and copper filings might be sprinkled on to give
a mottled effect. Just as Stamford ware in the late ninth century could be seen
to be strongly influenced by overseas products, so too in the late twelfth and
thirteenth centuries imports from Rouen in Normandy, and subsequently
from the Saintonge areas of Gascony, affected the English decorated wares.
The actual number of vessels of the former imported was not high – even in
London, it represents only 2 per cent or less of the total of pottery found – and
sherds from them are almost entirely found in ports, so they were not being
traded inland: nevertheless, they were copied in London and elsewhere in a
way never attempted of such twelfth-century imports as Rhenish 'Blue-grey'
handled bowls or red-painted wares. Also copied were high-quality metal
table wares, most strikingly the water jugs in the shapes of animals and
mounted men, known as 'aquamaniles', of which there were pottery equivalents in London by the mid thirteenth century. Many of these were produced
in Scarborough, and their coastal distribution around the east coast and as far
south as Sussex suggests that there was a wide demand for them. Some could
have reached their final breaking-places as gifts, others as the chattels of
peripatetic noble households, but there are enough of them to suggest at least
some intermittent trade, even if only as make-weights with other cargoes such
as coal. Other highly elaborate jugs include puzzle jugs (7,7), an insight into
medieval humour, and many with moulded figures, animals and human faces.
Imports of 'polychrome' Saintonge wares are sufficiently often found at castle
sites as to suggest that by the end of the thirteenth century that particular type
of pottery was, perhaps uniquely, being used at the tables of those of the highest status, and by few others except wealthy merchants in ports and occasional
inland houses. Although there is a single sherd at Wharram Percy, it was not

7, 7. Two late thirteenth-/early fourteenth-century Oxford jugs. The smaller one, on the left, is English, but in shape and decoration imitates contemporary imports from south-west France. The elaborate 'puzzle' jug, also English, has two separate compartments, the lower filled through the hollow handle. The stag's head is its spout: so an unwary drinker gets drenched when he tips up the jug - an insight into peasant humour. The elaboration of these vessels contrasts with the earlier tripod pitcher (**7, 2**) and suggests that many people already had a little more spending money. (Heights: 205 mm and (puzzle jug) 330 mm).

normally bought by rural dwellers, and almost certainly not by poorer townsmen, since there is not enough of it in urban rubbish pits to suggest regular shipments for sale to a wide market. English potters tried to copy it (**7,7**), not very successfully, as they could not achieve the necessary quality of clay.[65]

The scale of operation of many English potters was probably increasing: a single order for the royal castle at Winchester to the potters fifteen miles away at Laverstock, outside Salisbury, Wiltshire, was for 1,000 pitchers. They only cost the king twenty-five shillings, however, including transport. Laverstock

had another royal palace to supply, nearby at Clarendon, as well as the marketplace in Salisbury and other towns in the area. Few of their products have
actually been reported from Winchester, however, despite the orders from
the castle. Even over that distance, they may not have been competitive. This
seems to be fairly typical of known inland kilns: they could dominate a few
local markets, but not achieve long-distance distribution. Constraint by toll
charges may be shown at Bedford, where the pottery found north and south
of the river crossing comes from different supply sources. By such restraints
was the potters' capacity to expand limited.[66] One useful rôle of pottery
studies is to show that many villagers were not dependent on a single supplier
for their pots, since sherds from different kilns are usually found. This may
well mean that peasants and potters frequented more than one marketplace.
In the few cases where a particular pot-making centre did manage to exclude
virtually all competition from its nearest market, as Grimston succeeded in
doing at Lynn, its coastal location may have meant that it had some export
capacity, giving it a price advantage because of the scale of its production.

Although glazed jugs were getting into the countryside, the most highly decorated, and consequently presumably the most expensive, are proportionally
less likely to occur there than in towns. The village site at Goltho produced
two recognisable face-jug sherds and a few others with dots, pellets or horseshoes; Barton Blount, Derbyshire, did not produce any, nor did Seacourt,
and such results seem typical. Nevertheless the preponderance of cooking-
pots at these places may occur because they were much more prone to breakage, especially when used on open hearths. The assemblage from a thirteenth-century long-house at Dinna Clerks on Dartmoor is instructive,
because the building seems to have been destroyed by fire and no-one
bothered to retrieve its contents, which included a penny of the 1250s. There
were five cooking-pots, a glazed jug and two charred wooden dishes around
its hearth, but in an inner room were a cistern, two more jugs and another
cooking-pot. So the ceramic assemblage actually in use had a much higher
ratio of jugs to cooking-pots than a normal rubbish deposit contains.[67]

Did ordinary townspeople have any material advantage over their country
cousins? That the wealthy could prosper is shown by the stone houses, but it
is not so easy to gauge the access to high-quality goods of the artisans, nor to
be sure of their housing conditions. Sites such as St Peter's Street, Northampton, have substantial stone-founded buildings replacing timber, though
not on all the tenements, but few towns have yet produced evidence from
their central areas to give a clear idea of the different types of dwelling to be
found in them in the thirteenth century. Less intensive redevelopment in
subsequent centuries may mean that peripheral and suburban zones can be
expected to produce more complete evidence, although so far few towns have
yielded what might be widely anticipated, the one and two-roomed, probably
single-storey clay-walled houses found in fourteenth-century levels in Norwich.[68] In the Hamel, Oxford's west suburb, tenements were laid out at the
turn of the twelfth and thirteenth century (**7,8**). This site was near the flood-

plain of the River Thames on meadows which had been drained by ditches, one of which provided the boundary line for one of the new tenements. Although laid out in a single operation, the tenements were built on piecemeal. Stone seems to have been used at least for the foundations of all the buildings. Some of the different properties were joined together, suggesting terraced housing. Contiguous structures were not novel, of course, but the use of terracing may have been, suggesting maximum use of the available space, and a type of building particularly appropriate for towns. During the middle of the thirteenth century, there was also a much more substantial house in the Hamel, with walls a metre thick, clearly the property of someone wealthier than his neighbours. A seal owned by 'Adam the Chaplain' came from this tenement.[69]

Intermingling of social groups in towns meant that their rubbish became intermingled in the pits where much of it ended up, so that it is difficult to establish the extent to which the better foods and artefacts were the preserves of the wealthy. Nor is this problem helped by the friars, whose arrival in many towns in the thirteenth century brought a new factor into the urban community. Although they were supposed to espouse poverty, it is fairly clear from the sites of their houses in Oxford and Leicester that expenditure was more than basic, both in the scale of the building of their churches and in the food that

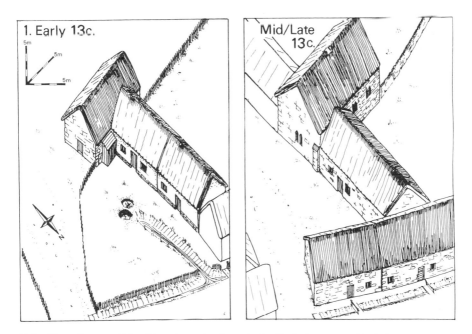

7, 8. Two phases at The Hamel, a suburban site in Oxford excavated by N. Palmer. Initially a terrace of buildings, the site was redeveloped intensifying occupation and creating a built-up street frontage. The presence of a more substantial house amongst the cottages shows the social 'mix' in the area.

they ate. The Dominicans at Oxford, despite being so far from the sea, were acquiring quantities of fish such as herring, cod and haddock, which may have been dried or salted, not fresh, and more than one sturgeon graced their tables over the years. Their Austin counterparts at Leicester were also acquiring such things, with large quantities of marine shell-fish being consumed, which can only have been eaten while fresh.[70]

It is possible to be reasonably certain that the fish in the pits and other contexts at the Oxford and Leicester friaries were actually consumed there because both sites were outside the towns, and it is not very likely therefore that their rubbish would have become mixed with others' to any great extent. Such exclusivity is unusual, however, for many friaries were intra-mural, as in Lincoln or Southampton, probably because powerful patrons were able to find them enough space, at least away from the main streets. This sort of patronage means that the location of friaries cannot be taken as a precise measure of a town's prosperity and consequent rent levels. They do, however, give some indication of which towns were considered the largest and most in need of the mendicants' missions.

Other measures of towns' thirteenth-century importance include their walls and gates, and the efforts that many put into maintaining and improving their streets and trading facilities. Particularly visible in archaeology are the quays and wharfs which have been found at a number of towns from the thirteenth century onwards, largely because the lower parts of their timbers are water-logged. In London, where the process of reclamation and improvement to the river frontage began earlier than elsewhere, the quays were not a municipal effort, uniformly constructed along the Thames, but seem to have been the initiatives of holders of narrow plots along the river bank, each having to compensate for what his neighbour had done, since each new extension into the water would cause the next-door stretch to silt up and lose its access.[71] The investment in these structures was not usually enormous, for the timbers did not have to be of great length: what they show is the need for new sorts of harbour facilities, with boats that were not simply unloaded onto a mud flat or shelving hard, with the risk of getting the cargo wet. Thirteenth-century seals indicate the use of high-sided capacious ships with a single main mast, relatively slow but reliable, and not requiring a very large crew. They needed to be able to ride in the water at quay-sides for unloading, or to anchor in mid-channel and use lighters. A good harbour was one where they did not have to lose time waiting for the high tide before they sailed, but as they were bulk carriers of wool, cloth, wine and other goods speed of delivery was not essential. But they were still quite small: the early fourteenth-century wine fleet needed a thousand ships to carry 72,700 barrels, an average load of *c.* 250 tons.[72]

Ships were expensive to buy, and to operate even with small crews. Investment in them had to be justified by efficient use; the provision of lighthouses is one way in which increased concern for safe navigation can be recognised.[73] Ports like London had to offer repair services as well as harbour and storage facilities. Financial expertise also developed as a result of shipping investments and transaction facilities had to be available. Consequently commercial activity increasingly concentrated at a few large ports rather than at a network of small harbours: 'beach markets', whether a Bantham or a Lynn, were no longer sufficient. Bigger ships were a reason for the decline of the river navigations, and several coastal places first mentioned late in the twelfth century grew to displace older-established ports, as Poole in Dorset did Wareham. At Portsmouth, Hampshire, traces of buildings close to the shore line attest the first use of the site soon after its foundation in the late twelfth century; a solidly-built timber-lined cistern dug to hold fresh water presumably partly supplied ships' water barrels.[74] Inland towns on river navigations were further affected by increased use of mills and fish-weirs, traces of which have been located in Nottinghamshire, for instance, which impeded the passage of boats:[75] rubbish dumping was another problem. Oxford and Lincoln are two towns whose trade may have suffered as much from this as from the recorded decline of their cloth industries, although loss of navigation may itself have been a cause of that decline.[76] Any problems that towns like these were facing are very difficult to establish from their archaeology. General commerce was sufficient to keep Oxford, for instance, buoyant, as the Hamel excavations show. No abandonments of property have been found, which would be the ultimate demonstration that a town was in difficulties. It must not be assumed, however, that walls and quays are necessarily a sign that a town was thriving; they might just as well have been built in a desperate attempt to keep up appearances or to win back lost trade.

Keeping up appearances may have been becoming more important after the middle of the twelfth century. Certainly high-cost items such as jewellery were increasingly evident. The simple twisted rings of the tenth and eleventh centuries passed out of use in the twelfth. New ring-wearing fashions appeared, partly under Church influence, because each priest had a gold ring set with a stone appropriate to his rank, semi-precious sapphires, garnets, turquoises and so on, each of which was considered to be endowed with special properties – to detect poison, to preserve the wearer from sudden death, or even to help an escape from prison. Neither the goldwork nor the quality of the stones are particularly impressive, but they are found in some number, often in ecclesiastics' graves, like that of Archbishop Walter de Gray of York. Secular usage, or at least import by a merchant if not for his own use, is demonstrated by a ring set with garnets found in a late twelfth-century pit in Southampton. Brooches were also changing, with ring-brooches coming into fashion, often set with stones like the finger-rings and with amorous or devotional inscriptions.[77] These things suggest more decorous behaviour and more courtly display as the well-to-do played out a subtler comedy of manners. Henry III was criticised in the middle of the thirteenth century for not acting his part by handing out festive dresses and costly jewels. Finds from Exeter and other towns show that those with shallower purses might have copper-alloy imitations set with glass or pastes, like the contemporary pottery, such copies suggest a unity of culture, divided not so much by birth as by wealth. To argue this is to argue that the rigid caste divisions of feudalism, dominated by inheritance and military service, were to some degree being broken down.

Concomitant with such social changes were changing ways of managing social relations, and the twelfth century is notable for the increased rôle that legislation and government administration played. The use of the abacus may not be attested archaeologically but the importance of legal processes is certainly shown by the increased numbers of seal-dies that are found. Even the poor had to have a personal seal with which to demonstrate their witness to documents: many of the cheapest dies were probably cut in lead and are occasionally found, as recently in Norwich, but copper-alloy seal-rings become quite frequent and probably exemplify the equivalent of Adam the Chaplain's well-cut handled die found at the Hamel.[78] Such seals are one way in which an increasing sense of a person as an individual was expressed. The late twelfth-century development of individual tomb effigies is another, at least for the highest ranks. There is an increase in memorial slabs generally, many carved with symbols like shears which seem to be indicators of professions.[79] Not only finger-rings, but also pewter chalices and patens were placed in priests' graves; it is as though these were ways of marking an individual's tomb, distinguishing its occupant from the anonymity of the mass cemetery.

Class distinctions became more important as they became even more prominently displayed. Class barriers could be crossed by the successful: an example is the Ludlow merchant Laurence's purchase of Stokesay Castle in 1281. The aim of acquiring wealth was to spend it, not to use it to accrue even more of it, and lavish expenditure included consumption of exotic foreign foods such as figs, the seeds of which are occasionally found, as well as elaborate display. The aim was to demonstrate the distance between those who could afford luxuries and those who could not, just as Laurence de Ludlow distanced himself physically from his fellow townsmen by buying his country property. It is distancing of this sort which probably accounts for many of the topographical changes in the countryside that mark the later twelfth and thirteenth centuries. At Goltho, for instance, the castle was abandoned, and its owners probably moved to a new site which took them half a mile away from their villagers.[80] Sometimes such abandonments may be for tenurial reasons: it is not unreasonable to link the demolition of the substantial stone structure at Wharram Percy in the thirteenth century to the sale of their manor there by the Chamberlain family in 1254.[81] Excavations are increasingly showing that moated sites came into use at this time, partly perhaps because of legal and economic prohibitions on castle building: a moat gave an echo of a castle without being seriously defensive, although some owners acquired licenses if they wanted something really big. A few moated sites, such as Milton, Hampshire, a late example, seem to have been laid out over existing peasant houses: more often it was the gentry who moved – at any rate, most of those excavated are either on previously unoccupied land, or overlie occupation that is as likely to come from a previous manor house as from some other building on the site. Not all moats were the property of gentry owners: sheer numbers in East Anglia suggest the work of better-off tenants. Many are in areas only recently brought into cultivation. As their numbers increased, no doubt their status claims declined, but they seem to have been part of a process which allowed a wider social stratum to proclaim its pretensions.[82]

At the same time as this process by which relative isolation in tight-knit enclaves was achieved by the wealthy was a tendency for their buildings to be conglomerated: instead of the separate halls, kitchens, sleeping-quarters and chapels of a site like Cheddar, a single building typically consisted of private apartments at one end of a hall, and service rooms at the other.[83] The great keeps in castles had perforce brought these together, but inconveniently: the new palaces and manor houses combined access and comfort, giving the owner accommodation separate from his servants, but also retaining the great hall in which he entertained and gave display to his gentility: private and public needs were satisfied.

By the end of the thirteenth century, housing at most social levels made this same fundamental provision for a central hall flanked by rooms used for other purposes. On Dartmoor and widely across England on higher ground, the long-house was one variation of it: the largest stone houses at Hound Tor (**7,5**) were of this type, each with a centrally placed entrance leading on one side into the hall, identifiable by its hearth, with access from it into a small inner room, and on the other side into a byre for livestock, often identifiable by a drain. Apart from a porch, a feature added to some of the Hound Tor houses during their period of use, this rectangular plan was generally used, and its adoption was probably one reason for the use in southern central, northern and western England of cruck construction, in which pairs of curved timbers along the length of the building gave substantial but flexible accommodation that allowed one end to be used, if required, for winter shelter of animals, perhaps with a loft space above; an open central hall, which might be two bays long if it could be afforded; and perhaps an end room to give further living and storage space. Radiocarbon and dendrochronology date the earliest surviving structures of this sort to the later part of the thirteenth century.[84]

Rectangularity of plan was not something that peasants would have observed on their visits to their landlord's manor house, where the end-blocks were usually at right angles to the hall and did not share its roof-line; it was the internal arrangement of the space that mattered. In areas where the cruck was not used, similar spatial provision was made. In Kent, for example, the types of joint used in its construction allow a thirteenth-century attribution to a house in Petham, which had an aisled hall and two end-rooms, its hipped roof showing that it had not had a full upper storey.[85] It may have been in order to provide first-floor space in such end-blocks that the 'Wealden' house and variations upon it came to be widely used in south-east England. All seem most suited to two- or temporarily three-generation nuclear family occupation, each house doing its own food preparation and so on without dependence upon outside support of the sort that a kin-group might provide. In towns, too, something of the same sort had come into use by the early fourteenth century, when the earliest surving 'burgess' housing is found, as at 58 French Street, Southampton. There, above a stone cellar which had its own separate access, there was provision for a shop on the street frontage, with a room above it, and a side passage which led into a central, open hall beyond which was another two-storey block. Kitchens, for safety reasons, often remained physically separate.[86] Similar plans characterise Chester's famous Rows, for which late thirteenth- and early fourteenth-century dates are now being obtained by dendrochronology.[87] Poorer townspeople had to be content with one- or two-roomed cottages, as in Norwich, or with terraced housing as in Oxford's Hamel (7,8), and there may have been poorly-built cots on the edges of hamlets and villages too, but the evidence of excavations is that the normal unit was rather better.

What seems to be suggested by all these buildings is that by the end of the thirteenth century there was an underlying unity in the concept of what a house should provide which permeated the whole of society. What was actually built varied both according to what could be afforded, and regional modes. The full-length cruck, for instance, has one of the most remarkable distribution patterns in archaeology, for it has a 'frontier' east of which are no examples. As there are no contemporary documents that state a reason for this, a variety of explanations – many somewhat improbable, such as survival of British traditions or Irish influence – has been offered, of which local carpentry techniques seems the best, although it does not explain how such preferences arose in the first place. Of more concern to the houses' occupants was the internal arrangement of the space that the different types of construction offered. The similarity of this arrangement at so many different social levels implies the same cultural unity that the pottery and the jewellery demonstrate.

The buildings also seem to have few variations on basic types: the cruck houses might be up to five bays long, but apparently never six; the 'Wealden' might have only one end-block if the owner could not stretch to a second, but they never had extra storeys added even when vertical extension was practised in towns. Wealth differences between owners meant that town houses had scope for different plans, but they are mostly adaptations within close-set limits. It is as though houses expressed the social place of their occupants as well as their income, so that they had to conform to what was regarded as appropriate. Although a few people bettered themselves, most sought to maintain rather than to advance their social position, behaving within parameters of expectation largely created by the basic teaching of the Church that all must perform their allotted tasks, not in order to acquire wealth but to secure sufficient for their needs. A house answered peoples' needs both because it provided shelter and because it proclaimed its occupants' social position. Similarity to the houses of others in that social position bolstered corporate identity and a sense of community. Too much variation in house types would have obscured those signals.

Chapter Eight

THE LATER THIRTEENTH AND FOURTEENTH CENTURIES

Luxury in a Cold Climate

In 1304, King Edward I refused to allow the Scots, whom he was besieging inside Stirling Castle, to surrender, mainly because he wanted to try out the *Warwolf*, a new weapon for which he was due to pay an engineer the large sum of £40; he also owed £20 to a Frenchman for gunpowder. The occasion was a bizarre mixture of courtly display and brutality, since a viewing gallery was erected for spectators, who included ladies. Tournament and real war rarely impinged upon each other so directly, but the siege of Stirling is an example of the latter's increasing costs. Although it would be some time before guns became indispensable, there were already other siege engines and specialist operatives to be paid for, and armies had to be more professional and better equipped. Even foot-soldiers needed long training if they were to be fully effective: an archer had to be able to fire some ten volleys per minute. Although campaigns could still be mounted by calling upon feudal levies, long-service contracts were needed to keep armies abroad for more than a few weeks at a time. All this put the Crown under pressure to raise its revenues through taxation and customs dues in order to meet the demands of war.[1]

Edward I's England was not really big enough to provide all that he would need if he were to be a major figure on the European stage. The English economy had expanded, but it had been growth primarily based on increased population and more intensive agricultural production, rather than increased productivity per head. The island remained balanced on the edge of the world, internally well enough supplied, but only tangential to most of the dynamic areas, such as northern Italy, and the ports of the German Hanse. Its economy was still basically manorial, as the archaeological record of the iron and other industries shows, even though the social system within which manorialism operated was changing. Edward I's wars with Wales and Scotland were in part a response to his need to expand in the only way open to him, enlargement of his kingdom. Similarly Edward III initiated the long series of campaigns in France to launch himself into a European involvement.

War was not all bad: successful war could be very profitable for some. Fortunes were to be made by campaigning soldiers, from ransoms paid by the captured enemy and from the money paid by the king to those who could raise a band of men-at-arms. Furthermore, the king's need for ships and weapons meant that suppliers stood to gain from his expenditure. It was also difficult to restrict piracy. In consequence, favoured individuals and places might thrive despite the pressures and uncertainties faced by the majority, and a delusion of general prosperity may be gained from the expenditure of the few. This problem is exacerbated by other external factors: worsening weather patterns, crop failures, animal deaths, and the mid fourteenth-century plague with its successors and its allies such as typhoid. Economically, socially and politically it was an unstable and uncertain era, and associating patterns of change with any particular cause is particularly difficult.

In a very few instances, changes in the archaeological record can plausibly be associated with specific events. In excavations in Southampton, large pits filled with burnt debris and burnt layers which interrupt building sequences have been found; material of that sort usually results from an unrecorded fire started by a domestic accident, but in Southampton's case there is so much of it that it can safely be identified as the residue of the rubble left behind after the catastrophe inflicted on the town in 1338 by the French and Genoese, whose destructive raid even affected its subsequent topographical history.[2] Some areas were not built on again for centuries, and when the next threat of French attack arose thirty years later, a defensive wall was built between the edge of the town and the sea, cutting off many of the merchants' warehouses from their direct access to the waterfront. Subsequently, everything had to go in and out through one of the town gates, putting a premium on properties near those and on the roads leading to them.[3]

Although as vulnerable as Southampton to French attack, Portsmouth shows no comparable interruption to its development. Activity on the water-front increased: a stone building associated with the late thirteenth-century cistern was enlarged, a stone well was dug, the cistern was reconstructed, and an attempt was probably made to reclaim part of the shore-line with stone walling. Most interesting of all, a six-metre wide dock for boats was cut into the shelving beach, constructed with wattle walls up to a metre thick woven round upright stakes. A gravel quay on one side gave loading facilities, and a sea wall was also constructed.[4] There is no indication here that Portsmouth was anything but flourishing: disruption to commercial trade could be made up by supplying the king's needs for a navy and transport.

The south coast of England was exposed to attack from France, but the east coast ports suffered too. The king demanded ships, which were liable to be impounded and taken away. Their owners did not even benefit from their need to be victualled and repaired. The effect on Yarmouth of the Hundred Years' War was particularly devastating, for losses of ships and trade were exacerbated by the building and upkeep of expensive town walls. Yarmouth's problems are not yet fully accessible from its archaeology, although the only large-scale excavation has an occupation sequence which fades out in the later Middle Ages and is concomitant with the failure of the town to revive its fortunes. War, however, was not Yarmouth's only problem, for the loss of its herring fishing to Dutch competition impeded its revival.[4]

Another of the effects of politics and war on Yarmouth involved the cessation of open hostilities against the Scots, for the port had benefited earlier as a supplier to Edward I's expeditions. This was of much more consequence to Berwick-upon-Tweed, on the Border itself. A poorly defended Scottish town with only a ditch and timber fence in the thirteenth century, it was sacked by Edward I, who then made it his major supply base.[5] His new, stone walls actually enclosed a smaller area than the old earthworks, presumably to create a more tight-knit defence. Three small sites have been excavated; two produced thirteenth-century and later activity, the third evidence of late twelfth-century use considerably enhanced by construction of stone buildings at the end of the thirteenth century. From the mid-fourteenth, however, this site was unoccupied, for by then royal interest in the town had waned and it was reverting to its earlier, limited rôle as a port for a hinterland which now had to contend with frequent cattle-raiding skirmishes as well as all the problems faced elsewhere in England. Hartlepool, further south, has also produced evidence which suggests royal patronage during the Scottish wars, with a stone dock being constructed.[6]

Although the north-eastern towns seem to have gained little in the long term from Edward I's Scottish campaigns, those in the north-west and west Midlands may have benefited from the peace which his Welsh expeditions brought to the area, at least for a century or so. In Shrewsbury, for instance, the authorities felt secure enough in the fourteenth century to allow houses to be built over the town walls. Streets were widened, and some previously open areas were enclosed.[7] At Chester, not only were the Rows being built, but money was also being spent on the Water tower, constructed in 1322, which stands forward from the walls to protect the river and to safeguard activity at the town's landing-place. The probability is that Chester was able to maintain its momentum well into the fourteenth century.[8] It is symptomatic of the security felt in the area that few of the gentry built defensible houses for themselves, as they felt compelled to do in the Scottish borders. Even the Welsh 'revolts' of the fifteenth century did not evoke a physical reaction.[9]

A town which has been extensively studied is Lynn, where continued development, particularly of the waterfront zone, is shown at one site by construction of a brick quay founded on timber, and at another by stone houses and warehouses. Silting at the water's edge was a problem that was partly countered by piles to stabilise the frontage. At the end of the fourteenth century, timber-framed buildings at one site collapsed and the hall there was rebuilt, but not the warehouses. Otherwise, the excavations show Lynn as consolidating its twelfth- and thirteenth-century growth; it was not adversely affected by the king's wars, though direct evidence of the Baltic and Hanse trade which was its livelihood is lacking from the archaeological record. There is practically no imported pottery, for instance, to indicate Lynn's connections with northern Europe.[10]

Fourteenth-century fluctuations are more apparent at Kingston upon Hull, established in 1293 as a borough 'grafted' upon a small existing village, with a street plan largely dictated by existing water-courses. Lines of stakes have shown how tenements close to the river were divided from each other, and many soon had buildings erected within them. One of these sites, however, fell into disuse again during the fourteenth century, perhaps a sign of failure to maintain early momentum. Similarly, a site near the town's walls away from the water-front produced post-holes which suggest an abortive attempt to establish buildings, the area subsequently being used for rubbish pits. It was probably waste areas like these that the corporation was seeking to buy in the early fourteenth century, hoping that they would be a good investment. Nevertheless, Hull was not a run-away success, and such success as it had may have been at the expense of neighbours like Beverley eight miles further up the river, although it also replaced a site on the river mouth lost to erosion.[11]

Hull's town walls are built of brick: a municipal brickyard recorded as early as 1303 continued in production until the middle of the fifteenth century. Brick had made occasional appearances before in England, but Hull marks its first significant bulk use. Some other east coast towns made similar use of it. A newly discovered tilery a mile outside Beverley has shown the very large scale of production involved in such enterprises.[12] Theoretically, brick had a huge potential market, but in practice it was in competition with stone in most districts, and its cost of production was too great even though the clay itself was cheap. Wage costs were high, both for skilled moulders and layers and for large numbers of unskilled labourers, and the kilns were voracious of fuel. Coal could be used, and has been found at a manufacturing site in Boston, but it had to be transported and so it was not cheap, probably even if carried as ballast by boats that had taken grain to the north-east. In the same way, bricks were too heavy for easy transport – in 1422, it cost £28 10 shillings to bring 114,000 bricks, themselves costing only £19, from Calais to Shene Palace, even though Shene is close enough to the Thames for overland carting to be minimal. With these sorts of expenses, production at a single centre for distribution over a wide area was not economic, which is the typically restrictive pattern of a medieval bulk industry. Another ceramic product, floor tiles, provides a comparable example. Boosted by royal patronage in the middle of the thirteenth century, they became widespread in churches, with their quality deteriorating as demand was met by less skilled makers. They continued to be bought for royal palaces such as Windsor, but they did not manage to establish a domestic market at a lower social level, presumably because cost prevented emulation.

Hull is another example of a port where excavations have shown the efforts that went into creating a stable quayside. Initially, clay layers were dumped on the shore-line and stakes were driven through them to create a platform; a vertical face to the water was cut, revetted by oak timbers. During the second quarter of the fourteenth century, this revetment was removed and replaced by a stone wall, probably part of the footings for a warehouse, and a new timber wharf was constructed further out into the river, with a stone hard in front of it on which boats could rest at low tide without getting stuck fast in the mud. Like Portsmouth's dock, these elaborate constructions emphasize the importance of providing adequate harbour facilities: although no trace of one may ever be found, the first reference to a crane in England dates to 1347. Presumably these were more efficient than the less sophisticated tilting arms, but were also more expensive and would only have been available at ports like Hull which made efforts to keep their quays up to date.

The earliest recorded docking point at Hull was the insalubriously but no doubt aptly named Rotten Herring Staithe. 'Rotenhering' was probably the original surname of an obscure Hull merchant who, under the more genteel name of de la Pole, sought his fortune in London: he prospered enough for his son in 1339 to be made a banneret (then a relatively new title, senior to a knight), his grandson an earl and his great-grandson a duke. This was a unique social climb, but it shows that men with luck, ability and, in the de la Poles' case, large sums of money – £100,000 in 1337 – to lend the king, could at least aspire to the nobility. Hull benefited from the family connection, since the de la Poles established a hospital there, a typical form of late-medieval charity which such people especially favoured as it helped them to buy their way into their new status. Chantries and colleges were other late-medieval pious foundations: the former are typical of a need felt by an uncertain élite both to create personal monuments and to establish recognition of their families, the latter are a sign of increasing concern for education as learned clerks and lawyers came to be more and more important to the administration of aristocratic estates and business affairs, which could less and less be run by relying upon servile customs and personal relationships.[13]

That the de la Pole family used building as a way of establishing status was of course not an innovation, but during the fourteenth century there are many examples of a trend that went somewhat beyond the mere purchase of a country house or the building of a castle by an aspiring social climber, such as Laurence de Ludlow exemplified in the later thirteenth century.[14] Even the king was building with more than architectural style and comfort in mind. Windsor Castle was reconstructed by Edward III in the middle of the fourteenth century so that it provided a setting for chivalric rôle-playing. The elaborate rituals of the Order of the Garter, which he created in 1348, partly served to form bonds of honour to weld together the élite group upon whose support he depended, and who in their turn depended upon him to supply the reassurance of corporate unity. 'Round Tables' had become particularly prestigious: that at Windsor has not survived, but it must have been on the scale of the one in the castle hall at Winchester, from which radiocarbon and dendrochronological dates have been obtained that suggest construction for Henry III or Edward I.[15] Normally, the king sat at the centre of a high table, with everyone arranged in strict order of rank down the room. At a 'Round Table' there was no precedence, creating an illusion that all those at the table were equal; but of course only those who had the qualifications of, or at least pretensions to, noble lineage could aspire to a seat as one of the king's chosen company at a 'Round Table'.

Few could emulate Windsor, though some tried. John of Gaunt, a member of the royal family, remodelled Kenilworth, Warwickshire (8, 1).[16] Ten miles away the Nevilles felt obliged to reconstruct Warwick Castle, giving it an elaborate 'show-front' with turreted towers and gate-house. The state apartments already built there may pre-date those at Windsor, causing the king to go one better. An important aspect of these structures was their provision of lodgings for members of the household and guests. Just as the king had his court, so a nobleman had to have a retinue of clients and dependents, some bound to him by annual payments, others by hope of favour and support. They were not bound to him by the old ties of service in return for land, however, and his need to accommodate them and to entertain them shows how the social bond had to be physically demonstrated. This was important even in areas where traditional ties might have been expected to last longer: the Courtenays were earls of Devon, but felt obliged to provide a new range of

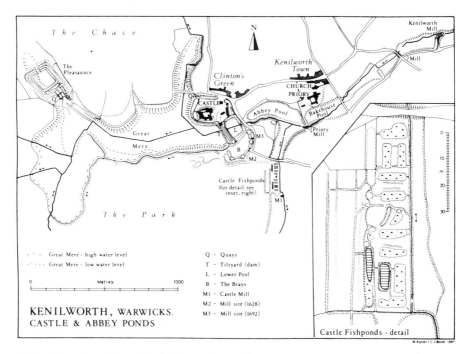

8, 1. The plan of the surrounding earthworks, by M. Aston and C. J. Bond, emphasises how Kenilworth Castle was defended by water on three sides, controlled by impressively engineered dams. The fishponds provided one of the varied foods which helped to distinguish the aristocracy from the rest of society, just as The Chase and The Park supplied them with venison as well as entertainment. The moated 'Pleasaunce' was constructed for the fifteenth-century equivalent of Glyndebourne picnics.

lodgings, each with an elegant first-floor chamber and a private lavatory, at their castle at Okehampton, so that they could offer hospitality there on an appropriate scale. Residences like these were increasingly likely to be built around a central courtyard, as though to give the effect that a monastic cloister had, of isolation and separateness from the rest of the world, enhancing the sense of belonging to a privileged clique.

One entertainment which the aristocracy offered their guests was hunting, and Okehampton is typical of many castles, particularly the royal ones, in that they were close to forests and served also as hunting lodges. A large number of barbed arrows, of types little used except in pursuit of game-animals such as deer (which they bring down by cutting the ham-strings), have been found at Okehampton Castle, and quantities of bones show that the guests were offered venison. A change from a predominance of red to roe deer bones can plausibly be linked to the known creation of a new park close to the castle at the end of the thirteenth century, which would have sheltered the roe: the red may have come mostly from the wider spaces of Dartmoor. The need to entertain guests was probably a more important reason for the creation of such parks than economic need: indeed, it has been suggested that to establish them on good agricultural land was a deliberate ploy by the wealthy to vaunt how they could afford to neglect opportunities to maximise their incomes.[17] Within Okehampton Park were settlements which the new regime would have disrupted. One hamlet there which excavations show to have come into use in the twelfth century seems to have been abandoned at about the time that the park was established,[18] although a few sherds suggest that at least some sort of occupation may have been maintained, if only as a lodge for the park keepers. Desertions caused by landlords' decisions to change land use were probably not very common until the fourteenth century: it is one thing to clear away a couple of farms, another to move out an entire, fully populated village, however supportive of the owner the law may be. A village already weakened by population loss might more easily be pressurised, and certainly clearance by landlords was to become more frequent as population pressures changed.

About twelve miles from Okehampton, but within the royal forest of Dartmoor, Hound Tor presents a number of contrasts (**7**, **5**). There is no documentation to suggest why that site should have been abandoned. Even its ownership is not certain, though it may have been part of the land held by a minor local family who in turn held it as tenants of another almost equally obscure family, who in their turn held it as tenants of Tavistock Abbey (who, to complete the story, would have held it ultimately from the king). If any of these had a motive to cause the abandonment of the site in the fourteenth century, it is not known what it was. More probably, an interplay of circumstances was involved and, as with most sites, whether any one factor outweighed others can be a matter of opinion. Is it significant, for instance, that Hound Tor had three barns into which drying-ovens were inserted, whereas the Okehampton site had none? Is this because the latter was abandoned before the weather had become so inclement that grain which could previously dry in the open air had to be brought indoors and dried artificially, despite the effort of gathering fuel? Or were there facilities elsewhere at Okehampton, such as a demesne oven, perhaps near an unlocated mill? Was grain even being grown at the Okehampton site, except on a minor scale? Near Hound Tor, a pollen sample has shown that both oats and rye were being cultivated during the thirteenth century, and there are lynchets resulting from ploughing around the site. But were crops being dried in field kilns which have not been detected, so that the barn driers merely represent the transfer of an existing activity to a new position, and were not a response to a new problem? Although a quantity of oats was found in one of the driers at Hound Tor, they might originally have been constructed in the vain hope that wheat could be grown on the exposed moors – and because they had been built, they were then used for the more sensible oats for which existing conditions might in fact still have been adequate. Or were there attempts to increase the quantity of oats being grown, perhaps because more horses were being used, which need more than just hay for their feed, unlike oxen and sheep? Cereals for animals would probably not have needed intensive drying, however, as they do not have to be threshed to separate the grain from the stalk. Unfortunately, in these acid Dartmoor soils, bones do not survive, so changes in the animals being kept cannot be identified. But it is important not to assume that the driers can only represent the Hound Tor farmers' desperate attempts to maintain their agriculture despite worsening weather.[19]

Cultural explanations have always to be considered as alternatives to climatic ones, as in the oft-quoted case of the documented decrease in English vineyards. This is at least as likely to be a tribute to the efficiency of the export trade from Gascony and elsewhere as of any further decline in the quality of the English product – much of which was never intended for drinking. It is incorrect to say that England simply could not produce wine in the fourteenth century because of the worsening climate, since Edward III was having it made from vines at Windsor Castle. That the climate did change is evidenced by glaciers and by a few pieces of evidence that do not seem to be affected by human choice, such as the disappearance from York of a nettle-eating bug which is sensitive to the cold. Certainly on some of the exposed uplands at the margin of cultivation, the effect of even slight changes to the climate or in weather patterns could have been to shorten the growing season to the point where arable farming ceased to be viable, or to create conditions too damp for animals to thrive. Most of the land of England was not so marginal, however. Other evidence that is sometimes adduced as indicative of greater rainfall creating damper conditions includes greater provision of drains and ditches – but these may simply result from an increase in building. With rain from roofs needing to be removed, any site had to improve its run-off system, whether it was an abbey like Battle with a rebuilt church and cloisters, or a village croft with a larger house and more out-buildings. Nor can higher river levels be used convincingly in the argument, since a greater water flow is as likely to result from forest clearance and other assarting in the catchment area as from greater precipitation. The flooding recognised in excavations at Bordesley Abbey was probably self-induced, since the monastery completely altered the stream systems to provide mill-leats, fish-ponds and drains.[20]

Pollen evidence does not seem to help with the problem of weather conditions on Hound Tor, for although it shows a regeneration of heather and bilberry at the expense of cereals and the weeds that flourish in their company, it does not seem to indicate an influx of cold or damp-loving species. What it does confirm is the evidence of the abandonment of agriculture during the first half of the fourteenth century at Hound Tor, which is broadly what the pottery indicates. Not far away from the main site, however, is a small complex of stone long-house, barn and grain-drier from which the pottery is of a type which may span the fourteenth century, but without any fabrics which seem to have been in use exclusively in its first half. This is quite likely therefore to represent a short-lived attempt to reuse the higher moor for more than just rough grazing, despite the adverse experience of those who had abandoned the bigger site. Would this have been undertaken if the weather had so obviously made it impossible to work the land? Just to muddy the picture further, there is the other Dartmoor site at Dinna Clerks where the stone long-house was burnt down in the later thirteenth century. Why should this site not have been reoccupied and the burnt building cleared away? Its desertion at what should have been the peak of demand for land, before the climate had worsened appreciably, and before any known population decline, shows the difficulty of making explanations in particular cases.

Because of the wide range of different pressures that affected different sites to different degrees, archaeological evidence is unlikely to be able to assess the effect of particular episodes like the known crop failures and animal mortality of 1315-21 upon settlements which did not go out of use entirely at such times. That pressures for the land remained despite records of waste in some areas is shown by West Whelpington, Northumberland, ravaged during Border raids in 1320 yet rebuilt and maintained despite its vulnerability to further attack. Long-term population decline after 1348–49 was probably the main reason for reduction in occupation at many sites, and total abandonment of others, but this does not mean that there was especially heavy mortality at the particular place where desertion occurred. In some instances documents which imply sudden change should not be taken at face value: at Wharram Percy, for instance, fifteen peasant households were recorded in 1323, thirty in 1368, and only twelve (perhaps) in 1377. Such violent fluctuations might not be apparent in the archaeological record, but the excavated crofts do not suggest anything but continuous use, and could indicate that the records are revealing tax avoidance or merely inefficiency by medieval accountants, not real population figures. Wharram in fact seems to have been less affected by fourteenth-century events than many sites. It has no evidence of amalgamated tenements; the two excavated clearly remained as units within their original boundaries throughout their lifetimes, and the earthworks of the others suggest that most also stayed the same size. This is in contrast to sites such as Gomeldon, Wiltshire, where properties were altered to give bigger plots.[21]

Fourteenth-century desertion at Gomeldon is argued largely on the evidence of a gold coin that must have been lost *c*. 1370 and which was found in the floor of one of the farm buildings – a remarkably valuable object to be in such a context. The pottery would suggest abandonment earlier in the fourteenth century, which prevents too close a date being attributed to the changes that took place within the site during its use. One significant observation was of a long-house modified by the removal of the partition between the living end and the byre or farm-storage end, with the latter being levelled presumably so that it could become part of the domestic accommodation. Separate barns and cow-houses became more standard, with buildings grouped around small yards. This is very different from Wharram Percy, where long-houses seem not to have been used until late in the fourteenth century, the earlier houses being shorter and therefore with less likelihood of domestic and farm activities having taken place under the same roof. The evidence seems to imply that this was becoming unfashionable in the south of England.

Not enough of Gomeldon has been excavated for it to be known whether the whole village was abandoned in the fourteenth century: at Foxcotte, one house site was not built on after the fourteenth century, but another came into use in the fifteenth. The extent of shrinkage at such places is hard to estimate without excavation of a substantial sample. There are, however, sites of isolated farmsteads that certainly went out of use – in the Weald, the Chilterns and the Peak District for instance. Reduction is not only in the most unfavourable territory, like Dartmoor, and it is noticeable that West Whelpington was not the only place in Northumberland to have survived well beyond the Middle Ages, despite the weather, Scottish devastations and remote locations. The high incidence of desertion on the Isle of Wight seems best explained by the island's rôle as the favourite target of French raids, rather than by any climatic or other environmental factor.[22]

Where amalgamations of properties took place, they presumably indicate spare capacity and quite often changing agricultural régimes. Cow-yards at Barton Blount and Goltho are plausibly attributed to greater emphasis being placed on stock-rearing than on arable, a process that would have saved labour.[23] Enclosing of ploughlands became widespread, although many settlements in lowland England did retain at least parts of their open fields. Demand for both cattle and sheep remained buoyant: the former increasingly for meat rather than as plough animals, the latter primarily for their wool. The growth of English cloth industries broadly compensated for the loss of wool exports, both being caused in large part by the collapse of the Flemish cloth manufactories. The industries provided a new demand for labour, at a time when it was becoming scarce, another reason for abandonment of labour-intensive vine production, and for other marginally profitable activities such as salt extraction. By the end of the fourteenth century wages generally had risen more than prices, an indication of increased spending-power among the less well-off. Nevertheless, not all peasants sought to improve themselves: the ethos that all should earn what was appropriate to their station in life meant that many simply did less work, leaving a minority to prosper through higher wages or cheaper land rents. But many could take advantage of increased demand for their products, in particular for meat, especially if the use of horse-drawn carts meant that there was rapid transport. Increased use of horses is suggested by frequent references to peasants owning them, though the bone evidence does not seem to point in the same direction. Horseshoes are commonly found from the twelfth century onwards on rural sites, and again do not clearly show that more horses were in use. The shoes do become bigger and heavier, however, which may indicate that better farriery made that use more efficient.[24]

Excavations at rural sites have not yet produced sufficient stratified deposits to allow precise statements on, for instance, changing food consumption patterns, although preliminary results on the bones from Wharram Percy did not indicate that any change to eating habits was likely to be found. What has been found generally at such sites is evidence of consumption of stock that had outlived its usefulness for other purposes, such as elderly cattle. The peasants' gardens, though small, would have provided peas and beans, with vitamins to add to the calories in their bread, meat and ale, but much of the food value can be lost in cooking. Fibrous foodstuffs that need to be boiled for a long time lose some of their nutritional usefulness, and the ubiquitous cooking-pots indicate that stews were indeed common. Ingenious analyses of residues trapped in some of these vessels show traces of flour, meat fibres and so on, though do not help in assessing the quality or the quantity of the stews. Herring and cod bones at Wharram Percy and oyster fragments at Seacourt show that at least some sea and shell-fish were available even at rural sites far inland, and that peasants involved in marketing could worry less about their own self-sufficiency, and risk more in production for sale, knowing that they could buy alternative foodstuffs in exchange. Deer bones at Lyveden have been taken as evidence of villagers prepared to help themselves to alternative foods, by poaching: if so, the Lyveden people were braver than those at Upton, Seacourt or Wharram Percy, where deer bone numbers range from nil to 3 per cent. In towns, there is evidence that fewer pigs and more domestic fowl were being eaten: if these reflect changes in the countryside, the former may result from more careful husbandry of woodland and pasture, which swine root up, the latter perhaps from more small-holdings.[25]

One source of protein was ale, weak though it often was. That a stronger brew, probably using hops, was becoming commoner than before is suggested by the increasing number of fairly small pottery cisterns, with bung-holes near the base so that the drink could be drawn off without disturbing the sediments. It is possible that these were merely replacing wooden casks, but their size is rather smaller than can conveniently be made with barrel staves. Beer brewed with hops keeps better than ale, so that it is a more saleable commodity, offering more opportunity to specialist producers and vendors. At the same time, there are more pottery baking-trays and frying-pans, which may mean a wider range of cooking methods being commonly practised, and better joints of meat more widely available. A decrease in pottery stew-pots becomes very marked after the thirteenth century. To some extent this is because more metal equivalents were in use: fragments of copper-alloy cauldrons are more frequently found, and clay potters were imitating the distinctive shapes of metal handles, so they were obviously a status symbol that had become common even at peasant level.[26] It is possible that there was a positive nutritional benefit from the use of at least iron cooking equipment, particles from which would help to counter anaemia, which is likely to have been a particular problem for women. *Cribra orbitalia* have been identified in five of some eighty skeletons from a hospital site at Newark, Nottinghamshire, founded *c.* 1135; this condition can result from iron deficiency. A healthy dollop of vegetables ought to be enough to prevent it – but medieval treatises reveal a belief that greenstuffs were medically suspect and only fit for the poor![27]

From skeletal evidence (8, 2) it is becoming possible to see something of the problems with which human bodies can cope. Most diseases are too rapidly mortal for them to affect the bones. Although there are a few cases where special conditions have preserved other parts of the body, such examples tend to be members of the aristocracy, for whom body-preservation was sought in the fourteenth and early fifteenth centuries by embalming and by the use of sealed lead coffins, an early example of which is the unknown knight found at St Bees Priory, Cumberland, whose skin had survived. He had died from blows to the neck and chest that he might have suffered in battle, a joust, when out hunting, or from some criminal assault. Sir Walter de Manny, who was buried in 1372 in the London Charterhouse which he had founded, still had his hair and beard in 1947. Despite his military career, his bones were free of the arthritis which was prevalent among most medieval adults. Elizabeth, Lady Audley, who was buried in 1400 at Hulton Abbey, Staffordshire, affected long, plaited hair – but it was probably a hair-piece. She was buried with a hazel staff, traditionally the sign of a pilgrim, though it is doubtful if she had visited any very distant shrines. Sir Hugh de Hastyngs at Elsing, Norfolk, may also have had a wig: cow-hair below his head could have been from a hat, but was certainly not from a pillow because the hair was full-length. He died in 1347; his precise date of birth is unknown, but documentary evidence places his age between thirty-seven and forty-two. This is useful, because physical anthropologists assessed his age at thirty-five to forty on the basis of his skeleton, which shows that modern dating methods are broadly reliable, something that had been called in question. He was a robust man, 5ft 9¾ ins tall, with very slight osteoarthritis, and shoulders

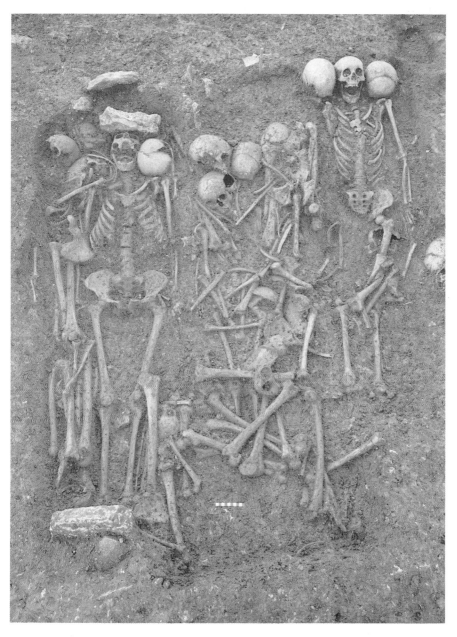

8, 2. A complex cemetery at Trowbridge, Wiltshire, excavated by the Trust for Wessex Archaeology. In a small graveyard there was presumably frequent disturbance of earlier graves, long-bones and skulls from which were returned so that the new grave became a charnel. Such circumstances militate against the establishment of a stratigraphical succession, but general evidence about the age range, diet and health of a medieval population can be obtained.

whose development suggested regular military exercises and training. Despite his status – son of Baron Hastyngs, grandson of the Earl of Winchester – his teeth had become very worn, from eating food that needed to be chewed, or from unrefined flour with grit in it: the Rhenish lava stones so often used for grinding are said to be very friable. His jaw had suffered a heavy blow at some time in his career. Twenty-two years after Hastyngs's death, Sir Bartholomew Burghersh was buried at nearby Walsingham Priory: he was a little older, between fifty and sixty, and the same height. Arthritis was not severe in him either, and he too had had bumps and blows consistent with a nobleman's hunting and soldiering career. He had also had a coarse diet. Some of these people are known because of the special care taken to mark their graves, as though to enhance their individuality and to ensure that their souls could be reunited to their bodies at the Resurrection. Concern over provision for the individual's soul to suffer less in Purgatory is also shown by the chantry tombs and the payments for perpetual obits that are distinctive of the later medieval aristocracy, secular and ecclesiastical.[28]

Although these aristocrats had had the injuries to be expected from their occupations, the increasing number of more ordinary skeletons that have now been analysed do not show many signs of violence, suggesting that there is a conflict between contemporary records of 'casual brutality' and the evidence of the bones. Eighty-five per cent of the recognisable skeletons in the Newark hospital were of adult males, nearly a quarter of whom had lived to over forty-five. Although these were men who would only have been in the sheltered environment of the hospital at the end of their lives, few had had injuries that showed in their bones. They may have had slightly privileged earlier lives, as hospitals were not always open to the poor, but they would not have been immune from life's knocks. Similarly, burials at a friary in Hartlepool, Cleveland, may have been of some of the brethren and better-off citizens, but only nine of the 150 skeletons even had fractures.[29]

At Newark, the average male height was 5 ft 8½ ins, with a range from 5 ft 6 ins to 6 ft: the women averaged 5 ft 4 ins, ranging from 4 ft 11 ins to 5 ft 7 ins. Osteoarthritis was relatively common. Few were obviously suffering from infections, though one may have had leprosy, which seems to have been waning during the later Middle Ages to judge from the closure of many hospitals. In one respect they had a great advantage over the modern English population, for few had serious dental problems: a fibrous, sugar-free diet at least prevented caries. This is fairly typical: similar results obtain at Hartlepool, and at Bordesley Abbey caries were almost entirely confined to the oldest men, who were mostly in their forties. Here, the average male height was 5 ft 8 ins, but many of the bones of the younger men looked frail, suggesting that they may have been sick visitors brought to the abbey for succour. 'Wormian' bones in several of the skulls at Leicester's Austin friary suggest a localised abnormality, indicating a population from a limited catchment area. If this is valid, it is interesting as an archaeological demonstration of the main geographical contacts of a town, comparable to that of personal names derived from place-names.[30]

Both Newark and Bordesley had a substantial element aged over forty, and Hartlepool had fifty-one adults who reached forty-five. Because these cemeteries may be biased to the wealthy, a higher than average life expectancy may result than from 'typical' populations such as at Raunds, with an expectancy of thirty-three for those who survived past the age of twelve. A small group of nineteen skeletons from a cemetery in Abingdon, Oxfordshire, where tenth- to thirteenth-century sherds and a thirteenth-century radiocarbon date are consistent with its recorded closure in 1284 when the Abbey asserted its mortuary rights, included at least three who had lived to over forty. There were only three children, so that the site is not representative of the total population, a bias against association of young with adults that has been noticed elsewhere. In the early phases at Raunds, children tended to be buried close to the walls of the church; at St Helen-on-the-Walls, York, 27 per cent of the 1,041 individuals were children, but even so they are thought to be under-represented. In particular, there were very few infants except for those buried with women, presumably their mothers (child-bearing being a time of particularly high risk). Occasional infant burials at rural farms could suggest exclusion of the very young from churchyards, perhaps because they had not been baptized. As many as 9 per cent of the St Helen's people lived to over sixty, with men over thirty-five out-numbering women. There were very few wounds and fractures visible in the bones, no more than would be expected to occur from normal everyday life: again, a violent society is not indicated, although hard work is, from the traces of osteoarthritis.[31]

All in all, it would seem that life was neither always so brief nor so violent as might be thought, and although there are some deficiencies, diet was adequate enough to produce robust skeletons of a good height. The population may not therefore have lived quite so close to starvation and collapse as some records suggest, though neither its diet nor its living conditions were able to do much to reduce the incidence of later-medieval bacterial attacks. The recorded fifteenth-century deaths among monks at Canterbury suggest that this really was a much worse problem than previously, despite the decline in leprosy. Their life expectancy was only twenty-eight, despite a high standard of food, shelter and hygiene. Plague, 'the sweat', dropsy and other ailments carried off most of the brethren. Syphilis seems to have been another new disease of the era, and if the weather was worse, sinusitis would have been more of a problem. A side-effect of the increase in provision of chimneys to replace open hearths would have been to reduce the incidence of cancer from woodsmoke, but that would only have affected the aristocracy, and then late in the period. Malaria affected low-lying areas. Concern over health, and attempts to recognise and cure disease, account for the number of glass urinals found particularly at monastic sites, where doctors tried to analyse their patients' problems by inspection of the water that they passed.[32]

Conscious attempts to ward off the plague by improving hygiene have been suggested as the explanation for such things as stone-lined drains and internal privies found in many later medieval towns, but they are as likely to result from more fastidious behaviour generally, part of the trend towards personal privacy that is emphasized by the many small rooms increasingly provided in houses at all social levels. Religious institutions with their elaborate water-supplies which also provided outflows for drains may have set a standard which others sought to emulate: an example recently investigated is the water supplied to Exeter from a network of wells and cisterns on high ground north of the city (8, 3). All such systems relied on gravity: not until the sixteenth century was even a wheel being used to scoop up river water in London, and suction pumps were known only in fifteenth-century Italy. The water was brought down to Exeter's Blackfriars in lead pipes laid in aqueducts, which in the fourteenth century were stone-lined to facilitate access for repairs. A well-house in the Close supplied the cathedral in the early fifteenth century, another religious house and, probably as a charitable act, a conduit for the citizens. A direct municipal supply came later: Exeter at that time was going through a prosperous era because of its new cloth industries.[33]

Stone-lined cess-pits were emptied regularly, the contents carted away to be dumped – much of it in local fields, but often its value as manure was lost by illicit dumping in rivers, impeding navigation. Because of this, there are fewer rubbish-pits to provide good examples of bones and pottery to compare with earlier assemblages. Sometimes back-land areas were used for dumping, as on a site in Norwich previously used for iron-smelting and brewing, where rubbish was used to fill up quarries. Changes in deposition patterns can make an absence of evidence seem more significant than it is: decline in numbers of Norwegian whetstones, for instance, may be an illusion. Certainly they have been reported in some quantity from sites like Battle Abbey since the suggestion was made that their import had ceased. But there are enough assemblages to show changes such as those in pottery forms that indicate new demands in cooking and brewing. Tableware was changing too, with large jugs no longer being almost the only glazed vessels. Instead, these were becoming plainer, and there were many more smaller drinking jugs, 'sauce bottles', bowls and dishes. Some of these changes became even more evident in the fifteenth century. They are concomitant with increasing use of pewter. Two saucers, from Southampton (8, 4) and Weoley Castle, near Birmingham, both have a stamped letter, presumably the maker's initial, and both have very high tin contents: the supposition is that they were made in the same workshop, quite probably in London, since it is from the City that records of the Pewterers' Guild come. There are no examples of pewter 'flatware' earlier than these, which date to the end of the thirteenth or first half of the fourteenth century.[34]

Although tin came from Devon and Cornwall, and provided a local source of employment which has left its mark in the great heaps of stone discarded in the 'streaming' process, it was not turned into finished objects in south-western England. Locally, the 'stannary' towns had some benefit, but otherwise it was the merchants who sold the tin, and the king who taxed it, who took

EXETER : CATHEDRAL AND TOWN MEDIEVAL AQUEDUCTS

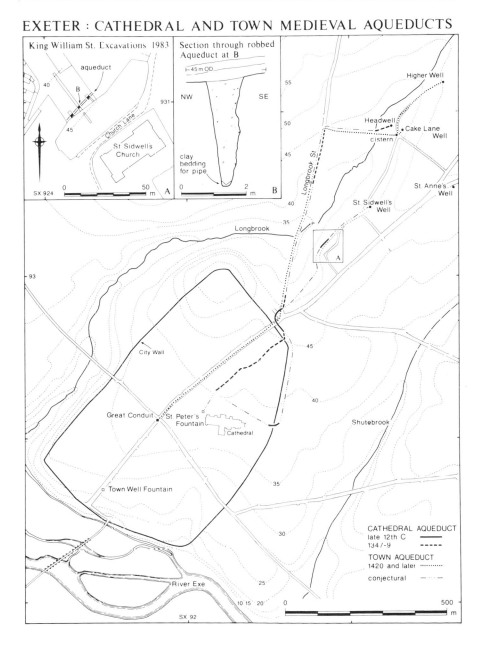

8, 3. Elaborate arrangements for bringing fresh water through pipes laid in aqueducts and through stone-lined passages to urban ecclesiastical establishments are shown by this plan of Exeter, Devon, prepared by C. G. Henderson. The cathedral's first supply from an extra-mural source was probably provided in the late twelfth century, and was replaced in 1347-48. The townsfolk benefited from a public conduit tapping the cathedral's water, until they established their own pipe-line in the fifteenth century.

the profits: the tinners themselves could not get their material to a market, and so could not hold out for higher prices against the middleman's control. Consequently, there is no material record of the industry recognisable in evidence of better local artisan housing or a wider range of goods than would otherwise have been available. Nor is the technology well understood: blowing-houses may have been introduced to improve smelting, but they are inferred from changes in taxation rather than because their sites have been located. The restricted impact that extractive industries had on their area is also seen in lead production, which provided some local employment in

8, 4. Late thirteenth-century pewter saucer, excavated by C. Platt in a pit in Southampton which contained other debris of the well-to-do mercantile class. The letter 'P' stamped on the rim is probably the maker's mark: a similar one has been found at a site near Birmingham. Pewter is a soft metal, and knife-marks made while the saucer was in use are clearly visible. (Shown slightly smaller than actual size).

Derbyshire and on the Mendips. The centres of output tended to shift as new 'rakes' were located, so that there was no concentration at a single site, causing extra demand for land or services at any one village for any length of time. Wage-earners therefore had only a temporary effect upon social and economic structures, even though they had quite a high spending power.[35]

That the pewterers were London-based is symptomatic of the capital's increased importance during the later Middle Ages, not least because the king's need for money concentrated financial and legal services there. Brass was another industry that was primarily based in London: from the later thirteenth century, there was increasing use of brass in churches, especially on funeral monuments. The distribution map shows that in the fourteenth century, lesser gentry and even yeomen might have a funerary brass if they lived close enough to London: further away, only those of the knightly or equivalent classes were commemorated in this way. At places at least a hundred miles away, local competitors could face London competition, but they did not have the craft skill to match the Londoners' products (8, 5). This had long been recognised on stylistic grounds, but has recently been confirmed by metallurgical analysis, which demonstrated that those brasses thought to have been made by a provincial workshop in Lincoln are indeed different from the London products, for the alloys used contain a much higher proportion of tin.[36]

Another thirteenth-century copper-alloy product was steelyard weights. These can be classified according to the coats of arms on them, and analyses have confirmed that the weights with the crudest coats are all composed of bronzes with a high lead content, as too are some of the better quality ones. But some of the better ones have a high proportion of zinc, giving them the lustre of a brass: these all seem to have one of two combinations of particular coats of arms. It is as though the quality of the alloy was carefully controlled and a better finish was given to some special types of weight.[37] Such control argues strongly for the sort of discipline that could be exercised at a single production centre, and London is obviously the most likely place. A number of moulds for buckles and other small items of dress have now been found in the City, and distribution of metalworkers' products from there may well have been increasing. Certainly the thirteenth-century decorative buckle-plates seem to have a uniformity to them which hints towards that sort of pattern, and another metal industry, iron knife-blade making, was moving in the same direction. The earliest makers' marks first occur *c.* 1300, and within a hundred years nearly half the blades were marked, as guild control and self-identity had their effect.[38]

London never had a monopoly of blade-making, but such products exemplify its increased rôle as a supplier. At the same time, the market that London offered was growing, not least because the royal household abandoned its tradition of buying at fairs and used London merchants instead.[39] Pottery was brought to the City from a distance: unlocated kilns close to it seem to have gone out of use in the thirteenth century, under pressure from

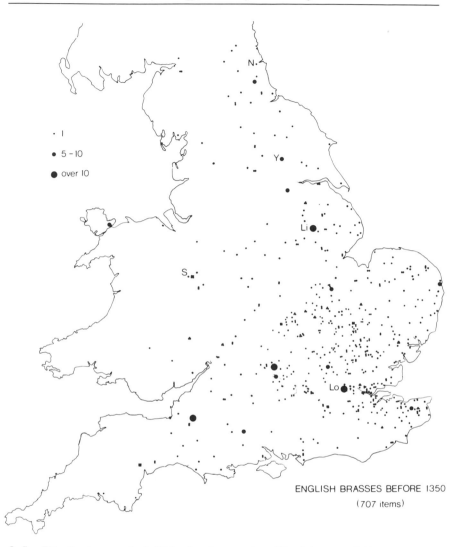

ENGLISH BRASSES BEFORE 1350
(707 items)

8, 5a. Distribution map by J. Blair of early examples of English memorial brasses, showing concentrations around London and other ecclesiastical centres.

demand for space even in the suburbs, although the fourteenth century may have seen some reversion. Wasters found in Southwark, however, were not accompanied by kiln debris, so they may have been brought from elsewhere and dumped to consolidate the river bank. If so, they were brought down the Thames from Kingston, where kilns have been found producing a white ware – perhaps trying to imitate the south-west French Saintonge polychrome. Kingston was rivalled by another Surrey industry at Cheam before the end of the fourteenth century, but both were subsequently outsold in London by un-located suppliers further south on the Surrey-Hampshire border: pre-

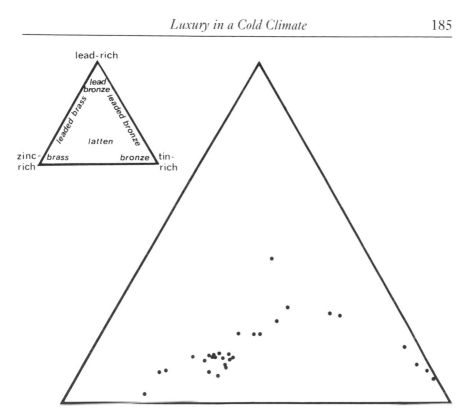

8, 5b. Scatter diagram by R. Brownsword of the metallic compositions of various letters from the inscriptions around memorial brasses. The group of four from Lincoln are picked out by their lower zinc content.

sumably they had less to pay for fuel and clay rents, and were able thus to offset higher transport costs. Together, these Surrey/North Hampshire industries were to account for two-thirds of the London market. The industries were never centralised, however, so that this market dominance could not be used to create capital accumulation. Nor did the products get redistributed through London to an even wider market: they are hardly found even down the Thames in Essex and Kent. They were being distributed southwards into Sussex and Hampshire, presumably mostly by overland routes, but were not able to oust local production from the south coast.[40]

All these commodities required cash: the longer the distance that any but the most prestigious object travels, the less likely it is that its exchange can be effected by any system depending on barter, kin networks or reciprocal gift. The relative infrequency of finds of single coins on excavations has already been mentioned, and it is difficult therefore to use them as a direct measure of the volume of cash transactions taking place. Nor, when there is an increase in the number of coins found, is it necessarily because more petty commodity sales were taking place: the later thirteenth-century increase in York, for instance, may be a consequence of Edward I's use of the town as a supply-base, with a roisterous soldiery reckless of its wages. Other towns do not show as great a proportional increase as York, although totals at Oxford, Southampton and elsewhere do grow. Unfortunately, actual numbers are too low for a trend to be very positively asserted – few totals even reach double figures. The same is broadly true of rural sites where numbers are even smaller, although written evidence suggests more market involvement and more cash in use. Were some peasants behaving like Pacific islanders after the Second World War, reluctant to deal in money despite increasing requirements for it in their transactions? Notwithstanding the paucity of finds, however, something in the order of three to four times more single late thirteenth-fourteenth-century coins seem to be found than of previous issues, whereas production at the mints is recorded as increasing by fifteen to twenty times.[41]

The mints were particularly busy in 1279–81 because of the new coins issued by Edward I, largely to raise money for his wars by recoinage profits. The high silver content and the heavy weight of the new pennies meant that they were sought after, and many left England as merchants' profits as well as in war expenditure. At the same time, foreign coins which imitated the English but were slightly lighter could not be prevented from entering the country and being circulated. These 'lushebournes', 'crockards' and 'pollards' are occasionally found – one in Canterbury, two in Oxford's Hamel site – where foreign coins are so few previously that their exclusion can be seen as nearly total. Occasional finds of coin balances, which were illegal for private use, show that people were well aware of the loss that they might incur from accepting low-weight coins. This was probably not such a serious problem as to cause rejection of coins as a means of exchange, but wariness over it may have been a factor restricting economic growth. Edward I also issued halfpennies and farthings, to ease the difficulties caused by a lack of sufficient low-value currency for everyday use. But these are not so common as to suggest that they were welcomed because they met a long-felt need, and there may be scarcely more of them than there are of the earlier, cut, halfpennies and farthings: the Hamel, for instance, produced five of the new farthings and a halfpenny, but also three earlier cut halfpennies, and Exeter one farthing and one halfpenny, against a single cut halfpenny.[42]

One of the numismatic problems of this period is to know the extent to which any deficiency in the official currency was made good by the use of base-metal tokens. It is suggested that these were introduced in the thirteenth century as a way of rewarding a task performed, such as by choirboys who had taken part in the services at Bury St Edmunds Abbey. Their increasing number indicates that they passed from the ecclesiastical into the secular world, reaching its murkiest depths as brothel tokens. Initially in pewter, they were almost invariably made of lead in the fourteenth century, and their uniformity of size, metal and range of design suggests that their issue was regulated, and that a production monopoly had been created even though they were not a governmental prerogative. The Pewterers' Guild may have been the beneficiaries. Quantities have been found in London, but many fewer elsewhere – only two or three from Oxford and none from Exeter. Their use may therefore have been localised and restricted to specific types of transaction. What do become very much commoner after *c.* 1325 are base-metal jettons, which are even more like coins in their design. Although they were supposed to be used only as 'reckoning counters' on accounting boards, their numbers suggest wider use than this – there are nine from the Hamel, dating before *c.* 1475 – and some have been defaced, as though to prevent their circulation.[43]

Official concern over high-value exchange transactions is a different aspect of the new denominations. The groat, valued at four pence, was introduced in 1279, and examples are occasionally found, as are half-groats: the numbers are small, but do suggest that circulation was achieved. Also new to the currency were gold coins, successfully introduced in 1351 after a couple of false starts – it was difficult to adjust their value in relation to silver equivalents. Gold coins were being minted elsewhere in Europe, since more of the metal was available from Hungary. Unsurprisingly, and despite the 'quarter-noble' from Gomeldon, they are hardly ever found as casual losses, although many are known from hoards. High-value coins were too much of a temptation for forgers to resist, however, and there is a fair amount of evidence to show that they were prepared to run the risks of drastic punishment if caught. A contemporary forgery of an Edward III groat was recently found in Rochester, and a Henry VI forgery is an old find from Exeter. Even more impressive are the two iron dies found, with a coin weight, in an Exeter rubbish pit. The dies were for use in counterfeiting the gold noble and half-noble issues of 1351–1412. They were probably made after 1412, as subsequent devaluation had made the older coins more valuable and therefore more profitable to forge. Sharp practice was not confined to towns, for there are surviving moulds from Strata Florida Abbey – and these give slight cause to doubt whether a weight found at Denny Abbey was not to be used in counterfeiting gold nobles, rather than just to check on the authenticity of any that the nuns received.[44]

Complexities in the currency can be studied through the intricacies of the interplay of alloys, weights and coin types. At times, shortages of silver are likely to have caused a shortage of coin, which would have kept prices artificially low. Any export of coin would have exacerbated this, and was made illegal, but there was a constant drain nevertheless. Deflation was consequently one of the economic problems of the period in the 1330s: inflation after 1350 may have been because more coin was circulating, with a lighter penny being introduced in 1351, or it could be because population decline meant that there were fewer people to use it. Surviving coins show that legislation introduced to prevent the king from debasing the coinage was not disregarded for the rest of the century, despite difficulties in obtaining silver, which became a general problem in Europe. Such legislation, forced on the king by Parliament in 1352, is significant of the way in which he could be persuaded not to adopt policies which did not suit the interests of his aristocracy and the Church: they were concerned about their fixed rental income, whose value would decline if paid in coins with a lower silver content.[45]

One reason why the king could not afford to flout the goodwill of the land-lord class was that he needed their support in campaigns against the French, which were increasingly expensive. During the second half of the fourteenth century, invasion was a recurring fear, and various counter-measures were taken to provide more effective coastal defences. The earliest known sys-tematic provision for gunnery in England occurs at Portchester Castle, where Assheton's tower of 1376–85 has, instead of cross-shaped arrowslits, special-purpose gunloops with a narrow viewing slit above a roundel through which the barrel could be fired. Assheton's tower provided cover both for the castle's wallwalks and of the area outside the walls (2, 4). Southampton's new town walls also provided a gun battery, which could rake the western shore-line. Canterbury was given a new gate with forward-projecting drum towers and three tiers of gun-loops (8, 6) which allow only a 45 degree traverse, showing that the guns would have had only quite short barrels. Guns were not yet very powerful, and many surviving gunloops show that they were not intended for heavy, floor-level cannons but for lighter weapons raised on trestles or even handguns held on poles, which were effective anti-personnel weapons. Guns had obviously become a necessity rather than a curiosity by the end of the fourteenth century.[46]

The gatehouse at Lord Cobham's Cooling Castle in Kent is very similar to Canterbury's West Gate, and may have had the same mason. Cobham was a soldier who had done well for himself and for his king in France, and could afford to build solidly. As he had official responsibilities for coastal defence, he was not just thinking about his status when he reconstructed Cooling. More enigmatic is Bodiam Castle, in Sussex, built on a low-lying site at the head of a navigable river. Its very picturesque moat would have served a prac-tical purpose, though if drained by a besieging army, could have been crossed on duck-boards. It has thick walls, a few gunloops in its gatehouse though not in its wall towers, and it dispensed with portcullises which took up much space because of the counter-weights that had to be built in, disfiguring the interiors of the rooms in which they were housed. Bodiam could have stood up to a lightning raid of the sort feared in the 1370s and 1380s from the fast-moving oared French galleys, but not to a long siege. It was built by Sir Edward Dalyngryge, another successful soldier: was he being serious when he requested a license on the basis that it was 'for the defence of the local neighbourhood', or was this just a conventional formula, and he wanted a castle to give him status in an area in which he had no established ties? Its internal arrangements with guest suites and provision for servants certainly emphasize comfort and style rather than military function.[47]

So far as documentary sources can tell, Bodiam had no direct part to play in arrangements for coastal defence, which concentrated more upon garrisoned towns and royal bases such as Portchester – and Corfe, which seems to have had virtually no provision for gunnery despite its status. Simi-larly, Bramber Castle in Sussex was not maintained, despite its suitable

8, 6. Exterior view of the West Gate, Canterbury, built in the 1370s/1380s when French raids were feared. The prominent drum towers contain several 'inverted keyhole' gun-loops, the round openings being for short barrelled guns, the slits above them for viewing. The gate makes little concession to civic pride by displaying heraldic emblems, unlike many. The increasing importance of gunnery can also be seen at Portchester (**2, 4**). There would have been a drawbridge in the foreground over the River Stour. Additional protection for the gateway is provided by machicolations, built out on corbels, through which stones could be dropped. The small square 'put-log' holes are for scaffold poles.

position. Some measures were taken that probably owed more to tradition than to reality: it is difficult to believe that the abbot of Battle Abbey was really the best person to be put in charge of the defence of Winchelsea, even though his house's income could be used to advantage: but he had to do it because William I three hundred years earlier had intended that the abbey should defend that stretch of coast. The abbot of Quarr had similar responsibilities on the Isle of Wight: hence the gunports built into his abbey.[48]

If Bodiam is enigmatic, no such doubts need really apply to other new castles erected by successful campaigners in the later fourteenth and fifteenth centuries. Farleigh Hungerford and Nunney in Somerset are both comfortable houses castellated to give the illusion of defensibility, as were Wressle, Bolton and Sheriff Hutton in the north, where emphasis was on a quadrangular plan, a fashion which allowed separate entrances to the lodgings and guest suites, but could be adapted to include an existing structure, like the Norman keep at Middleham, a Neville stronghold in Yorkshire.[49] All, however, emphasise the importance of the non-feudal household, with the hall as the main focus of entertainment and display. They are as good an indication as any of how society was changing, but within circumscribed conventions.

Chapter Nine

THE LATER FOURTEENTH, FIFTEENTH AND EARLY
SIXTEENTH CENTURIES

Into a New Age?

The unfortunate monks who died at such a young age in Canterbury Cathedral Priory in the fifteenth century exemplified one of the period's problems for such institutions, that of maintaining a reasonable number of inmates. Fewer monks meant lower costs, however, which was some compensation for hard-pressed estate managers in a period of increasing wages, reduced rents and unstable prices. Nevertheless, although some abbeys contracted, and the Cistercians rearranged their houses because they could no longer find lay-brothers, buildings had to be maintained and many new works were undertaken: at the cathedral, for instance, transepts were rebuilt and a new library was constructed. Then, at the end of the fifteenth century, the great central tower, 'Bell Harry', celebrated the archbishopric of Cardinal Morton, and was followed by a new gatehouse between the precinct and the town. Gatehouses, abbots' lodgings and other refurbishments expressed the status of a great late-medieval magnate of the Church. Greater comfort and privacy for a community's other inmates were also sought, as they were in the secular world.

The cathedral priory's income seems to have halved in the first half of the fifteenth century, yet it was not acceptable to counter such problems by any reduction in building. To try to recoup the position, the priory was prepared to make considerable outlays, such as in the drainage of Appledore Marsh. Another investment was 'The Bull', a building project apparently of *c.* 1449–68 immediately outside the precinct, where timber-framed ranges were erected over cellars round a courtyard; there were probably shops on the ground floor, and ten or a dozen lodging chambers above, each reached by a separate stair. If these were for visitors, they were built at a time when pilgrims to Canterbury were beginning to become fewer, with the waning in popularity of Thomas à Becket's tomb. The appeal of his shrine from the end of the twelfth century is shown by the large number of lead *ampullae* and badges that pilgrims took home with them, which other shrines sought to emulate. They provide an excellent indication of the quantities of travellers that there were on the medieval roads.[1]

Houses were also a form of investment. A remarkable terrace of nine

'Wealden'-type houses has recently been recognised in Battle, built by the abbey to attract tenants. They were probably intended as accommodation for craftsmen, whose small workshops would front the street. Shops could be very profitable, and there are examples like those at Tewkesbury, Gloucestershire, where nineteen of the original row of twenty-four survive. Behind the front room was a small two-storey hall with an open hearth, and a single-storey room behind that. The terrace runs along the edge of the abbey churchyard, so that the houses had only very short gardens. Fourteenth-century terraces in York had similarly been allowed to encroach on churchyards. Licensed encroachment of another sort can often be recognised in market-places where previously open space has been taken up by permanent buildings, as lockable shops gave a greater security and stability than did stalls. This was part of a process of sedentarism which affected towns throughout late-medieval Europe and can be seen also in the decline of the great fairs, although smaller ones continued. Inns were much-favoured investments. In Gloucester the 'New Inn' is a courtyard building constructed as a benefaction for St Peter's Abbey by one of its community. Although it must have been built by 1441, it was still referred to as 'lately built' in 1455, which cautions against taking such phrases too literally. The arrangement of the lodgings was different from that at 'The Bull' in Canterbury, for the division was horizontal, with chambers entered from corridors. The 'New Inn' and their ilk were organised as commercial lodgings that could provide travellers with an individual room. Merchants and pilgrims no longer felt safe in the communal dormitories of a monastic guest-house, from fear presumably of both infection and theft; nor did traditional accommodation offer the privacy that was becoming the social norm, as is shown by the guest-suites in castles. Furthermore, the monasteries could less well afford to offer hospitality to visitors: there were more people on the roads, many of them probably rootless, taking advantage of the opportunities offered by low rents and high wages to leave places where their lord might try to enforce customary obligations upon them. Others, however, were well-to-do merchants, particularly those involved in the wool and cloth trades. Revival of the cloth industry meant that there were native producers to be supplied, with dyes and raw or spun wool. As their houses show, be it in a small town like Lavenham, Suffolk, or in the country round Halifax, West Yorkshire, they were working in small units, and although many were wage-earning 'out-workers' weaving the yarn that others supplied, there were only a few men who controlled large units and bought in huge quantities. Consequently there were many individual transactions to be effected, with more opportunities for both markets and middlemen. Moreover, many monasteries were by the fifteenth century leasing a greater proportion of their estates, reducing their own direct involvement with great merchants like the Italian Peruzzis and Bardis of the later thirteenth and earlier fourteenth centuries. Some therefore closed their guest-houses altogether, and many saw inns as a sound investment, not only in big towns like Gloucester but also in smaller markets such as Norton St Philip, Somerset, where a local charterhouse built 'The George' in the late fourteenth century and found it well worth maintaining and reconstructing in the fifteenth (**9,1**). Norton is an example of a small place which had the added attraction of two annual, three-day fairs of the sort that remained profitable despite the decline of the longer and larger fairs.[2]

Documents that refer to the 'New Inn' at Gloucester are part of an excellent archive about that town in the late fourteenth and fifteenth centuries. It was an active port, with overseas as well as internal contacts. Several wealthy citizens were investing in house ownership, and were rebuilding their properties to attract tenants, as Battle Abbey was doing. Such investment did not bring in a high return, but it was relatively safe and the buildings could be used as loan security. Because of such factors, analysis of a town's buildings may not be an absolute guide to its late-medieval prosperity. The Gloucester citizens' caution was probably typical of a general reluctance to invest in trade and industry, which would have been a severe limitation on economic growth.

9, 1. The George Inn, Norton St Philip, Somerset. Originally a completely stone-walled building, it was altered *c.* 1500 when the jettied timber framing was added to the two upper storeys. At this time the top floor may have been used for storage of wool and cloth, with guest chambers below for the dealers. The Fleur de Lis represents a more ordinary licensed village ale-house, of the sort proliferating in the later Middle Ages as the peasantry tended to have more money to spend and were less likely to brew in their own houses.

Unfortunately the Gloucester documents are less detailed after the middle of the fifteenth century, but there are complaints about decaying property and inability to pay taxes, and a fall in population by about a third has been suggested. Such complaints were frequently made by towns in the fifteenth and early sixteenth centuries, and their validity has been much discussed. Although it seems that nearly all suffered population loss, the extent of this varied and the relative prosperity of the surviving citizens can only be measured by comparisons between incomplete sources. Until a range of evidence becomes available from a wider spectrum of towns than at present, a series of individual case-studies has to be evaluated within an inadequate overall pattern. Many of the period's problems stemmed from its politics, such as difficulties of dealing in international markets during the French wars, and internal disruption of the Wars of the Roses, in which a town could be seriously disadvantaged if it supported the wrong side. Towns might also be more susceptible than the countryside to bacterial disease, despite many impovements to drains and water-supplies, because infection could spread more quickly from contact to contact.[5]

Towns which did not have a significant cloth industry seem to have been less likely to thrive, but there is no uniformity. In Oxford, for instance, the suburban site in the Hamel remained in occupation (**9,2**); there was no significant new building until the very end of the fifteenth century, nor were

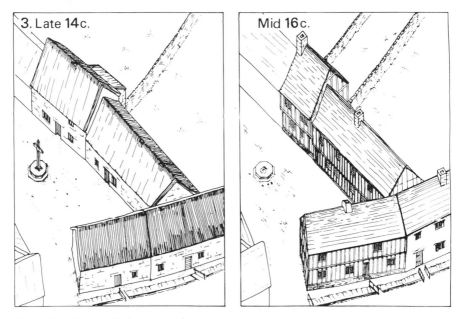

9, 2. The Hamel, Oxford. In its late fourteenth-century phase, the site was still predominantly composed of single-storey houses (cf. **7, 8**). The early sixteenth century saw a change to more substantial, two-storey timber-framed houses, each with a chimney stack allowing fire-places to heat four rooms.

stone-lined drains or cess-pits constructed, but evidence of post-holes and internal walls shows that buildings were kept in repair, and one large tenement was even sub-divided. Around 1500, some completely new cottages were erected, with stone-wall footings that probably supported timber-framed, two-storey superstructures with fireplaces and chimneys. They were built for tenants, not owner-occupiers. Close by, however, there was at least one very much larger and more substantial house, of 'Wealden' type, quite probably built in the middle of the fifteenth century, which is known only from nineteenth-century pictures. In another of Oxford's suburbs, the evidence is very different: structural evidence included one fifteenth-century building, but vacant properties are also recorded, and there was much less fifteenth-century than earlier pottery. In an unrestricted area, where pit-digging was still practised in the post-medieval period, different methods of rubbish disposal are unlikely to be the cause of the paucity of late-medieval wares. The area only recovered slowly during the sixteenth century.[4]

Intra-mural Oxford also has its contrasts. The main commercial area was maintained, and one property was probably divided into two towards the end of the fifteenth century, showing that investment was still worthwhile. The 'new tenement' of Henry Mychegood in the 1480s seems to have been semi-detached and timber-framed, with two shops over cellars, and two full-height storeys above. Behind them, the existing hall may have been retained. There was a particular demand in Oxford for halls and chambers, because of the university, and many seem to have had a fringe of shops in front. The university would obviously have contributed to Oxford's trade, but its establishment is in part a symptom of the town's economic difficulties as early as the thirteenth century, as only low rents would have permitted the students to lodge in the town. By the fifteenth century, pressure on space had reduced to the point that some colleges could be established on main-street frontages, albeit not in central locations.[5]

Like Oxford, Canterbury has a suburban 'Wealden' house, in this case still surviving. Here too, therefore, not all the substantial citizens lived within the walls. Excavations in the centre of Canterbury have not produced a great deal of late-medieval evidence, but such as there is suggests stone buildings constructed in the fourteenth century being maintained in the fifteenth. There does not seem to have been much competition for space, however, as one area only a block away from a main street remained vacant, although used for pit digging.[6]

One town which was certainly prospering on the cloth industry was Lavenham, where timber-framed buildings include shops and the houses of very wealthy merchants and of weavers earning high wages. Although one of the country's most highly taxed towns, Lavenham had a population of under a thousand people. Those who lived there could proclaim their advantages by their display in building, but there were not very many of them overall. Nor, of course, do surviving buildings give an indication of short-term fluctuations, since material evidence of that sort is not normally recognisably responsive to such things as cloth-price variations. Only long-term decay, which came to Lavenham in the sixteenth century, can be identified, in that case because stagnation brought new building to a halt.

Another, larger, town which benefited from the cloth industry was Norwich: excavations away from the town centre have shown late-medieval pressure on space even in back-land areas, some of which had not been intensively used until the fourteenth century; indeed, on one site, Pottergate, there is some conflict between documentary and archaeological evidence, for whereas the former indicates the existence of 'cottages' even in the thirteenth century, the latter shows structures only from well into the second half of the fifteenth, with a range of houses and cellars. The objects recovered included windowglass and Italian terracotta, suggesting occupants wealthy enough to obtain well-lit housing with superior internal decoration. The whole site had been burnt, an episode plausibly attributed to the known fire of 1509, when nearly half of Norwich was said to have been destroyed: certainly what had occurred at Pottergate was not a piecemeal fire, affecting only one or two properties. Complete rebuilding did not take place there for a century. A similar fire ravaged St Peter's Street, Northampton, which was also not rebuilt in the early sixteenth century. This failure to rebuild contrasts with the evidence from two sites north of the river at Norwich, apparently untouched by the 1509 fire or any other. At Alms Lane, six fifteenth-century tenement plots with clay-walled houses were recognisable in the archaeological record; these were rebuilt at the start of the sixteenth century with brick and rubble dwarf walls suggesting more substantial timber-framed superstructures, a process similar to one that occurred a little earlier on a site near-by. As in Canterbury and Oxford, open hearths were replaced by fireplaces, which imply chimneystacks. This indicates abandonment of the open hall as the principal room and two- or three-storey houses becoming general, the beginning of a process that became increasingly common during the course of the sixteenth century, and which is part of the trend in living conditions to greater personal privacy.[7]

The differences between the various Norwich sites demonstrate the need to have an adequate sample within a town, as well as between towns, to obtain a representative picture. It would seem that even Norwich had some problems in the early sixteenth century, with insufficient buoyancy in the richer area to recover completely from the 1509 fire. It was not that wealthy citizens abandoned the town, while lesser artisans prospered, for some very fine private houses survived such as 'Strangers Hall' and the 'White Swan'. Many of them were set back from the street, which is not usual in England, and suggests that there could still be considerable variations in building arrangements between different towns. Similarly, Norwich has a large number of undercrofts which could not be entered directly from the street, unlike most of those in other towns. The undercrofts are not usually closely datable. Another form of building of which Norwich again has many survivals is churches: thirty-two remain of the sixty known to have existed in the late thirteenth century. The structure of the great majority is later-medieval: neither their fabric nor their fittings suggest any general diminution in building around the end of the fifteenth century.[8]

Although churches may be one general guide to a town's ability to maintain its profitability their rebuilding is as likely to result from individual benefactions as from those of congregations acting collaboratively, particularly since tax returns indicate what the quality of private houses like 'Strangers Hall' and the 'White Swan' also demonstrates, that towns such as Norwich had a small upper stratum of outstandingly wealthy citizens. Nor can abandonment of urban churches, which occurred quite widely in the fourteenth and fifteenth centuries, be an absolute guide to poverty or population loss, since some parish amalgamations may have resulted from ecclesiastical reorganisation to create bigger units, not directly from changes in local demography. The same is broadly true of guildhalls, which have also been used as an index of urban prosperity. Norwich, for instance, has one surviving from the first half of the fifteenth century, which is typical because it is claimed that few if any were built anywhere after *c.* 1450. This could possibly, however, be from lack of need, not a declining ability to maintain the guilds, which were certainly fundamental to urban life, with their feasts, mystery plays and manipulation of commerce. Their 'good unity, concord and charity' stressed social order and harmony.[9]

The condition of town defences is potentially another physical indicator of urban prosperity, but again it is one of which the significance is hard to evaluate. Norwich, for instance, already had a complete wall circuit: there are few references to it in the fifteenth-century records, suggesting that maintenance was minimal. This need not have been from poverty, however: there was less threat of invasion on the east coast, and the walls were probably seen as enough to deter roaming bands of pillaging soldiers skulking home from defeats in France. Against sustained bombardment, walls would no longer suffice. Norwich constructed towers on both sides of the River Wensum so that a boom could be strung between them, and at the end of the fourteenth century built what has been claimed as the earliest purpose-built detached gun tower in England. This, the Cow Tower, had two internal floors and also allowed for quite heavy guns to be mounted on the roof. The intention was probably primarily to fire upon ships attempting to get up-river to the landing stages. Twenty years later, Southampton was providing itself with an artillery tower which projected from one corner of the walls so that ships coming up Southampton Water could be prevented from getting close to the town. Emphasis was upon stopping an enemy from landing or from bombarding a town from ships. As cannonry increased in effectiveness, so this became more of a threat and, in consequence, walls became less useful as they could not resist sustained pressure unless strengthened with earth ramparts, which were both costly and used up a lot of space.[10]

Only three or four towns are recorded as in receipt of privileges to enable them to build completely new walls in the fifteenth century, such as Alnwick, on the coast near the Scottish border, and Poole in Dorset. The latter was a growing south coast port which was thoroughly ravaged by the French and Spanish in 1405, and was a base for English expeditions into France in the 1420s and 1430s. The 'Town Cellars', surviving though diminished, may well have been rebuilt to accommodate war supplies. How much defensive wall was actually constructed is not clear, though there was certainly a town gate by 1524, the massive foundations of which have been investigated. Poole also has Scaplen's Court, a very fine example of a stone-built courtyard house, probably fifteenth-century in origin, and assumed to have been the property of a rich townsman. It was not inevitable that a busy port like Poole should have such housing, for it could often happen that the main profits of trade were controlled by outsiders, giving a port many small service tasks to perform, but not necessarily giving its citizens the opportunity to create the sort of wealth that would purchase a Scaplen's Court. Warehouses like the 'Town Cellars', even if not Crown property, could also be built and owned by outsiders. It may be symptomatic of change that a large stone warehouse built in Southampton at the end of the fourteenth century by one of its wealthiest merchants had become a property of Beaulieu Abbey by 1454.[11]

Evidence of the upkeep of town walls in the fifteenth century is extremely sparse: the Wars of the Roses do not seem to have caused many flurries of repairs, although the rubble that still blocks Canterbury's Queningate is so irregular that it looks as though it was hastily done, and may well be the work recorded in 1466/68. Excavations have shown that some of the walltowers are fifteenth-century work also. Evidence of this sort is spasmodic from other towns; Southampton's 'Catchcold' Tower is documented and it is also one of the very few which is horseshoe-shaped, the most effective design for cover of the base of the walls. If this was a specifically fifteenth-century plan, then its rarity suggests that very few other towns added walltowers, just as very few bothered to insert gunloops. All this need not have been from inability to pay the costs as much as from recognition that walls were obsolescent in serious warfare, and what existed already was enough for local peace-keeping. Lack of interest in maintenance is strongly suggested by the way that Canterbury's town ditch had been allowed to fill with rubbish by the sixteenth century.[12]

One element in the defences which were more likely to be maintained were gatehouses. The town gate was a traffic control and a toll-collecting point, and the rooms over the gate might serve as guildhall, jail or other civic function. Furthermore, travellers approaching a town gained their first impression of it from its gate, so that a display of heraldry, banners and even models of sentries on the roof all proclaimed a town's status. Southampton remodelled the façade of its main road gate, which was projected forward without regard to the detrimental effect this had on the defensive rôle of the flanking fourteenth-century drumtowers. Lynn also altered one of its main gates. It may be a real measure of urban problems in the fifteenth and sixteenth centuries that few other towns went to such lengths.

Another way in which towns' provisions for war might be used as a measure

of their prosperity is consideration of the rôle of the urban castle. Four of
these in shire towns were privately-owned, including Warwick, which shows
that some great lords felt it worthwhile to maintain a presence in towns, retaining an alliance which integrated mercantile and aristocratic interests.
Most shire-town castles were royal and, as they were not well sited for hunting expeditions, had had less money spent on their accommodation facilities
than many rural palaces. At the same time, centralisation of government reduced the kings' need to travel to administer justice. Nevertheless, castles
were retained as much for administrative as for defensive reasons, since law-
court sessions were held in them and they also served as jails. Sometimes, part
of the castle was ceded by the Crown to the town: in 1345, some of the bailey
area at Norwich was transferred in this way, although other parts were kept
even though only for meadow grazing. This sort of encroachment might have
become more frequent if towns had continued to grow, but Norwich seems
to have been exceptional: in Gloucester, for instance, a zone called 'Bareland'
apparently added to the castle in the thirteenth century was not thereafter
handed back to the town despite its important position adjoining the quay
area. One reason why Norwich was exceptional was that the castle was in the
centre of the city, whereas most castles were peripheral, abutting the wall circuit: consequently there was less demand for their space, which might remain
unbuilt on even though 'void' as Bedford's was in the fourteenth century.

Castles in a few smaller towns had already been abandoned. Dorchester,
Dorset, although a shire town, had an outer bailey ditch which has been
shown to have been filled at least in part by the fourteenth century, and was
compacted sufficiently to be built over in the fifteenth. This was permissible
because the castle had been sold off before 1309, when it was donated for use
as a friary, a similar situation to that recorded at Chichester. These cases do
not therefore really throw light on the late-medieval position. The difficulty
of interpreting the evidence from documents alone is shown by another Dorset town's castle, Wareham. A lease of the site in 1461 might seem the most
likely moment for the outer bailey ditch to have been filled in and built over.
Excavations, however, suggested that this had happened much earlier, in the
thirteenth century, perhaps when the castle passed from the Crown into
baronial ownership. Whether the ditch was built over then by private houses,
as it is today, is not known. At Devizes there is a strong possibility that the
outer bailey of the castle was used in the later Middle Ages as the town's
marketplace, in preference to an older market area outside the castle. This
may have been a thirteenth-century development, however, not one which reflects later-medieval pressures. Devizes Castle was a property of the bishops
of Salisbury, who presumably did not feel a need to maintain such a large
area. In Banbury, however, the bishops of Lincoln retained their castle
despite any temptation to rent out new tenements in a town which, though
small, was doing very well as a market for a cloth-producing area. Excavations
here have shown that after rebuilding in the thirteenth or fourteenth centuries, the castle remained at its full size, however ruinous the buildings, with

its outer ditch not filled in until the seventeenth century: this was despite fronting directly onto the marketplace.[13]

Less archaeological work has been carried out within 'the Banburys of England' than in larger towns. Results from them are likely to vary as much: in Newbury, Berkshire, which like Banbury was doing well on cloth, excavation has shown that adjoining tenements had very different histories. One which had had structures on it in the thirteenth century lay vacant as garden space in the fourteenth, but was rebuilt towards the end of the fifteenth. The other had a building sub-divided in the fourteenth century which remained in use until the seventeenth. Excavation on the edge of the market area in another small town, Alton in Hampshire, produced a rather more uniform picture, with four tenements developed as a terraced row in the late fifteenth or early sixteenth century, an indication of commercial pressure near the central focus of the town.[14]

Towns which had neither cloth industry nor port had only a commercial function left to them, and reduction in population was bound to affect the volume of trading even if there was some compensation to be had from any greater purchasing capacity within the surviving population. Very many places, both boroughs and villages, which had received a market grant did not emerge as active markets in the post-medieval period, and a considerable shake-up in the commercial network must have occurred even if a lot of the grant recipients had never established much of a market in the first place.[15] Some indication of the sort of evidence that might be expected comes from recent work in Yarm, Yorkshire, a small port founded in the thirteenth century, where an area initially used for building had reverted to open backland for wells and pits by the end of the Middle Ages. Another site in Yarm produced an iron-smelting furnace, which ceased operations in the early fifteenth century.[16]

For a town to have had even a small-scale iron-producing capacity seems to have remained unusual. Reduced pressure on space did not lead to industries being established on the vacant properties in early sixteenth-century Norwich or Northampton, although even anti-social activities might have been allowed if a worthwhile rent could have been achieved. Iron-smelting was not reintroduced to Norwich, despite production there in the early fifteenth century. Presumably higher quality or more cheaply refined ores were available from elsewhere. The same is true of salt in the 'wich' towns: the Nantwich excavations suggested sporadic production continuing into the sixteenth century, but on a much reduced level, presumably because imports from the Bay of Bourgneuf were cheaper than the native product. Although many towns were known for particular products, none but London seems to have been sufficiently specialised to give it a rôle as a centre of enough significance to exist independently of its cloth industry and its retail and exchange function. Sheffield was already known for its knives, for instance, Walsall for its horse-bits and spurs, Chellaston, Nottinghamshire, for its alabaster carvings, but none sustained a large or steadily expanding population.[17]

Some of the problems of English industrial output in the later Middle Ages are epitomised by Wealden iron. Only Chingley has yet produced incontrovertible evidence that water power was being used, although over thirty sites have been located where ore residues occur with later medieval pottery: some of these may just be dumps, not production centres, but they suggest a fair number of small operations, quite probably moving from site to site as woodland management created new areas for charcoal production, as seems to have happened earlier in Northamptonshire. One site which has been excavated, at Rotherfield, Sussex, was in use long enough for its original furnaces to have been replaced. In its final phase, it was a fairly substantial complex, with a roasting hearth, a smelting furnace enclosed within a stone-footed timber-framed building, a hut, and bins for storing charcoal. The furnace was bigger than some of the bowl furnaces known from earlier centuries, but was only just over a metre wide internally even so, and the technology was not fundamentally different. Indeed, limestone found at the site is thought to have been used simply as walling material, not as a flux, which is how it can be utilised if the technology is understood. Although Rotherfield is larger than Alsted had been, and suggests production of ore for more than just use on the owner's estate, its activity was brief, and despite its location beside a small stream, it does not appear to have utilised water power. It was probably typical of the low-output, small individual units operating in the Weald in the fourteenth and fifteenth centuries. This is a considerable contrast to documentary evidence from the north-east of England, where the bishop of Durham set up a large estate industry at Weardale, capable of producing twenty-four tons of iron in a week, using thirteen tons of charcoal in the process; but it did not thrive. There was probably still insufficient demand to sustain production in such quantity, and thus to justify the expenditure in setting up the plant and paying for specialised craftsmen to operate it. Extraction pits still survive, demonstrating the efforts that went into obtaining the ores, with concomitant labour costs.[18]

Demand for iron did increase, but not because of internal economic growth. Instead it was the king's wars which were to make investment worthwhile, as guns and cannonballs came increasingly to be demanded. Even so, it was not until 1496 that the first English blast furnace is recorded, at Newbridge, initially to make fittings for artillery carriages and shot. Cast-iron guns followed soon afterwards. Many French immigrants were involved in the Wealden industry, although its development during the early sixteenth century remains difficult to assess, and archaeologically obscure. Proximity to the naval bases in the Thames and on the south coast gave the Weald an advantage over iron producers in northern England.

The best evidence about early sixteenth-century guns is from the *Mary Rose* which sank in 1545 almost as publicly as she was raised again in 1982. On board when she foundered were guns of cast bronze, and of both wrought and cast iron. The number of wrought-iron guns was surprising, since they should seemingly have been obsolete by 1545: presumably replacing them was a slow process. The quantity of yew-wood bows, and arrows for them, suggests that gunnery had by no means replaced older weaponry in English minds. Nevertheless, the importance of heavy guns on fighting ships is very clearly brought out by the adaptation of the *Mary Rose* in 1536 from her original construction of overlapping ('clinker') to edge-to-edge ('carvel') planks. This would have facilitated the piercing of the ship's sides for gunports, so that she was in effect a floating, tiered artillery platform. New hull designs were also needed for more elaborate rigging and multi-masted ships. An earlier royal naval vessel, Henry V's *Grace Dieu*, parts of which lie in mud in the River Hamble, was triple-clinkered, but not yet fully adapted to bombard as well as to resist bombardment. She was, however, too large and heavy to sail economically as a commercial vessel, so that she could not be hired out to merchants in times of peace. This increasing specialisation, although never absolute, emphasizes royal expenditure on warfare, as well as the increasing size of ships generally.[19]

The *Mary Rose* was originally completed in 1510, a year after another royal vessel, the *Sovereign*, is recorded as having been rebuilt. What little survives of the latter indicates that either then or later she too was converted from clinker to carvel construction. A smaller vessel which sank outside Plymouth in about 1530 was carvel-built from the first. This process involved building the 'skeleton' of the ship, its keel and ribs, before the planks were attached, rather than adding the ribs into a 'carcase' of planks as in clinker building, a considerable change in construction methods, which increased strength and rigidity; uncertainty in them is apparently indicated by the use of both iron and wooden nails. It is, of course, difficult to be sure of the country of origin of an unnamed wreck, but the Plymouth vessel had English stones in her ballast, and was probably primarily a coasting vessel, able to carry some two or three hundred tons of cargo.[20]

There were wrought-iron guns aboard the Plymouth wreck, as she would have had to be prepared to repel pirates. Building and equipping individual ships became more and more expensive as efforts were made both to reduce bulk carrying-costs and to ensure that vessels were large enough to avoid easy capture. More complex sails as well as defensive needs meant that larger crews had to be carried, with higher wage costs, and greater losses would be incurred if entire cargoes were lost at sea. These inter-connected factors had led to joint-stock funding ventures in Italy and other countries, a major development in mercantile risk-spreading. Facilities such as insurance and bills of exchange made international trade more flexible, and could also be used to get round any canonical bans on usury. But despite England's strong Italian connections from the second half of the thirteenth century onwards, English merchants took little part in such early capitalistic activities, allowing other nations not only to discover new worlds but to usurp most of the existing world's carrying-trade in the fifteenth century. Although in the early fourteenth century England had been able to muster a thousand ships to carry wine from Bordeaux, import levels fluctuated violently, and in the fifteenth century never reached even half of the early fourteenth-century quantity, partly because of the widespread consumption of strong beer, as the pottery cisterns show. It is estimated that only half even of England's own exports and imports were transported in English ships during the earlier part of the sixteenth century.[21]

One factor which may have limited English interest in commercial complexities was the high quality of the English coinage, which was readily acceptable overseas and thus obviated part of the need for paper transactions.[22] This perhaps dubious advantage was not entirely lost even though the weight of the penny was eventually reduced to fifteen grains in 1411 and twelve in 1464. Despite some native production, for instance in Devon, shortage of silver was part of a general European problem, and gold supplies were erratic. There were still some poor-quality European coins being imported, but there seem to be fewer of these found in excavations than of the earlier 'crockards' and their ilk, which does not suggest that they created any more of a problem. There is a possibility that fewer coins were circulating generally in the fifteenth century: although there are plenty of jettons, actual coins are perhaps scarcer in coin lists—in Exeter, only a Scandinavian 'sterling'; a single Edward IV penny from two sites in Northampton; a halfpenny and a quarter noble in the Trig Lane waterfront, London; a half groat of Henry VI from Oxford's Hamel; York has only ten fifteenth-century English coins, against some twenty-two of the previous century. These totals tend to confirm that silver shortages and population decline meant that there were fewer coins in use in the fifteenth- and early sixteenth-century towns.[23] Whether jettons and tokens were circulating as unofficial currency remains unknown, but is correspondingly more likely as actual coins became scarcer. Furthermore, greater awareness of coins and coin-use is demonstrated by the large number of metal frames from purses, and of money boxes that are one of the new ceramic products of the period (9,3). Indeed, Oxford has produced a novel type of hoard—a hoard of money boxes of the fifteenth/sixteenth century, found in a pit behind one of the main commercial streets.[24]

The Oxford money boxes did not all come from the same source: some were from Brill, Buckinghamshire, which had long traded its pottery over the ten-mile trip into Oxford, but others had come from the Surrey/North Hampshire potting area which was now making inroads into what was a fairly distant market, particularly with small tableware such as mugs and bowls in fine white wares. Especially distinctive are the misnamed 'Tudor Green' wares, actually made from at least a century before Henry VII's accession, which were used for vessels such as finely-made lobed cups with glossy green glazes, the most technically accomplished English pottery since Stamford ware (9,3). Another contemporary fineware, but using red clays, suffers another misnomer as 'Cistercian ware', because it was first recognized on Cistercian abbey sites: it was, however, no more made by monks than any other pottery, being a normal commercial venture. The wide distribution of these products may be evidence of a change in marketing patterns, a reversion

9, 3. A selection of fifteenth-/early sixteenth-century pottery products, typically smaller and more delicate than earlier types (cf. **7, 2** and **7, 7**). They include (left to right) a tripod handled bowl, perhaps for warming food; a small drinking-jug; a lamp; a money-box with a thin slit for the coins - it had to broken to get at them again; a whistle; a drinking-beaker; and a 'Tudor Green' lobed cup.

to the late Saxon Stamford type of organisation, since the distances involved are too great for potters to have travelled in a day in order to sell their own wares in a local market. Middleman involvement is implied—and this may have quickened responsiveness to change, since such men would want what was regarded as the most desirable, fashionable product.[25] Even so, fashions did not necessarily spread quickly: Exeter never made use of bowls like those quite common further east, and was slow to adopt the use of drinking mugs, which only appeared there towards the end of the fifteenth century. Despite this relative parochialism, early sixteenth-century kiln waste found in Exeter shows a range of vessel forms most comparable to pots from the Low Countries. It would seem that an immigrant may have tried and failed to set up a business.[26]

Exeter's is among the few urban kilns known in the late Middle Ages. The town was getting most of its pots from north Devon and south Somerset, trade which must have used overland routes. The Somerset industry was centred at Donyatt, and is one of a number of such industries becoming established in the late Middle Ages which were to continue for a long period. Others, however, were closing down, and no very obvious explanation for such volatility is forthcoming, although it may well be seen as a sign of the instability of the period generally. If middlemen were involved in the wider sale of the potters' wares, they would have been more interested in involvement with producers sited where distribution was easy: it is argued that Donyatt's location was partly caused by proximity to a well-used main road. It may also have been important further north to be close to coal supplies, as multi-flue kilns suggest that this was increasingly used as fuel. If there were no seams near the kilns, an adequate transport system for bringing the coal would have been

needed. There is also fairly good general evidence that decoration was important again. More uniform and evenly spread glazing was applied to the fine
wares, requiring specialist skills which would have tended to concentrate at
particular centres, cutting down on the proliferation of kilns seen earlier in
the villages of Northamptonshire and Bedfordshire. Even so, small-scale
operations still occurred: Lower Parrock, East Sussex, is an example of an
attempt early in the sixteenth century to establish a small industry, copying
northern French pottery from the Beauvais area, sherds found there perhaps
being from pots that functioned as models. Like its nearest known rival,
Hareplain, it was not sited with an obvious market to target, and was probably
one of several small-scale operations in the Weald forest. By contrast, West
Sussex had at Graffham a much bigger industry, which dominated its local
markets. The East Sussex potters may have expected to take advantage of any
established system for distributing Wealden iron by pack transport. If so, they
had only a limited success because of differences in demand between the two
products. A distinction also needs to be made between the likely distribution
of the fine wares and the presumably cheaper kitchen earthenwares such as
the baking trays, which would have been much more difficult to transport.[27]

Despite transport costs, pottery was being imported in relatively large
amounts during the fifteenth century, for the first time since the Roman
period, and not only tablewares.[28] Stoneware drinking vessels from the
Rhineland are the most commonly found, but there are also Dutch 'red-
wares'–the stonewares were also probably transported by Dutch carriers,
since they would have been found in bulk earlier if traded by the German
Hanse merchants who dominated North Sea trade until the fifteenth century.
Even in the east coast towns, however, the proportions of German and Dutch
imports are not enormous–probably no more than 10 per cent except at a few
waterside landing sites. This is, however, considerably more than the 1 or 2
per cent of earlier centuries, and there is more imported pottery inland also,
suggesting that there was a definite trade in it, not that just a few vessels were
scattered accidentally by travellers. There is, however, no obvious pattern,
such as a proportion of imports diminishing as a factor of distance. Lynn, for
instance, has produced almost no pottery from overseas even though it is a
port, perhaps because the local Grimston potters managed to stave off the
competition, by lower prices or possibly by restraint, if they were sufficiently
structured into the town to uphold a monopoly.

In London, German and Dutch imports increased in quantity from the
middle of the fourteenth century. Imports from France and Iberia–the latter
high-quality tin-glazed lustreware, probably brought in by Italian merchants–continued to arrive; there are sherds of pottery from Italy itself, and
from Egypt or Syria, also probably coming in via Italy. The actual quantities
of these southern wares do not increase, however, and although they are an
indication of occasional luxuries and exotica, they are not like the north European wares which are frequent enough in the fifteenth century to suggest bulk
importing. A comparable pattern has been found in Exeter, but over a diffe-

rent time-scale. In the thirteenth century, there were in effect no Low Countries or German pottery imports, just as there were no lava querns from the Mayen area or Norwegian honestones, a factor of distance. Jugs from France were not uncommon, although never more than 10 per cent of the pottery in use in the town. Saintonge pottery from the Bordeaux region was still 5 per cent of the total in the fifteenth century, but was down to just over 1 per cent in the sixteenth, which is in line with records of declining wine imports from that part of France. There are also occasional sherds from Iberia. Dutch redware pottery was never introduced, and even German stonewares did not arrive until the end of the fifteenth century, but they then became quite common. There is a very interesting contrast between the sources of continental pottery used in sixteenth-century Exeter, and the records of the places with which its merchants were actually trading. The excavated pottery gives little indication of the latter: almost all of it must have been brought into London or another port, and then redistributed. This was probably also happening in the fifteenth century, which would help to explain why different ports have such different proportions of imports. Inland towns may have fewer imports, but nevertheless have enough to show that such pottery was more likely to be taken away from the ports for resale than previously.[29]

Because of abandonments, fifteenth-century evidence from rural sites is less than complete, but at Wharram Percy, where occupation on both the crofts so far excavated extended to around 1500, it is notable that the village was receiving some of its pottery from further away than it had done previously, with York becoming a supplier. Three sherds of French pottery are recorded from two Wharram house sites in the thirteenth or early fourteenth century, but there are some thirty-one Rhenish stonewares of the fourteenth and fifteenth centuries. A similar though less clear-cut trend is shown at Goltho, where one sherd of Dutch redware and one of stoneware are late-medieval finds – there is also a single undated French sherd – and the village may have reduced its reliance on Toynton products since 'Humber ware' is found. At Foxcotte, the thirteenth-fourteenth-century deposits produced pottery sherds from east Wiltshire, north Hampshire and Berkshire, a fifteen-mile radius, whereas a fifteenth-sixteenth-century house yielded pottery from west Sussex, and 'Tudor Green' from the north Hampshire/Surrey industry, twice as far away. Although there were no imports, there were several fragments of copper-alloy skillets and other metal vessels, and none of the earlier coarse cooking-pots. There were also three fifteenth-century coins as well as jettons. Evidence like this points towards higher rural living standards, and greater involvement in the market system and a money economy. The distances travelled by, and the quality of, the goods obtained could indicate not only a greater choice of markets, but also more use of the markets at the larger and more specialised centres. Far more evidence is needed, since another possibility is that itinerant middlemen were bringing such goods directly to the rural sites, thus in fact bypassing at least the smaller markets, partly accounting for the disappearance of many of them.[30]

Similarly, more evidence is needed to assess whether villages were becoming more self-reliant than previously. A smithy building at Goltho, for instance, could be taken as a response to a greater peasant demand for iron products caused by their greater expenditure levels and the reduction in manorial requirements, creating a rôle for a specialist craftsman, perhaps at the expense of urban production. A saw pit at Goltho may indicate more village carpenters at work – or it may just indicate that the saw pit was a new phenomenon, introduced as splitting and adzing gave way to sawing, which makes more economical use of timber at the cost of weakening the grain structure. If there was a time when village-based specialists should have flourished, it was the fifteenth century. More buildings for storage and more grain-drying facilities may indicate greater ability to benefit from processing and retaining agricultural products that could then be released onto the market when higher prices could be obtained than at harvest time. Diversification from agriculture is not demonstrated, however, activities such as lead mining in Somerset and Derbyshire, or coal mining in the Midlands, remaining as marginal rural activities. Evidence of cloth weaving, recorded in some villages in the second half of the fifteenth century, has not been recognised in excavations, although it may account for rural buildings and prosperity in East Sussex and elsewhere.[31]

Changes in the rural economy are shown by the evidence of increased emphasis on livestock farming. The 'cow yards' for cattle at Barton Blount and Goltho are examples; further north, Low Throston in Northumberland seems to have evidence of a fenced cattle yard associated with a fifteenth-century farm unit. Direct evidence of this sort is generally lacking: more frequently the evidence is indirect, with the abandonment of farms, villages and hamlets, and of their associated field systems. This landscape change is usually associated with the enclosure movement – although without excavation it would be very difficult to prove in most cases that there was no time interval between the two processes, and thus that they are causally linked; the assumption is made because documentary records provide evidence. The same dating question applies in many cases where settlements survived, but with their ploughlands reduced, as the ridge and furrow remaining visible in pasture fields in many parts of England demonstrates. Many parks, too, were reduced in size or converted from their original purpose.[32]

The large number of surviving substantial houses is an indication that changed agricultural régimes were to the advantage of many producers. It was not only wool sales that they benefited from, for any reduction in bulk demand caused by population loss could be compensated for by the increased purchasing power of wage earners for better cereals and more meat. Environmental analyses sometimes indicate what was required. Increased consumption of wheat in fourteenth- and fifteenth-century Winchester is reported to have been accompanied by a decline in the quantities of coarser cereals. In Exeter, there were rather more younger cattle, suggesting that less tough beef was eaten. Carcase size increased slightly, but this may not be significant, just as the introduction of some long-horned cattle cannot be taken as evidence that new breeds were being developed to cater for the meat market by producing animals that would fatten quickly and not be needed for cart and plough haulage. A decrease in pig bones may indicate that swine were not being allowed onto the pastureland which had previously been arable and grazed by them when it was fallow. Increased numbers of deer bones at castles may be because consumption of venison had become more prestigious at a time when other meat was more widely available to the rest of the population. The cooking vessels and sauce bottles indicate new ways of preparing food, emphasizing that it was not profligate consumption that marked status, but also lavish expenditure on creating rarified flavours. The symbolic importance of the table can be seen in more refined use of cutlery. Pewter spoons became quite common, and it has been noticed that in London there are many fewer scabbards in the later Middle Ages, as people kept their eating knives at home rather than carrying them round all the time.[33]

One animal which is quite frequently recorded in bone assemblages is the cat, kept as a vermin-hunter and as a pet, and which could then as now provide acceptable fur: bones with skinning marks have been found in several towns. Fur was much sought after and is one commodity which late-medieval sumptuary laws sought to restrict: anyone could wear cat or rabbit, but imported skins were for the élites, carefully graded by rank. Such laws are difficult to evaluate: they may reflect real concern that status should be maintained and made visible, or they may just be part of a general European concept of what was proper, since sumptuary legislation emanated from Italy and was widely copied. Nevertheless, they are an important expression of social values: *noblesse* must survive in an age of opportunity. The sumptuary laws also laid down prohibitions on the wrong people wearing precious-metal jewellery, and there are enough fourteenth- and fifteenth-century gold finger-rings to suggest that they at least were worn without too much fine regard for the letter of the law. This sort of concern about display and personal appearance probably accounts for the wearing of pointed rather than rounded leather shoes and for the large number of small mirrors that have been found. The earliest known portraits, of Edward III and Richard II, suggest the same awareness of self.[34]

One jewel which in particular expresses the ethos of the period is the Dunstable Swan, a gold and enamel brooch which was the badge of the Bohun family, becoming a Lancastrian emblem after Henry IV had taken the throne from Richard II. Richard's use of badges to foster courtly cliques was one reason for his downfall: these things were not just tokens to be worn at tournaments as they had been under Edward III, but were political symbols which expressed factional allegiances. The hoards of coins and jewellery from Thame, Oxfordshire (**9, 4**), and Fishpool, Nottinghamshire, show the huge sums available to be spent on lavish display, but they were also portable, and their owners could take them out of the country if the world turned against them. They were not just a sign of wealth, but of insecurity, since the retribution of a rival faction could mean loss of life and land in a way that had not pertained under the feudal régime. There was also the insecurity of new blood: despite emphasis on lineage and family honour, few old-established families managed to survive. Those achieving noble status from the ranks of the lesser gentry needed to display their new position. Hence the continued building of new houses, many called castles though their military capacity was only skin deep, like Lord Cromwell's keep at Tattershall, Lincolnshire, built in brick and stone so that it was an essay in polychromy on a huge scale, as the jewels were in miniature. Expenditure on these edifices was another reason for high wages, since even unskilled labourers were in demand.[35]

The jewellery of the fifteenth century also demonstrates the continuing social importance of the long-distance supply of luxuries: pearls, semi-precious stones and by now even diamonds from the Far East. Much of the gold for the settings came from West Africa, via Spain. Was it a contemporary exchange network that took a fine copper-alloy jug, made in London during Richard II's reign and decorated with his badges, to the 'Gold Coast' where it was found in the palace of the Ashanti King Prempeh in 1895? Italian glass, increasingly found at least in ports like London and Southampton, and tin-glazed pottery are other examples; the internal distribution of these is not yet fully established, nor is the extent of native glass production in the Weald.

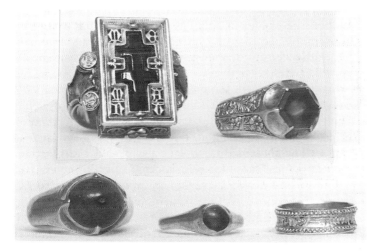

9, 4. The gold rings found in the Thame hoard. Although with coins which show that they were not deposited before *c.* 1457, the rings may all have been fifty years old or more. The biggest has a bezel which can be opened for use as a reliquary; the ring next to it has flowers engraved on the hoop, and a hexagonal peridot in a claw setting. Below left is another claw setting, holding a toadstone - actually a fossilised tooth, though popularly believed to come from a toad's mouth. Next to it is a very common type of later medieval ring, a stirrup-shaped hoop holding a stone, in this case a turquoise. The final ring is inscribed with a common-place love motto '*Tout pour vous*' (All for you), and sprays of flowers, probably originally enamelled

Consequently the balance between the importance, or value, to towns of their rôle as suppliers of luxury goods to the élite and of domestic consumables to the wider populace cannot be quantified.[36]

The importance of London as the principal distributor of luxury goods reflects its importance as more than just the largest city, for by the later Middle Ages it was in every sense the capital of the nation: hence the royal and other palaces grouped in and around it – Shene, Kensington, Savoy, Westminster. Access to the king's favour, to Parliament and to courts of law was more important in the rise of most new families than was involvement in the City's commerce. As such people advanced, they did not invest in trade or industry but bought land to secure status, just as they had in the fourteenth century. With land went houses and 'castles' such as Cromwell's Tattershall of the 1430s or Buckingham's Thornbury which was unfinished when he was executed in 1521, its size having alarmed the jealousy of Henry VIII. Men like this clearly thought of themselves as magnates striving for territorial dominance. The use of brick at Tattershall made a stronger statement by the way its colour contrasted with the grey stone of surrounding buildings. Cromwell also built a vast country mansion at Wingfield, Derbyshire, to a double-courtyard plan: 'castles' were not the only houses that such men built, although nearly all made a 'castle' their first priority. Some placed them in a parkland setting, as Lord Hastings intended to do at Kirby Muxloe, out of appreciation of the concept of landscape, to emphasize scale of expenditure, and to extend the distance between noble and folk. What survives today at Kirby Muxloe shows considerable provision for gunnery: many late fifteenth-century houses were more defensible than their predecessors, a reflection of the reality of the period's politics.[37]

Despite their new status, the Cromwells and the Buckinghams were thinking along conservative lines in their buildings and their jewellery. Their burial fashions changed a little, with tombs stressing the corruptibility of the flesh rather than seeking its perpetuation, but chantries received the same emphasis as before. The choice of burial place also usually continued to stress a family's associations and its landed rôle: alternatively, they might seek burial in London because of the capital's particular status. Embellishments, such as the use of terracotta at the end of the fifteenth century for decoration, might change, but underlying ambitions did not alter from the pursuit of position through control of resources that gave status and supporters, but through patronage not ties of service. When new estates were acquired, the new owners did not invest in them by trying to increase agricultural productivity or to encourage new industries. Consequently the ultimate profit on cloth exports and such other advantages as late-medieval England had did not make social changes as fundamental as those brought about by demographic processes.

Only in the Church can new ideas be seen. Structurally, this is not apparent. Although the Perpendicular style is different from Gothic in its use of glass, fan vaulting and tall towers, it is difficult to see it as qualitatively different. When Canterbury Cathedral built its new gatehouse in the early sixteenth century, it was doing no more than to maintain the same separation of the town from the ecclesiastical enclave that Salisbury had established in the thirteenth century. But it was in the churches that new, scientific thought was being adopted: an understanding of 'the inner meaning of hidden things' was being actively sought. The evidence of broken alembics used in distilling at Selborne Priory and other houses is an indication of the sort of experimentation being practised. Other evidence at least of education is not just the foundation of schools and colleges, but more widespread ownership of books: larger numbers of late-medieval copper-alloy clasps are not simply the result of new binding methods. Printing, higher standards of music – facilitated by increased use of glass which improved resonance in buildings – and knowledge of Greek were beginning to make inroads and to spread 'Renaissance' concepts. Arabic numerals show access to new concepts in mathematics; clocks introduced new ideas about the regularity of time, independent of the length of daylight; the use of the vernacular for funerary inscriptions suggests that literacy was spreading. A remarkable example of the use of the vernacular at all social levels is the recent discovery of a door jamb at a peasant's house in Warwickshire at Burton Dassett with the owner's family name, Gormand, inscribed on it (**9, 5**).[38]

To a large degree, Henry VIII delayed the progress of the Renaissance by his split with Rome and his dissolution of the monasteries. England was still on the edge of the world, despite the discovery of America, and remained there until the New World became economically exploited by more than just a brief attempt at cod fishing off Newfoundland by Bristol merchants. The Crown's politics did nothing to build England's continental contacts, and the dynamic potential of the Church was vitiated. Some of the most efficient medieval estate management had been by the monasteries: their rôle could have redeveloped as sixteenth-century population growth swung the advantage in labour control back to the landlords. As it was, Henry VIII handed most Church land over to private individuals whose ambitions with it remained much as they would have been in the fifteenth century; investment received no spur, nor did the Crown increase its long-term buying power by any permanent increase in its revenues. The coastal defences that the king built against yet another threat of French invasion took up most of the immediate profit.[39]

The Henrician 'castles' such as Camber and Hurst which are strung out along the south coast are very different from medieval residential castles, as they are elaborate artillery works with no function other than defence, foreshadowed by municipal enterprises such as Norwich's Cow Tower. The Crown built them without relying on its subjects to assist by building personal castles of their own, in the way that Cooling and perhaps Bodiam had been built in the fourteenth century. Potentially, therefore, the new fortifications could have been as symbolic of a new order as eleventh- and twelfth-century castles had been of feudalism, but in this case of a growing state monopoly. But Henry VIII sold off and gave away monastic estates without ensuring first

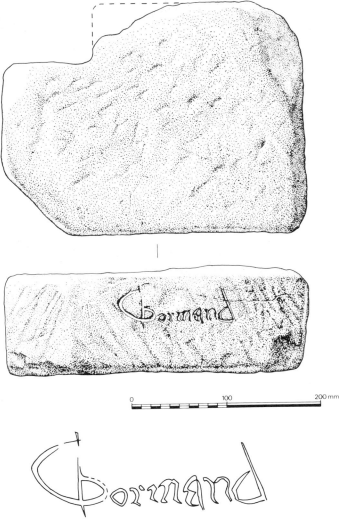

Above and opposite: **9, 5**. Drawing and photograph of a stone door-jamb inscribed with the name 'Gormand', found in excavations at Burton Dassett, Warwickshire, by N. Palmer in 1987. The Gormands were a family named in thirteenth - to fifteenth - century records from various local parishes. Even though the inscription does not prove their literacy, it shows that they could expect many of those passing their house to have sufficient familiarity with letters to recognise their name.

that he had new sources of taxation revenue from which to recoup his loss. Consequently he had no funds with which to continue the momentum of war-related investment, be it in building or in armament industries, and so he failed to achieve any monopolistic control. The first half of the sixteenth century therefore saw England only superficially different. Fundamentally, social relations were scarcely affected by Henry's politics and protestantism: physical evidence shows how deeply-rooted society remained in the traditional attitudes of the past.

Notes

Chapter One
THE FIFTH AND SIXTH CENTURIES

1. P.J. Casey (ed.), *The End of Roman Britain* (Oxford, British Archaeological Reports British Series 71, 1979) still seems to contain the best discussions – see especially the essays by J.P.C. Kent, J.P. Gillam and M. Fulford.

2. P.A. Barker, 'The latest occupation of the site of the baths basilica at Wroxeter', 175–81 *ibid*.

3. Issues like these are considered by C.J. Arnold, *Roman Britain to Saxon England* (London/Sydney, Croom Helm, 1984). See also C. Wickham, 'The other transition: from the ancient world to feudalism', *Past and Present*, 103 (May 1984), 3–36.

4. S. West, *West Stow. The Anglo-Saxon Village* (Ipswich, East Anglian Archaeology Report 24, 1985), including the specialist reports in it by P. Crabtree, A. Russel, V.I. Evison *et al*.

5. In addition to her summary on the bones in *ibid*., see P. Crabtree, 'The archaeozoology of the Anglo-Saxon site at West Stow, Suffolk', 223–35 in K. Biddick (ed.), *Archaeological Approaches to Medieval Europe* (Kalamazoo, 1985).

6. L. Mortimer, 'Anglo-Saxon copper alloys from Lechlade, Gloucestershire', *Oxford Journal of Archaeology*, 7ii (1988), 227–34.

7. P.J. Drury and N.P. Wickenden, 'An early Saxon settlement within the Romano-British small town at Heybridge, Essex', *Medieval Archaeology*, 25 (1982), 1–40. For the evidence of towns generally, D.A. Brooks, 'A review of the evidence for continuity in British towns in the 5th and 6th centuries', *Oxford Journal of Archaeology*, 5i (March, 1986), 77–102.

8. York: R. Hall, *The Viking Dig* (London, Bodley Head, 1984) and *id*., 'The making of Domesday York', 233–47 in D. Hooke (ed.), *Anglo-Saxon Settlements* (Oxford, Blackwell, 1988); Gloucester: T. Darvill, 'Excavations on the site of the early Norman castle at Gloucester, 1983–84', *Medieval Archaeology*, 32 (1988), 1–49 and C. Heighway, 'Saxon Gloucester', 359–83 in J. Haslam (ed.), *Anglo-Saxon Towns in Southern England* (Chichester, Phillimore, 1984).

9. R. MacPhail, 'Soil and botanical studies of the "Dark Earth" ', 309–32 in M. Jones and G. Dimbleby, *The Environment of Man: The Iron Age to the Anglo-Saxon Period* (Oxford, British Archaeological Reports British Series 87, 1981).

10. For 'opportunism', see C. Thomas, *Celtic Britain* (London, Thames and Hudson, 1988), chapter 3.

11. H. Hurst, 'Excavations at Gloucester: Third interim report – Kingsholm 1966–75', *Antiquaries Journal*, 55ii (1975), 267–94, especially the specialist section by D. Brown, 290–94.

12. B. Hope-Taylor, *Yeavering: an Anglo-British Centre of Early Northumbria* (London, Her Majesty's Stationery Office, 1977).

13. C.J. Arnold, *An Archaeology of the Early*

Anglo-Saxon Kingdoms (London/New York, Routledge, 1988), chapter 5, discusses this further.

14. N. Higham, *The Northern Counties to AD 1000* (London, Longman, 1986).

15. P. Rahtz, 'Celtic Society in Somerset AD 400–700', *Bulletin of the Board of Celtic Studies*, 30i and ii (Nov. 1982), 176–200.

16. For dates, see Thomas, above, note 10, 58–60.

17. Higham, above, note 14, 243 *seq.*, summarizes recent work and makes the interesting point about slave raids.

18. Hampshire: P.J. Fasham, 'Fieldwork in Micheldever Wood, 1973–80', *Proceedings of the Hampshire Field Club and Archaeological Society*, 39 (1983), 5–45, at 33. Nottinghamshire: T. Unwin, 'Townships and early fields in north Nottinghamshire', *Journal of Historical Geography*, 9iv (1983), 341–46; Wharram Percy: C.C. Taylor and P.J. Fowler, 'Roman fields into medieval furlongs', 159–62 in H.C. Bowen and P.J. Fowler, *Early Land Allotment* (Oxford, British Archaeological Reports British Series 48, 1978). See also now contributions by P. Warner, T. Unwin and T. Williamson in Hooke (ed.), above, note 8.

19. C. Scull, 'Further evidence from East Anglia for enamelling on early Anglo-Saxon metalworking', *Anglo-Saxon Studies in Archaeology and History*, 4 (1985), 117–24.

20. D. Miles, *Archaeology at Barton Court Farm, Abingdon, Oxfordshire* (London, Council for British Archaeology Research Report 50, 1984).

21. W.J. and K.A. Rodwell, *Rivenhall: Investigations of a Villa, Church and Village 1950–1977* (London, Council for British Archaeology Research Report 55, 1985) and dating caveats by M. Millett, 'The question of continuity: Rivenhall reviewed', *Archaeological Journal*, 144 (1987), 434–44.

22. P. Drury and W. Rodwell, 'Settlement in the later Iron Age and Roman periods', 59–75 in D.G. Buckley (ed.), *Archaeology in Essex to AD 1500* (London, Council for British Archaeology Research Report 34, 1980); T. Williamson, 'Settlement chronology and regional landscapes: the evidence from the claylands of East Anglia', 153–75 in Hooke (ed.), above, note 8.

23. E.-J. Pader, *Symbolism, Social Relations and the Interpretation of Mortuary Remains* (Oxford, British Archaeological Reports International Series 130, 1982).

24. J.D. Richards, *The Significance of Form and Decoration of Anglo-Saxon Cremation Urns* (Oxford, British Archaeological Reports British Series 166, 1987).

25. *Ibid.*

26. S.M. Hirst, *An Anglo-Saxon Inhumation Cemetery at Sewerby, East Yorkshire* (York, University of York Archaeological Publication 4, 1985).

27. Precise ageing of older skeletons is difficult, however.

28. A.M. Cook and M.W. Dacre, *Excavations at Portway, Andover, 1973–75* (Oxford, University Committee for Archaeology Monograph 4, 1985).

29. Rahtz, above, note 15.

30. A. Ellison, 'Natives, Romans and Christians on West Hill, Uley: an interim report on the excavation of a ritual complex of the first millennium AD', 305–28 in W. Rodwell (ed.), *Temples, Churches and Religion in Roman Britain* (Oxford, British Archaeological Reports British Series 77, 1980).

31. S. Foster, 'Early medieval inscription at Holcombe, Somerset', *Medieval Archaeology*, 32 (1988), 208–11 for west Somerset and bibliography.

32. Thomas, above, note 10, 71–76; work by Cornwall Archaeological Unit summarized in S.M. Youngs, J. Clark and T. Barry, 'Medieval Britain and Ireland in 1986', *Medieval Archaeology*, 31 (1987), 110–91, entry 19. M. Fulford, 'Byzantium and Britain: a Mediterranean perspective on post-Roman Mediterranean imports in western Britain and Ireland', *Medieval*

Archaeology, 33 (1989), 1–6 emphasizes the direct contact between Britain and the eastern Mediterranean which can be implied from the nature and range of the imported pottery.

33. R.J. Silvester, 'An excavation on the post-Roman site at Bantham, North Devon', *Devon Archaeological Society Proceedings*, 39 (1981), 89–118; F.M. Griffith, 'Salvage operations at the Dark Age site at Bantham Ham, Thurlestone, 1982', *ibid.*, 44 (1986), 39–58.

34. A. Preston-Jones and P. Rose, 'Medieval Cornwall', *Cornish Archaeology*, 25 (1986), 135–85.

35. L. Alcock, 'Cadbury-Camelot: a fifteen-year perspective', *Proceedings of the British Academy*, 68 (1982), 356–88.

36. Ulwell: work by Wessex Archaeological Committee (now Trust for Wessex Archaeology) summarized in S.M. Youngs, J.Clark and T.B. Barry, 'Medieval Britain and Ireland in 1982', *Medieval Archaeology*, 27 (1983), 161–229, entry 36 (and now also P.W. Cox, 'A seventh-century inhumation cemetery at Shepherd's Farm, Ulwell near Swanage, Dorset', *Proceedings of the Dorset Natural History and Archaeological Society*, 110 (1988), 37–47); Cannington: Rahtz, above, note 15.

37. V.I. Evison, 'The Anglo-Saxon finds from Hardown Hill', *Dorset Natural History and Archaeological Society Proceedings*, 90 (1968), 232–40.

38. V.I. Evison, *The Fifth-Century Invasions South of the Thames* (London, Athlone Press, 1965).

39. T. Capelle, 'Animal stamps and animal figures on Anglo-Saxon and Anglian pottery', *Medieval Archaeology*, 31 (1987), 94–96 and references.

40. J. Hines, *The Scandinavian Character of Anglian England in the pre-Viking period* (Oxford, British Archaeological Reports British Series 124, 1984) and review by G. Speake, *Medieval Archaeology*, 30 (1986), 203–04.

41. B.M. Ager, 'The smaller variants of the Anglo-Saxon quoit brooch', *Anglo-Saxon Studies in Archaeology and History*, 4 (1985), 1–58.

42. T.M. Dickinson, 'Fowler's Type G penannular brooches reconsidered', *Medieval Archaeology*, 26 (1982), 41–68.

43. R.A. Chambers, 'The late and sub-Roman cemetery at Queenford Farm, Dorchester-on-Thames, Oxfordshire', *Oxoniensia*, 52 (1987), 35–70.

44. C. Sparey Green, *Excavations at Poundbury 1964–1980. Volume I: The Settlements* (Dorchester, Dorset Natural History and Archaeological Society Monograph 7, 1987).

45. A point of debate – see S. James, A. Marshall and M. Millett, 'An early medieval building tradition', *Archaeological Journal*, 140 (1984), 182–215.

46. D. Dumville (ed.), *Gildas: New Approaches* (Woodbridge, Boydell Press, 1984) shows that Gildas's work should not be thought to establish a precise chronology in this period.

47. J.R. Kirk and E.T. Leeds, 'Three early Saxon graves from Dorchester, Oxfordshire', *Oxoniensia*, 17–18 (1952/53), 63–76.

Chaper Two
THE LATER SIXTH AND SEVENTH CENTURIES

1. S.C. Hawkes, 'Anglo-Saxon Kent *c.* 425–725', 64–78 in P.E. Leach (ed.), *Archaeology in Kent to AD 1500* (London, Council for British Archaeology Research Report 48, 1982), 72–77.

2. G.R. Owen-Crocker, *Dress in Anglo-Saxon England* (Manchester, University Press, 1986), 57–63.

3. J.W. Huggett, 'Imported grave goods and the early Anglo-Saxon economy', *Medieval Archaeology*, 32 (1988), 63–96.

4. A. Ozanne, 'The Peak dwellers', *Medieval Archaeology*, 6–7 (1962/63), 15–52.

5. The phrase is borrowed from J. Coy, 'The animal bones', 41–51 in J. Haslam, 'A middle Saxon iron smelting site at Ramsbury, Wiltshire', *Medieval Archaeology*, 24 (1980), 1–68.

6. Cf. W.R. DeBoer, 'Pillage and production in the Amazon', *World Archaeology*, 18ii (Oct. 1986), 231–46. There are Anglo-Saxon objects on the Continent, but in contexts which associate them with people of some social standing.

7. Cf. Pader, chapter 1, note 23.

8. R.F. Tylecote and B.J.J. Gilmour, *The Metallography of Early Ferrous Edge Tools and Weapons* (Oxford, British Archaeological Reports British Series 155, 1986).

9. D. Powlesland, 'Excavations at Heslerton, North Yorkshire', *Archaeological Journal*, 143 (1986), 53–173, at 163.

10. J. Shephard, 'The social identity of the individual in isolated barrows and barrow cemeteries in Anglo-Saxon England', 47–79 in B.C. Burnham and J. Kingsbury (eds), *Space, Hierarchy and Society* (Oxford, British Archaeological Reports International Series 59, 1979).

11. R. Bradley, 'Time regained: the creation of continuity', *Journal of the British Archaeological Association*, 140 (1987), 1–17.

12. R. Bruce-Mitford, *The Sutton Hoo Ship-Burial*, 3 volumes (London, British Museum, 1975–83).

13. Swindon: R. Canham, pers. comm.; Chalton: P.V. Addyman and D. Leigh, 'The Anglo-Saxon village at Chalton, Hampshire: second interim report', *Medieval Archaeology*, 17 (1973), 1–25, pl. vi; Puddlehill: C.L. Matthews and S.C. Hawkes, 'Early Saxon settlements and burials on Puddlehill, near Dunstable, Bedfordshire', *Anglo-Saxon Studies in Archaeology and History*, 4 (1985), 59–115 – building 6.

14. M. Millett with S. James, 'Excavations at Cowdery's Down, Basingstoke, Hampshire, 1979–81', *Archaeological Journal*, 140 (1983), 151–279, at 196–97.

15. J. Hinchliffe, 'An early medieval settlement at Cowage Farm, Foxley, near Malmesbury', *Archaeological Journal*, 143 (1986), 240–59.

16. N. Brooks, *The Early History of the Church of Canterbury* (Leicester, University Press, 1984); S.S. Frere *et al.*, *Archaeology of Canterbury* series (Maidstone, Kent Archaeological Society, 1982 *et seq.*); T. Tatton-Brown, 'The towns of Kent', 1–36 in Haslam (ed.), chapter 1, note 8; J. Rady, 'Excavations at St Martin's Hill, Canterbury, 1984–85', *Archaeologia Cantiana*, 114 (1987), 123–218.

17. M. Biddle, 'The study of Winchester: archaeology and history in a British town, 1961–1983', *Proceedings of the British Academy*, 69 (1983), 93–136.

18. Hall, chapter 1, note 8; D. Phillips, *The Cathedral of Thomas of Bayeux: Excavations at York Minster Volume II* (London, Her Majesty's Stationery Office, 1985), 1–2 and 44.

19. P.J. Bidwell, *The Legionary Bath house and Basilica and Forum at Exeter* (Exeter Archaeological Reports volume 1: Exeter, City Council and University of Exeter, 1979).

20. W. Rodwell, 'Churches in the landscape: aspects of topography and planning', 1–23 in M.L. Faull (ed.), *Studies in Late Anglo-Saxon Settlement* (Oxford, University Department of Extra-Mural Studies, 1984).

21. See Rodwell, above, for all these except the last: N. Doggett, 'The Anglo-Saxon see and cathedral of Dorchester-on-Thames: the evidence reconsidered', *Oxoniensia*, 51 (1986), 49–61.

22. M. Biddle, 'The archaeology of the Church: A widening horizon', 65–71 in P. Addyman and R. Morris (eds), *The Archaeological Study of Churches* (London, Council for British Archaeology Research Report 13, 1976); Burgh Castle: S. Johnson *et al.*, *Burgh Castle, Excavations by Charles Green*

1958–61 (Gressenhall, East Anglian Archaeology Report 20, 1983).

23. H.M. Taylor and D.D. Yonge, 'The ruined church at Stone-by-Faversham: a re-assessment', *Archaeological Journal*, 138 (1981), 118–45.

24. J.R. Magilton, *The Church of St Helen-on-the-Walls, Aldwark* (Archaeology of York 10/1, London, Council for British Archaeology, 1980), 16–17; and see Rodwell, above, note 20.

25. R. Morris, *The Church in British Archaeology* (London, Council for British Archaeology Research Report 47, 1983).

26. Work by A. Down reported in S.M. Youngs, J. Clark and T. Barry, 'Medieval Britain and Ireland in 1986', *Medieval Archaeology*, 31 (1987), 110–91, entry 205 and previous volumes.

27. For more discussion, see Morris, above, note 25.

28. M. Welch, 'Rural settlement patterns in the early and middle Anglo-Saxon periods', *Landscape History*, 7 (1985), 13–25; Arnold, chapter 1, note 13, has much of interest on this in chapter two.

29. Raunds: *Current Archaeology*, 106 (1987), 325–27; Walton: M. Farley, 'Saxon and medieval Walton, Aylesbury. Excavations 1973–74', *Records of Buckinghamshire*, 20 ii (1976), 153–290.

30. This increasingly controversial subject was brought into focus by A. Goodier, 'The formation of boundaries in Anglo-Saxon England: a statistical study', *Medieval Archaeology*, 28 (1984), 1–21. Several papers in Hooke (ed.), chapter 1, note 8 are also highly relevant.

31. For the political implications, H. Mayr-Harting, *The Coming of Christianity to Anglo-Saxon England* (London, Batsford, 1972).

32. P. Grierson and M. Blackburn, *Medieval European Coinage I. The Early Middle Ages* (Cambridge, University Press, 1986), 160 *seq.*

33. Cf. P. Wormald, 'Viking Studies: where and whither?', 128–56 in R.T. Farrell (ed.), *The Vikings* (Chichester, Phillimore, 1982), at 132.

34. S.C. Hawkes, 'The Amherst brooch', *Archaeologia Cantiana*, 100 (1984), 129–51, at 141–43 with references.

35. An up-to-date distribution map of Ipswich ware would be welcome. See R. Hodges, *The Hamwih Pottery* (London, Council for British Archaeology Research Report 37, 1981), 58–60 for a discussion. (A map has now been provided! K. Wade, 'Ipswich', 93–100 in R. Hodges and B. Hobley, *The Rebirth of Towns in the West* (London, Council for British Archaeology Research Report 68, 1988), fig. 54: Essex has four find-spots, as has Kent.)

36. Drury and Rodwell, chapter 1, note 22; P. Warner, 'Pre-Conquest territorial and administrative organisation in East Suffolk', 9–34 in Hooke (ed.), chapter 1, note 8 draws an interesting contrast in the archaeological record from Blything and Wicklaw hundreds.

37. B. Cunliffe, *Excavations at Portchester Castle Vol. II: Saxon* (London, Society of Antiquaries, 1976).

38. The summary and references by M. Sparks and T. Tatton-Brown, 201–05 in Rady, above, note 16 are a good introduction to an important topic, which can then be pursued through G. Astill, 'Archaeology, Economics and Early Medieval Europe', *Oxford Journal of Archaeology*, 4ii (July 1985), 215–32 with references.

39. I. Stewart, 'The early English denarial coinage, *c.* 680–*c.* 750', 5–26 in D. Hill and D.M. Metcalf, *Sceattas in England and on the Continent* (Oxford, British Archaeological Reports British Series 128, 1984); but D.M. Metcalf, 'Monetary circulation in southern England in the first half of the eighth century', 27–69, *ibid.*, reaffirms the Kentish origin for Series A questioned by Stewart.

Chapter Three
THE LATER SEVENTH AND EIGHTH
CENTURIES

1. D.H. Hill, 'The construction of Offa's Dyke', *Antiquaries Journal*, 65i (1985), 140–62 and references; M. Gelling (ed.), *Offa's Dyke Reviewed by Frank Noble* (Oxford, British Archaeological Reports British Series 114, 1983); recent work by D. Hill and the Offa's Dyke Project is summarized in S.M. Youngs, J. Clark and T. Barry, 'Medieval Britain and Ireland in 1985', *Medieval Archaeology*, 30 (1986), 114–98, entry 114.

2. Mersea: P. Crummy, J. Hillam and C. Crossan, 'Mersea Island: the Anglo-Saxon causeway', *Essex Archaeology and History*, 14 (1982), 77–93; Oxford: B. Durham, 'Archaeological investigations in St Aldates, Oxford', *Oxoniensia*, 42 (1977), 83–203, at 176–79; Tamworth: P.A. Rahtz, 'Medieval Milling', 1–15 in D. Crossley (ed.), *Medieval Industries* (London, Council for British Archaeology Research Report 40, 1981). For contemporary Irish mills, C. Rynne, 'The introduction of the vertical watermill into Ireland: some recent archaeological evidence', *Medieval Archaeology*, 33 (1989), 21–31.

3. R. Shoesmith, *Excavations on and close to the Defences. Hereford City Excavations Volume 2* (London, Council for British Archaeology Research Report 46, 1982), 29–31.

4. C.R. Salisbury, 'An Anglo-Saxon fish-weir at Colwick, Nottinghamshire', *Transactions of the Thoroton Society*, 85 (1981), 26–36.

5. Haslam, chapter 2, note 5.

6. J.H. Williams, M. Shaw and V. Denham, *Middle Saxon Palaces at Northampton* (Northampton, Development Corporation, 1985). Arnold, chapter 1, note 13 makes some good points about this site – arguments over interpretation are only possible because of the clarity and quality of the excavation report.

7. M. Audouy, 'Excavations at the church of All Saints, Brixworth, Northamptonshire (1981–82)', *Journal of the British Archaeological Association*, 137 (1984), 1–44.

8. P.J. Huggins, 'Excavation of a Belgic and Romano-British farm with Middle Saxon cemetery and churches at Nazeingbury, Essex, 1975–76', *Essex Archaeology and History*, 10 (1978), 29–117.

9. M. Biddle *et al.*, 'Coins from the Anglo-Saxon period from Repton, Derbyshire', 111–32 in M.A.S. Blackburn (ed.), *Anglo-Saxon Monetary History* (Leicester, University Press, 1986); H.M. Taylor, 'St. Wystan's Church, Repton, Derbyshire: a reconstruction essay', *Archaeological Journal*, 114 (1987), 205–45.

10. Metcalf, chapter 2, note 39; Grierson and Blackburn, chapter 2, note 32.

11. M.M. Archibald, 'The coinage of Beonna in the light of the Middle Harling hoard', *British Numismatic Journal*, 55 (1985), 10–54.

12. M.M. Archibald, Fiche 57 in Williams *et al.*, above, note 6. Archaeologists owe a great debt of thanks to numismatists for coin identifications, and it is regrettable that the important information derived from them is nowadays often consigned to microfiche reports.

13. D.M. Metcalf, 'The coins', 17–59 in P. Andrews (ed.), *The Coins and Pottery from Hamwic* (Southampton, City Museums, Southampton Finds Volume 1, 1988); much of the preceding paragraph derives from Metcalf's work, e.g. chapter 2, note 39. For pottery, Hodges, chapter 2, note 35 and J. Timby, 'The Middle Saxon pottery', 73–124 in Andrews (ed.), this note.

14. P. Holdsworth, *Excavations in Melbourne Street, Southampton, 1971–76* (London, Council for British Archaeology Research Report 33, 1980), 39; the shroud hooks are not yet published.

15. J. Hunter, 'The glass', 59–71, *ibid.* and (with M. Heyworth), pers. comm.

16. Burrow Hill: V. Fenwick, '*Insula de Burgh*; excavations at Burrow Hill, Butley, Suffolk, 1978–81', *Anglo-Saxon Studies in Archaeology and History*, 3 (1984), 35–54; Brandon: R.D. Carr, A. Tester and P. Murphy, 'The Middle-Saxon settlement at Staunch Meadow, Brandon', *Antiquity*, 62 no. 235 (June, 1988), 371–77; Medmerry: D.M. Goodburn, 'Medmerry: a re-assessment of a Migration Period site on the south coast of England, and some of its finds', *International Journal of Nautical and Archaeological Underwater Exploration*, 16iii (1987), 213–24.

17. Southampton: J. Bourdillon and J. Coy, 'The animal bones', 79–120 in Holdsworth, above, note 14; Portchester: A Grant, 'Animal bones', 262–95 in Cunliffe, chapter 2, note 37, at 277–78; Ramsbury: Coy, chapter 2, note 5. See also now J. Bourdillon, 'Countryside and town: the animal resources of Southampton', 177–95 in Hooke (ed.), chapter 1, note 8.

18. P. Wade-Martins, *Excavations in North Elmham Park, 1967–72* (Gressenhall, East Anglian Archaeology Report 9, 1980).

19. D. Seddon *et al.*, 'Fauna', 69–71 in P.V. Addyman, 'A dark-age settlement at Maxey, Northamptonshire', *Medieval Archaeology*, 8 (1964), 20–73.

20. C.F. Tebbutt, 'A Middle-Saxon iron-smelting site at Millbrook, Ashdown Forest, Sussex', *Sussex Archaeological Collections*, 120 (1982), 19–36.

21. M. Biddle and B. Kjølbye-Biddle, 'The Repton Stone', *Anglo-Saxon England*, 14 (1985), 233–92.

22. M. Budny and J. Graham-Campbell, 'An eighth-century bronze ornament from Canterbury and related works', *Archaeologia Cantiana*, 97 (1981), 7–25; for other objects and discussion, D.M. Wilson, *Anglo-Saxon Art from the Seventh Century to the Norman Conquest* (London, Thames and Hudson, 1984), chapter 3.

23. Work by the York Archaeological Trust summarized in S.M. Youngs, J. Clark and T.B. Barry, 'Medieval Britain and Ireland in 1982', *Medieval Archaeology*, 27 (1983), 161–229, entry 143 and plates 15–18.

24. J.G. Hurst, 'The Wharram research project: results to 1983', *Medieval Archaeology*, 28 (1984), 77–111.

25. D. Coggins, K.J. Fairless and C.E. Batey, 'Simy Folds: an early medieval settlement site in Upper Teesdale', *Medieval Archaeology*, 27 (1983), 1–26.

26. G.R. Gilmore and D.M. Metcalf, 'Consistency in the alloy of the Northumbrian stycas: evidence from die-linked specimens', *Numismatic Chronicle*, 144 (1984), 192–98.

27. I. Stewart, 'The London mint and the coinage of Offa', 27–43 in Blackburn (ed.), above, note 9; H. Pagan, 'Coinage in Southern England, 796–874', 45–66; *ibid.*; Archibald, above, note 11; Grierson and Blackburn, chapter 2, note 32, 169 and 275 *seq.*

28. J. Haslam, 'Market and fortress in England in the reign of Offa', *World Archaeology*, 19 i (June, 1987), 76–93 has a number of interesting ideas, some of which are questioned in these paragraphs.

Chapter Four
THE NINTH AND EARLY TENTH CENTURIES

1. C.F. Battiscombe (ed.), *The Relics of St Cuthbert* (Oxford, University Press, 1956).

2. R. Cramp, 'Excavations at Wearmouth and Jarrow, Co. Durham: an interim report', *Medieval Archaeology*, 13 (1969), 21–66; *ead.*, 'Monastic sites', 201–52 in D.M. Wilson (ed.), *The Archaeology of Anglo-Saxon England* (Cambridge, University Press, 1976).

3. N.P. Brooks, 'The development of military obligations in eighth- and ninth-century England', 69–84 in P.

Clemoes and K. Hughes (eds), *England before the Conquest* (Cambridge, University Press, 1971).

4. Metcalf, chapter 3, note 13.

5. W.A. van Es and W.J.H. Verwers, *Excavations at Dorestad 1. The Harbour: Hoogstraat I* (Amersfoort, Berichten van de Rijksdienst voor hat Oudheidkundig Bodemonderzoek 9, 1980).

6. J. Booth, 'Coinage and Northumbrian history *c.* 790–*c.* 810', 57–90 in D.M. Metcalf (ed.), *Coinage in Ninth-century Northumbria* (Oxford, British Archaeological Reports British Series 180, 1987), at 74.

7. D.M. Metcalf, 'Introduction', 1–10 in *ibid.*; Pagan, chapter 3, note 27; N.P. Brooks and J.A. Graham-Campbell, 'Reflections on the Viking-Age silver hoard from Croydon, Surrey', 91–110 in Blackburn (ed.), chapter 3, note 9; also note 15, below.

8. P. Rahtz, *The Saxon and Medieval Palaces at Cheddar* (Oxford, British Archaeological Reports British Series 65, 1979); Tamworth: Rahtz, chapter 3, note 2.

9. G. Beresford, *Goltho: The Development of an Early Medieval Manor* (London, English Heritage Archaeological Report 4, 1987).

10. P. Wade-Martins, 'The origins of rural settlement in East Anglia', 137–59 in P.J. Fowler (ed.), *Recent Work in Rural Archaeology* (Bradford-on-Avon, Moonraker Press, 1975) and comments by A.J. Lawson, *The Archaeology of Witton near North Walsham, Norfolk* (Gressenhall, East Anglian Archaeology Report 18, 1983), 70–71.

11. Addyman, chapter 3, note 19.

12. A. King, 'Gauber High Pasture, Ribblehead – an interim report', 21–25 in R.A. Hall (ed.), *Viking Age York and the North* (London, Council for British Archaeology Research Report 27, 1978).

13. R.L.S. Bruce-Mitford, 'A Dark-Age Settlement at Mawgan Porth, Cornwall', 167–96 in R.L.S. Bruce-Mitford (ed.), *Recent Archaeological Excavations in Britain* (London, Routledge and Kegan Paul, 1956).

14. Tylecote and Gilmour, chapter 2, note 8; J.R. Watkin, 'A late Anglo-Saxon sword from Gilling West, North Yorkshire', *Medieval Archaeology*, 30 (1986), 93–98.

15. D.M. Metcalf and J.P. Northover, 'Debasement of the coinage in southern England in the age of King Alfred', *Numismatic Chronicle*, 145 (1985), 150–76; Metcalf, above, note 7; Brooks and Graham-Campbell, above, note 7.

16. Nazeingbury: Huggins, chapter 3, note 8; North Elmham: Wade-Martins, chapter 3, note 18.

17. Brooks, chapter 2, note 16, at 168.

18. K. East, 'A lead model and a rediscovered sword, both with Gripping Beast decoration', *Medieval Archaeology*, 30 (1986), 1–7; G.G. Astill, *Historic Towns in Berkshire: An Archaeological Appraisal* (Reading, Berkshire Archaeological Committee, 1978), 75–86.

19. C.D. Morris, 'Viking and native in northern England: a case study', *Proceedings of the Eighth Viking Congress* (Odense, 1981), 223–44; M.L. Alexander, 'A "Viking-Age" grave from Cambois, Bedlington, Northumberland', *Medieval Archaeology*, 31 (1987), 101–05.

20. Biddle *et al.*, chapter 3, note 9.

21. A. Stirling, 'Human bones', 49–57 in B. Ayers, *Excavations within the North-East Bailey of Norwich Castle, 1979* (Gressenhall, East Anglian Archaeological Report 28, 1985), 57. R. Hodges, 'Anglo-Saxon England and the origins of the modern world economy', 291–304 in Hooke (ed.), chapter 1, note 8, at 302 should perhaps not have succumbed to the temptation to quote the late Calvin Wells!

22. R. Bailey, *Viking Age Sculptures in Northern England* (London, Collins, 1980), 209–13.

23. P.H. Robinson, 'A pin of the later

Saxon period from Marlborough and related pins', *Wiltshire Archaeological Magazine,* 74–75 (1979/80), 56–60.

24. There is a useful summary on this difficult topic by C.D. Morris 'Aspects of Scandinavian settlement in northern England: a review', *Northern History,* 20 (1984) 1–22.

25. V. Smart, 'Scandinavians, Celts and Germans in Anglo-Saxon England: the evidence of moneyers' names', 171–84 in Blackburn (ed.), chapter 3, note 9.

26. Hall, chapter 1, note 8 and the growing series of York fascicules, as chapter 2, note 24.

27. Work by the Norfolk Archaeological Unit summarized in S.M. Youngs, J. Clark and T. Barry, 'Medieval Britain and Ireland in 1985', *Medieval Archaeology,* 30 (1986), 114–98, entry 133.

28. A. Rogerson and C. Dallas, *Excavations in Thetford 1948–59 and 1973–80* (Gressenhall, East Anglian Archaeological Report 22, 1984).

29. C. Mahany, A. Burchard and G. Simpson, *Excavations in Stamford, Lincolnshire 1963–1969* (Society for Medieval Archaeology Monograph 9, 1982).

30. P. Crummy, *Anglo-Saxon and Norman Colchester* (London, Council for British Archaeology Research Report 39, 1981).

31. D. Perring, *Early Medieval Occupation at Flaxengate, Lincoln* (London, Council for British Archaeology, Archaeology of Lincoln IX-1, 1981); J.E. Mann, *Early Medieval Finds from Flaxengate, Lincoln I: Objects of Antler, Bone, Stone, Horn, Ivory, Amber, and Jet* (Same series, XIV-1, 1982); M. Blackburn, C. Colyer and M. Dolley, *Early Medieval Coins from Lincoln and its Shire* (Same series, VI-1, 1983).

32. D.J.P. Mason, *Excavations at Chester: 26–42 Lower Bridge Street 1974–76: The Dark Age and Saxon Periods* (Chester, City Council, Grosvenor Museum Archaeology Excavation and Survey Report 3, 1985).

33. J. Schofield, *The Building of London* (London, British Museum, 1984); T. Dyson and J. Schofield, 'Saxon London', 285–314 in Haslam (ed.), chapter 1, note 8.

34. C. Morris, 'Note on iron objects 331–42', 32–39 in Darvill, chapter 1, note 8.

35. Winchester: Biddle, chapter 2, note 17; Chichester: A Down, *Chichester Excavations 5* (Chichester, Phillimore, 1981), 136 *seq.*; Bath: B. Cunliffe, 'Saxon Bath', 345–58 in Haslam, chapter 1, note 8; Exeter: J.P. Allan, *Medieval and Post-Medieval Finds from Exeter, 1971–1980* (Exeter, Exeter Archaeological Report 3, 1984); Canterbury: P. Bennett, 'Rescue excavations in the Outer Court of St Augustine's Abbey, 1983–84', *Archaeologia Cantiana,* 103 (1986), 79–117 and Rady, chapter 2, note 16.

36. Cunliffe, chapter 2, note 37.

37. S. Keynes and M. Lapidge, *Alfred the Great* (Pelican, Harmondsworth, 1983), 193–94 and notes; D. Hill, 'Towns as structures and functioning communities through time: the development of central places from 600 to 1066', 197–212 in Hooke (ed.), chapter 1, note 8, summarizes his many important contributions to this topic.

38. Shoesmith, chapter 3, note 3, 74–80.

39. B. Durham, T. Hassall, T. Rowley and C. Simpson, 'A cutting across the Saxon defences at Wallingford', *Oxoniensia,* 37 (1972), 82–85.

40. N.P. Brooks, 'England in the ninth century: the crucible of defeat', *Transactions of the Royal Historical Society,* 5th ser. 29 (1979), 1–20.

41. P. Crummy, 'The system of measurement used in town planning from the ninth to the thirteenth centuries', *Anglo-Saxon Studies in Archaeology and History,* 1 (1979), 149–64.

42. B.A.E. Yorke, 'The bishops of Winchester, the kings of Wessex and the development of Winchester in the ninth and early tenth centuries', *Proceedings of the Hampshire Field Club and*

Archaeological Society, 40 (1984), 61–70.

43. Wilson, chapter 3, note 22; G.A. Kornbluth, 'The Alfred Jewel: reuse of Roman *spolia*', *Medieval Archaeology*, 33 (1989), 32–37.

44. T.A. Heslop, 'English seals from the mid ninth century to *c.* 1100', *Journal of the British Archaeological Association*, 133 (1980), 1–16.

Chapter Five
THE TENTH CENTURY

1. Rogerson and Dallas, chapter 4, note 28.
2. K. Kilmurry, *The Pottery Industry of Stamford, Lincolnshire* c. *AD 850–1250* (Oxford, British Archaeological Reports British Series 84, 1960), 177.
3. *Ibid.*; Mahany, Burchard and Simpson, chapter 4, note 29.
4. L. Adams, 'Early Islamic pottery from Flaxengate, Lincoln', *Medieval Archaeology*, 25 (1979), 218–19.
5. A.G. Vince, 'The Saxon and Medieval pottery of London: a review', *Medieval Archaeology*, 29 (1985), 25–93, at 34.
6. *Ibid.*, 34–36; P. Jones, 'The pottery', 36–85 in R Poulton, 'Excavations on the site of the Old Vicarage, Church Street, Reigate, 1971–82, Part I', *Surrey Archaeological Collections*, 77 (1986), 17–94, questions at 71–73 whether the source has to be the Oxford area, but I am told that there does seem to be some fossil shell in the clay.
7. E.g. N. Macpherson-Grant, 105–112 in Bennett, chapter 4, note 35.
8. Down, chapter 4, note 35, 136, 190.
9. M. Biddle and K. Barclay, 'Winchester ware', 137–66 in V.I. Evison, H. Hodges and J.G. Hurst (eds), *Medieval Pottery from Excavations* (London, John Baker, 1974). The dating evidence for clamp kilns found in Winchester has yet to be published.
10. Vince, above, note 5, 34–35.
11. G. Hutchinson, 'The bar-lug pottery of Cornwall', *Cornish Archaeology*, 18 (1979), 81–104.

12. British Museum Laboratory Report, 441–42 in J.R. Fairbrother, 'Faccombe, Netherton: archaeological and historical research', unpublished M. Phil. thesis, University of Southampton, 1984.
13. P. Nightingale, 'The London Pepperers' Guild and some twelfth-century English trading links with Spain', *Bulletin of the Institute of Historical Research*, 58 no. 138 (Nov. 1985), 123–32.
14. V. Fenwick, *The Graveney Boat* (Oxford, British Archaeological Reports British Series 53, 1978); *ead.*, 'A new Anglo-Saxon ship', *International Journal of Nautical Archaeology*, 12ii (1983), 174–75.
15. J. Moulden and D. Tweddle, *Anglo-Scandinavian Settlement South-West of the Ouse* (London, Council for British Archaeology, Archaeology of York 8/1, 1986); Hall, chapter 1, note 8.
16. E.J.E. Pirie, *Post-Roman Coins from York Excavations, 1971–1981* (London, Council for British Archaeology, Archaeology of York 18/1, 1986).
17. Owen-Crocker, chapter 2, note 2, 147.
18. D.M. Metcalf, 'The monetary history of England in the tenth century reviewed in the perspective of the eleventh century', 133–57 in Blackburn (ed.), chapter 3, note 9.
19. Dyson and Schofield, chapter 4, note 33.
20. Perring, chapter 4, note 31.
21. M. Atkin, B. Ayers and S. Jennings, 'Thetford-type ware production in Norwich', 61–104 in P. Wade-Martins (ed.), *Norfolk: Waterfront Excavations and Thetford Ware Production* (Gressenhall, East Anglian Archaeology Report 17, 1983).
22. J.H. Williams, 'A review of some aspects of late Saxon urban origins and development', 25–34 in Faull (ed.), chapter 2, note 20.
23. Biddle, chapter 2, note 17.
24. J. Allan, C. Henderson and R. Higham, 'Saxon Exeter', 385–414 and P. Holdsworth, 'Saxon Southampton',

331–43 in Haslam (ed.), chapter 1, note 8.

25. Shoesmith, chapter 3, note 3; A.G. Vince, 'The ceramic finds', 34–82 in R. Shoesmith, *The Finds* (London, Council for British Archaeology Research Report 56, 1985), 79.

26. C.M. Heighway, A.P. Garrod and A.G. Vince, 'Excavations at 1 Westgate Street, Gloucester, 1975' *Medieval Archaeology*, 23 (1979), 159–213: the textile discussion is Appendix 6, by J.W. Hedges, 190–96.

27. M. Carver, 'Medieval Worcester: an archaeological framework', *Transactions of the Worcestershire Archaeological Society*, 3rd ser. 7 (1980).

28. E.g. *Oxoniensia*, 36 (1971), plate III, B.

29. Mason, chapter 4, note 32; Metcalf, above, note 18, 142–44.

30. J. Graham-Campbell, 'Some archaeological reflections on the Cuerdale hoard', 329–44 in Metcalf (ed.), chapter 4, note 6.

31. Bailey, chapter 4, note 22; J.T. Lang, 'The hogback', *Anglo-Saxon Studies in Archaeology and History*, 3 (1984), 85–176.

32. T. O'Connor, *Animal Bones from Flaxengate, Lincoln* c. *870–1500* (London, Council for British Archaeology, Archaeology of Lincoln XVIII-1, 1982): an excellent study from which all this paragraph is derived.

33. E.g. D. Baker, E. Baker, J. Hassall and A. Simco, 'Excavations in Bedford, 1967–77', *Bedfordshire Archaeological Journal*, 13 (1979), 1–309.

34. Farley, chapter 2, note 29.

35. Raunds: chapter 2, note 29 and G.E. Cadman, 'Raunds 1977–1983: an excavation summary', *Medieval Archaeology*, 27 (1983), 107–22.

36. A number of studies on this topic have been published recently by J. Blair, such as 'Secular minster churches in Domesday Book', 104–42 in P. Sawyer (ed.), *Domesday Book: A Reassessment* (London, Edward Arnold, 1985) and 'Minsters in the landscape',

35–58 in Hooke (ed.), chapter 1, note 8.

37. Work by B.K. Davison and R. Mackey, in D.M. Wilson and S. Moorhouse, 'Medieval Britain in 1970', *Medieval Archaeology*, 15 (1971), 124–79 at 130–31.

38. Biddle, chapter 2, note 17 and references.

39. Magilton, chapter 2, note 24 and Rodwell, chapter 2, note 20.

40. B.J.J. Gilmour and D.A. Stocker, *St Mark's Church and Cemetery* (London, Council for British Archaeology, Archaeology of Lincoln XIII-1, 1986).

41. A. Boddington and G. Cadman, 'Raunds: an interim report on excavations 1977–1980', *Anglo-Saxon Studies in Archaeology and History*, 2 (1981), 103–22.

42. Work by G. Scobie, summarized in S.M. Youngs, J. Clark and T.B. Barry, 'Medieval Britain and Ireland in 1983', *Medieval Archaeology*, 28 (1984), 203–65, entry 51.

43. C. Heighway and R. Bryant, 'A reconstruction of the 10th-century church of St Oswald, Gloucester', 188–95 in L.A.S. Butler and R.K. Morris (eds), *The Anglo-Saxon Church* (London, Council for British Archaeology Research Report 60, 1986) and references.

44. A.W. Klukas, 'The architectural implications of the *Decreta Lanfranci*', *Anglo-Norman Studies*, 6 (1984), 136–71. For architecture generally, B. Cherry, 'Ecclesiastical architecture', 151–200 in Wilson, chapter 4, note 2 and E. Fernie, *The Architecture of the Anglo-Saxons* (London, Batsford, 1983).

45. All these books and objects are discussed and illustrated in J. Backhouse, D.H. Turner and L. Webster (eds), *The Golden Age of Anglo-Saxon Art* (London, British Museum Publications, 1984), as are those which follow.

46. D. Buckton, 'Late 10th- and early 11th-century *cloisonné* enamel brooches', *Medieval Archaeology*, 30

(1986), 8–18.

47. Baker *et al.*, above, note 32.
48. Bruce-Mitford, chapter 4, note 13.
49. Cunliffe, chapter 2, note 37.
50. Rahtz, chapter 4, note 8. (R. Holt, however, in *The Mills of Medieval England* (Oxford, Blackwell, 1988), 18–19 prefers the original interpretation of the 'fowl-house' as a mill because of its size and the find of a large piece of stone suitable for milling. Certainly the Northampton mortar-mixers show that rotary man- or animal-power was applied in the period.)
51. Wade-Martins, chapter 3, note 18.
52. Waltham: E. Lewis, 'Excavations in Bishops Waltham 1967–78', *Proceedings of the Hampshire Field Club and Archaeological Society*, 41 (1985), 81–126; Goltho: Beresford, chapter 4, note 9; Netherton: above, note 12.

Chapter Six
THE ELEVENTH CENTURY

1. G. Beresford, 'Three deserted medieval settlements on Dartmoor: a report on the late E. Marie Minter's excavations', *Medieval Archaeology*, 23 (1979), 98–158, at 110–12.
2. Goltho: G. Beresford, *The Medieval Clay-land Village: Excavations at Goltho and Barton Blount* (Society for Medieval Archaeology Monograph 6, 1975), 21 and 37–40; Walton: chapter 2, note 29, 228; North Elmham: Wade-Martins, chapter 3, note 18.
3. E.g. now D. Hooke, 'Regional variation in southern and central England in the Anglo-Saxon period and the relationship to land units and settlements', 123–51 in Hooke (ed.), chapter 1, note 8.
4. Bruce-Mitford, chapter 4, note 13, 194–96.
5. This paragraph grossly oversimplifies much work by many people: see summaries e.g. by D. Hall, 'The late Saxon countryside: villages and their fields', 99–122 in Hooke (ed.), chapter 1,

note 8; C. Hayfield, *An Archaeological Survey of the Parish of Wharram Percy, East Yorkshire: 1. The Evolution of the Roman landscape. Wharram: A study of Settlement on the Yorkshire Wolds Volume V* (Oxford, British Archaeological Reports British Series 172, 1987), 195; R.A. Dodgshon, *The origin of British Field Systems: An Interpretation* (London/New York, Academic Press, 1980); C.J. Dahlman, *The Open Field System and Beyond* (Cambridge, University Press, 1980).
6. Goltho: Beresford, chapter 4, note 9, period 5; Cheddar: Rahtz, chapter 4, note 8, 57–60; Portchester: Cunliffe, chapter 2, note 37; Netherton: Fairbrother, chapter 5, note 12; Bishop's Waltham: Lewis, chapter 5, note 51; Raunds: Cadman, chapter 5, note 34, 116–18.
7. B.K. Davison, 'Excavation at Sulgrave, Northamptonshire, 1960–76', *Archaeological Journal*, 134 (1977), 105–14.
8. P.J. Huggins, 'The excavation of an eleventh-century Viking hall and fourteenth-century rooms at Waltham Abbey, Essex, 1969–71', *Medieval Archaeology*, 20 (1976), 75–133, esp. fig. 31; *id.*, 'A note on a Viking-style plate from Waltham Abbey, Essex, and its implications for a disputed late-Viking building', *Archaeological Journal*, 141 (1984), 175–81.
9. Wilson, chapter 3, note 22, chapter 5.
10. Beresford, chapter 4, note 8, period 6.
11. Davison, above, note 7.
12. S. Rahtz and T. Rowley, *Middleton Stoney: Excavation and Survey in a North Oxfordshire Parish, 1970–1982* (Oxford, Department of Extra-Mural Studies, 1984).
13. P.V. Addyman, 'Excavations at Ludgershall Castle, Wiltshire', *Château-Gaillard*, 4 (1969), 9–12.
14. R.J. Ivens, 'Deddington Castle, Oxfordshire and the English honour of Odo of Bayeux', *Oxoniensia*, 49 (1984), 101–19.
15. B. Cunliffe and J. Munby, *Excavations*

at Portchester Castle Volume IV: Medieval, The Inner Bailey, (Society of Antiquaries of London, 1985), 73 *seq.*

16. M. Hare, 'The Watergate at Portchester and the Anglo-Saxon porch at Titchfield: a reconsideration of the evidence', *Proceedings of the Hampshire Field Club and Archaeological Society,* 40 (1984), 71–80.

17. J.G. Coad and A.D.F. Streeten, 'Excavations at Castle Acre Castle, Norfolk, 1972–77: country house and castle of the Norman earls of Surrey', *Archaeological Journal,* 139 (1982), 138–301.

18. Norwich: Ayers, chapter 4, note 21; Barnstaple: T. Miles, 'The excavation of a Saxon cemetery and part of the Norman castle at North Walk, Barnstaple', *Devon Archaeological Society Proceedings,* 44 (1986), 59–84; Colchester: P.J. Drury, 'Aspects of the origins and development of Colchester Castle', *Archaeological Journal,* 139 (1982), 302–419; for urban castles in general, C. Drage, 'Urban Castles', 117–32 in J. Schofield and R. Leech (eds), *Urban Archaeology in Britain* (London, Council for British Archaeology Research Report 61, 1987).

19. The word 'borough' was deleted from this sentence because of the discussion by S. Reynolds, 'Towns in Domesday Book', 295–309 in J.C. Holt (ed.), *Domesday Studies* (Woodbridge, Boydell Press, 1987).

20. Rahtz, chapter 4, note 8, chapter 1.

21. Alcock, chapter 1, note 35.

22. A. Borthwick and J. Chandler, *Our Chequered Past: The Archaeology of Salisbury* (Trowbridge, Wiltshire Library and Museum Service, 1984), 38–39.

23. B. Ayers and P. Murphy, 'A waterfront excavation at Whitefriars Street Car Park, Norwich, 1979', 1–60 in Wade-Martins (ed.), chapter 4, note 21; Ayers, chapter 4, note 21.

24. D. Brothwell, 'British palaeodemography and earlier British populations', *World Archaeology,* 4 (1972), 75–87, at 82.

25. Gilmour and Stocker, chapter 5, note 39.

26. Perring, chapter 4, note 31; O'Connor, chapter 5, note 31.

27. Mason, chapter 4, note 32, period 5.

28. Allan, chapter 4, note 35, 30.

29. M. Maltby, *Faunal Studies on Urban Sites: The Animal Bones from Exeter, 1971–1975* (Sheffield, University Department of Prehistory and Archaeology, Exeter Archaeology Reports 2, 1979).

30. M. Blackburn and S. Lyon, 'Regional die-production in Cnut's quatrefoil issue', 223–72 in Blackburn (ed.), chapter 13, note 9.

31. Blackburn, Colyer and Dolley, chapter 4, note 31.

32. Pirie, chapter 5, note 16.

33. Hall, chapter 1, note 8.

34. Kilmurry, chapter 5, note 2.

35. F.A. Pritchard, 'Late Saxon textiles from the City of London', *Medieval Archaeology,* 28 (1984), 46–76.

36. Beresford, chapter 4, note 9, 55.

37. P. Nightingale, 'The origin of the Court of Husting and Danish influence on London's development into a capital city', *English Historical Review,* 404 (July 1987), 559–78.

38. P. Sawyer, 'Anglo-Scandinavian trade in the Viking Age and after', 185–99 in Blackburn (ed.), chapter 3, note 9.

39. M.O.H. Carver, 'Three Saxo-Norman tenements in Durham City', *Medieval Archaeology,* 23 (1979), 1–80.

40. P. Nightingale, 'The Ora, the Mark and the Mancus: weight-standards in eleventh-century England', *Numismatic Chronicle,* 144 (1984), 234–48.

41. A. Freeman, *The Moneyer and the Mint in the Reign of Edward the Confessor, 1042–66* (Oxford, British Archaeological Reports British Series 145, 1985).

42. D.M. Metcalf, 'Continuity and change in English monetary history, *c.* 973–1086, Part I', *British Numismatic Journal,* 50 (1980), 20–49, especially for silver and quantities; *id.*, 'Part II', *ibid.,* 51 (1981), 52–90 for foreign coins (at 57–58) and individual mint outputs;

Exeter: N. Shiel, with contributions by M. Archibald *et al.*, 'The numismatic finds', 248–57 in Allan, chapter 4, note 35.

43. Morris, chapter 4, note 34; C.A. Morris, 'A late Saxon hoard of iron and copper-alloy artefacts from Nazeing, Essex', *Medieval Archaeology*, 27 (1983), 27–39.

44. Tylecote and Gilmour, chapter 2, note 8.

45. I. Peirce, 'The knight, his arms and armour in the eleventh and twelfth centuries', 152–64 in C. Harper-Bill and R. Harvey, *The Ideals and Practice of Medieval Knighthood* (Woodbridge, Boydell Press, 1986).

46. W.A. Seaby and P. Woodfield, 'Viking stirrups from England and their background', *Medieval Archaeology*, 24 (1980), 87–122.

47. Heslop, chapter 4, note 44.

48. S.A. Heslop, 'A walrus ivory seal matrix from Lincoln', *Antiquaries Journal*, 66ii (1986), 371–72.

49. Fernie, chapter 5, note 43; E. Fernie, 'The effect of the Conquest on Norman architectural patronage', *Anglo-Norman Studies*, 9 (1987), 71–85; and R. Gem, 'How should we periodize Anglo-Saxon architecture?', 146–55 in Butler and Morris (eds), chapter 5, note 42 are the main sources for this and subsequent paragraphs.

50. R. Gem and L. Keen, 'Late Anglo-Saxon finds from the site of St Edmund's Abbey', *Proceedings of the Suffolk Institute of Archaeology and History*, 35 (1981), 1–30 at 20–30; Backhouse, Turner and Webster (eds), chapter 5, note 44, at 44 and 135–37.

51. Although S. Ridyard, '*Condigna Veneratio*: post-Conquest attitudes to the saints of the Anglo-Saxons', *Anglo-Norman Studies*, 9 (1987), 179–206 has shown that cults were respected. For York Minster, Phillips, chapter 2, note 18.

52. W. Rodwell and E. Clive Rouse, 'The Anglo-Saxon rood and other features in the south porch of St Mary's Church, Breamore, Hampshire', *Antiquaries Journal*, 64ii (1984), 298–325.

53. Norwich: Stirling, chapter 4, note 21; North Elmham; C. Wells in Wade-Martins, chapter 3, note 18; York: J.D. Dawes and J.R. Magilton, *The Cemetery of St Helen-on-the-Walls, Aldwark* (London, Council for British Archaeology, Archaeology of York 12–1, 1980); Raunds: Boddington and Cadman, chapter 5, note 40 and A. Boddington, 'Raunds, Northamptonshire. Analysis of a country churchyard', *World Archaeology*, 18iii (Feb. 1987), 411–25; Portchester: B. Hooper, 'The Saxon burials', 235–61 in Cunliffe, chapter 2, note 37.

54. M.R. McCarthy and C.M. Brooks, *Medieval Pottery in Britain, AD 900–1600* (Leicester, University Press, 1988), 123.

55. W. Rodwell and K. Rodwell, 'St Peter's Church, Barton-upon-Humber: excavation and structural study, 1978–81', *Antiquaries Journal*, 62ii (1982), 283–315.

56. E.g. Sewerby: Hirst, chapter 1, note 26.

57. E.g. Lincoln: Gilmour and Stocker, chapter 5, note 39.

58. B. Golding, 'Anglo-Norman knightly burials', 35–48 in Harper-Bill and Harvey, above, note 45.

Chapter Seven
THE TWELFTH AND THIRTEENTH CENTURIES

1. I.J. Stewart, 'Note on the *Tabula* set', 31–35 in Darvill, chapter 1, note 8; I. Stewart and M.J. Watkins, 'An eleventh-century *tabula* set from Gloucester', *Medieval Archaeology*, 28 (1984), 185–90.

2. R. Eales, 'The game of chess: an aspect of medieval knightly culture', 12–34 in Harper-Bill and Harvey, chapter 6, note 45.

3. Work by Trust for Wessex Archaeology, pers. comm. S.M. Davies and P.J. Woodward. Publication on Grey-

hound Yard excavation tee-shirt, 1984.

4. Coad and Streeten, chapter 6, note 17.

5. A. Grant, 'Animal resources', 149–87 in G. Astill and A. Grant (eds), *The Countryside of Medieval England* (Oxford, Blackwell, 1988) effectively replaces all previous summaries. Nevertheless, her implication (at 181) that special cuts are unique to Okehampton does not seem to me to take acocunt of A. Ellison, 'Animal skeletal material', 146–51 in P.L. Drewett, 'Excavations at Hadleigh Castle, Essex 1971–1972', *Journal of the British Archaeological Association*, 38 (1975), 90–154, at 147. This report and those from Castle Acre by P.J. Lawrance do however bear out Dr Grant's suggestion that less venison was consumed on the eastern side of the country.

6. A. Grant, 'The large mammals', 244–56 and A. Eastham, 'Bird bones', 261–69 in Cunliffe and Munby, chapter 6, note 15.

7. D.J. Rackham and A. Wheeler, 'The faunal remains', 146–53 in P.V. Addyman and J. Priestley, 'Baile Hill, York', *Archaeological Journal*, 134 (1977), 115–56.

8. D. Austin, 'The castle and the landscape: annual lecture to the Society for Landscape Studies', *Landscape History*, 6 (1984), 69–81.

9. J.M. Steane, 'The royal fishponds of medieval England', 39–68 in M. Aston (ed.), *Medieval Fish, Fisheries and Fishponds in England* (Oxford, British Archaeological Reports British Series 182, 1988); E. Roberts, 'The Bishop of Winchester's fishponds in Hampshire, 1150–1400', *Proceedings of the Hampshire Field Club and Archaeological Society*, 42 (1986), 125–36.

10. P. Barker and R. Higham, *Hen Domen, Montgomery, Volume One* (Royal Archaeological Institute, 1982).

11. S. Margeson, 'Worked bone', 241–55 in Coad and Streeten, chapter 6, note 17.

12. The phrase is by R. Allen Brown,

English Castles (London, Batsford, 3rd ed. 1976), 27. This book remains fundamental to castle studies.

13. Darvill, chapter 1, note 8; H. Hurst, 'The archaeology of Gloucester Castle: an introduction', *Transactions of the Bristol and Gloucestershire Archaeological Society*, 102 (1984), 73–128.

14. A.P. Garrod and C. Heighway, *Garrod's Gloucester: Archaeological Observations 1974–81* (Western Archaeological Trust, n.d.)

15. D. Bates, 'The building of a great church: the abbey of St Peter's Gloucester, and its early Norman benefactors', *Transactions of the Bristol and Gloucestershire Archaeological Society*, 102 (1984), 129–32.

16. Heighway and Bryant, chapter 5, note 42.

17. Ayers and Murphy, chapter 6, note 23.

18. R.W. Unger, *The Ship in the Medieval Economy* (London, Croom-Helm, 1980) has some errors of detail, but is excellent on the wider issues. S. McGrail, *Ancient Boats in North-West Europe*, (London/New York, Longman, 1987) also has a wide range of topics.

19. D.M. Owen, 'Bishop's Lynn: the first century of a new town', *Proceedings of the Battle Conference*, 2 (1979), 141–53.

20. A. Rogerson, 'Excavations on Fuller's Hill, Great Yarmouth', 131–245 in P. Wade-Martins (ed.), *Norfolk* (Gressenhall, East Anglian Archaeology Report 2, 1976).

21. Rogerson and Dallas, chapter 4, note 28; S. Dunmore and R. Carr, *The Late Saxon Town of Thetford* (Gressenhall, East Anglian Archaeology Report 4, 1976).

22. E.g. M.B. Rowlands, *The West Midlands from AD 1000* (London/New York, Longman, 1987), 35–45: 40 of the 140 West Midlands 'new towns' of 1100–1300 were on 'frontiers'.

23. M. Biddle, 'Early Norman Winchester', 311–31 in J.C. Holt (ed.), *Domesday Studies* (Woodbridge, Boydell Press, 1987).

24. Atkin, Ayers and Jennings, chapter 5,

note 21 and references.

25. McCarthy and Brooks, chapter 6, note 54, 88–89.

26. J. Le Patourel, 'Pots and potters', *Medieval Ceramics*, 10 (1986), 3–16.

27. A. Vince, 'The medieval and post-medieval ceramic industry of the Malvern region: the study of a ware and its distribution', 257–306 in D.P.S. Peacock (ed.), *Pottery and Early Commerce* (London, Academic Press, 1977); McCarthy and Brooks, chapter 6, note 54, especially 79.

28. Work by Canterbury Archaeological Trust summarized in S.M. Youngs, J. Clark and T. Barry, 'Medieval Britain and Ireland in 1986', *Medieval Archaeology*, 31 (1987), 110–91, entry 136. Other references in McCarthy and Brooks, chapter 6, note 54.

29. M. Atkin, A. Carter and D.H. Evans, *Excavations in Norwich 1971–1978 Part II* (Gressenhall, East Anglian Archaeology Report 26, 1985), especially the Alms Lane site.

30. Mahany, Burchard and Simpson, chapter 4, note 29, part three.

31. H. Howard, 'Fabric analysis of crucible sherds in early medieval contexts', 34–37 in Allan, chapter 4, note 35.

32. R. McNeil, 'Two 12th-century wich houses in Nantwich, Cheshire', *Medieval Archaeology*, 27 (1983), 40–88; J. Oxley, 'Nantwich: an eleventh-century salt town and its origins', *Transactions of the Historical Society of Lancashire and Cheshire*, 131 (1981), 1–19.

33. M.W. Beresford and J.G. Hurst (eds), *Medieval Villages* (Guildford/London, Lutterworth, 1971).

34. Iron-smelting continued into the 12th century at Simy Folds, but by then the excavated buildings seem to have been abandoned: K. Brown, 'The metal-working residues', 18–20 in Coggins *et al.*, chapter 3, note 25.

35. C. Dyer, 'English peasant buildings in the later Middle Ages', *Medieval Archaeology*, 30 (1986), 19–45 at 34–37 argues that this would have become

more important after *c.* 1200 because of stone foundations: see below.

36. The Fens: B. Silvester, 'The Norfolk Fens', *Antiquity*, 62 no. 235 (June, 1988), 326–30; Raunds: Cadman, chapter 5, note 34; Broadfield: E.C. Klingelhöfer, *Broadfield Deserted Medieval Village* (Oxford, British Archaeological Reports British Series 2, 1974); Wharram: Hurst, chapter 3, note 24; Goltho: Beresford, chapter 6, note 2.

37. R.D. Bell, M.W. Beresford *et al.*, *Wharram Percy: The Church of St Martin*, J.G. Hurst and P.A. Rahtz (eds), *Wharram: A Study of Settlement on the Yorkshire Wolds, Volume III* (Society for Medieval Archaeology Monograph 11, 1987).

38. Oxford: J. Blair, 'Frewin Hall, Oxford: a Norman mansion and a monastic college', *Oxoniensia*, 43 (1978), 48–99, especially figs. 1, 2 and 7; London: Schofield, chapter 4, note 33, 52–56; Southampton: P.A. Faulkner, 'The surviving medieval buildings', 56–125 in C. Platt and R. Coleman-Smith, *Excavations in Medieval Southampton 1953–1969* (Leicester, University Press, 1975); Lincoln: J.W.F. Hill, *Medieval Lincoln* (Cambridge, University Press, 1948), chapter 11.

39. M.E. Wood, *The English Medieval House* (London, Phoenix, 1965).

40. E.g. R.H.C. Davis, 'An Oxford charter of 1191 and the beginnings of municipal freedom', *Oxoniensia*, 33 (1968), 53–65.

41. Pers. comm. Peter Stone.

42. D. Stephenson, 'Colchester: a smaller medieval English jewry', *Essex Archaeology and History*, 16 (1985), 48–52; N. Crummy, *The Coins from Excavations in Colchester 1971–79* (Colchester Archaeological Report 4, 1987), 70, 71, 76.

43. Northampton: J.H. Williams, *St Peter's Street, Northampton: Excavations 1973–1976* (Northampton, Development Corporation, 1979) and F. Williams, 'Excavations on Marefair, North-

ampton, 1977', *Northamptonshire Archaeology*, 14 (1979), 38–79; Winchester: M. Dolley and C.E. Blunt, 'Coins from the Winchester excavations 1961–1973', *British Numismatic Journal*, 47 (1977), 135–38; York: Pirie, chapter 5, note 16.

44. E.W. Holden, 'Slate roofing in medieval Sussex', *Sussex Archaeological Collections*, 103 (1965), 67–78.

45. A.J. Gurevich (trans. G.L. Campbell), *Categories of Medieval Culture* (Henley, Routledge and Kegan Paul, 1985), 140 *seq.*

46. G. Astill, 'Rural settlement: the toft and the croft', 36–61 in Astill and Grant (eds), above, note 5.

47. Beresford, chapter 6, note 1; Astill, above, note 46, stresses the lay-out's suitability for pastoral rather than arable farming. He also emphasizes the importance of different regions generally.

48. Dyer, above, note 35 and references.

49. Goltho: I.H. Goodall *et al.*, 'Metalwork from Goltho', 76–96 in Beresford, chapter 6, note 2; Seacourt: D.B. Harden, 'Note', 185 in M. Biddle, 'The deserted medieval village of Seacourt, Berkshire', *Oxoniensia*, 26/27 (1961/62), 70–201.

50. J.S. Otto, 'Artifacts and status differences – a comparison of ceramics from Planter, Overseer and Slave sites on an antebellum plantation', 91–118 in S. South (ed.), *Research Strategies in Historical Archaeology* (New York, Academic Press, 1977).

51. J. Langdon, 'Agricultural equipment', 86–107 in Grant and Astill (eds), above, note 5.

52. P.D.E. Smith *et al.*, 'The investigation of a medieval shell midden in Braunton Burrows', *Devon Archaeological Society Proceedings*, 41 (1983), 75–80.

53. Work by J.M. Steane and G.F. Bryant is conveniently summarized by S. Moorhouse, 'The medieval pottery industry and its markets', 96–125 in Crossley (ed.), chapter 3, note 2. See also LePatourel, above, note 26, for this paragraph.

54. Mill Green: D.C. Mynard, M.R. Petchey and P.G. Tilson, 'A medieval pottery at Church End, Flitwick, Bedfordshire', *Bedfordshire Archaeology*, 16 (1983), 75–84; Nash Hill: M.R. McCarthy, 'The medieval kilns on Nash Hill, Lacock, Wiltshire', *Wiltshire Archaeological Magazine*, 69 (1974), 97–160.

55. Malting-kilns are better known from towns, e.g. D.W. Williams, '16, Bell Street, Reigate', *Surrey Archaeological Collections*, 74 (1983), 47–89, and it was expensive to buy e.g. lead pans: B.A. Hanawalt, *The Ties that Bound: Peasant Families in Medieval England* (Oxford/New York, Oxford University Press, 1986), 134. For a pottery two-bushel cistern, see *Oxoniensia*, 33 (1968), 66–70.

56. Foxcotte: A.D. Russel, 'Foxcotte: the archaeology and history of a Hampshire hamlet', *Proceedings of the Hampshire Field Club and Archaeological Society,*. 41 (1985), 149–224; Hartfield: C.F. Tebbutt, 'A deserted medieval farm settlement at Faulkners Farm, Hartfield', *Sussex Archaeological Collections*, 119 (1981), 107–16.

57. L. Stevens, 'Some windmill sites in Friston and Eastbourne, Sussex', *Sussex Archaeological Collections*, 120 (1982), 93–138.

58. R. Holt, 'Whose were the profits of corn milling? The abbots of Glastonbury and their tenants 1086–1350', *Past and Present*, 116 (Aug. 1987), 3–23; textiles: M.C. Higham, 'Some evidence for 12th- and 13th-century linen and woollen textile processing', *Medieval Archaeology*, 33 (1989), 38–52.

59. This gem is from a University College, London undergraduate thesis. Grenville Astill kindly answered my questions on the work at Bordesley, summarized in S.M. Youngs, J. Clark and T. Barry, 'Medieval Britain and Ireland in 1986', *Medieval Archaeology*, 31 (1987), 110–91, entry 124 and earlier volumes. Abbotsbury: A.H. Graham, 'The Old Malthouse, Ab-

botsbury, Dorset: the medieval water-mill of the Benedictine Abbey', *Proceedings of the Dorset Natural History and Archaeological Society*, 108 (1986), 103–25.

60. G. Coppack, 'The excavation of an outer court building, perhaps the Woolhouse, at Fountains Abbey, North Yorkshire', *Medieval Archaeology*, 30 (1986), 46–87.

61. Alsted: L. Ketteringham, *Alsted: Excavation of a Thirteenth/Fourteenth-century Sub-manor Site with its Ironworks in Netherne Wood, Merstham, Surrey* (Surrey Archaeological Society Research Volume 2, 1976); Waterley: D. Hall, 'The excavation of an iron-smelting site at Easton Mauduit, Northamptonshire', *Bedfordshire Archaeology*, 16 (1983), 65–74; Chingley: D. Crossley, *The Bewl Valley Ironworks* (Royal Archaeological Institute, 1975). For the industry generally, H. Cleere and D. Crossley, *The Iron Industry of the Weald* (Leicester, University Press, 1985).

62. R.F. Tylecote, 'Metallurgical report', 81–82 in Beresford, chapter 6, note 2. For what follows, Cleere and Crossley, above, note 61.

63. J.R. Hunter, 'The medieval glass industry', 143–50 in Crossley (ed.), chapter 3, note 2.

64. D.W. Williams, 'Islamic glass vessel fragments from the Old Vicarage, Reigate, Surrey', *Medieval Archaeology*, 27 (1983), 143–46.

65. The work of A.G. Vince, P.G. and N.C. Farmer, S. Moorhouse, the late G.C. Dunning and others is now summarized in McCarthy and Brooks, chapter 6, note 54.

66. G.G. Astill, 'Economic change in later medieval England: an archaeological review', 217–47 in T.H. Aston *et al.* (eds), *Social Relations and Ideas: Essays in honour of R.H. Hilton* (Past and Present Society, 1983) – an important contribution in a *festschrift* for a scholar whose work has been highly influential. For Bedford, Baker *et al.*, chapter 5, note 32, 294.

67. Beresford, chapter 6, note 1, 135–36 and 147–50.

68. Atkin, Carter and Evans, above, note 29, 245 *seq.*

69. N. Palmer, 'A beaker burial and medieval tenements in The Hamel, Oxford', *Oxoniensia*, 45 (1980), 124–225.

70. Leicester: J.E. Mellor and T. Pearce, *The Austin Friars, Leicester* (London, Council for British Archaeology Research Report 35, 1981), Oxford: G. Lambrick, 'Further excavations on the second site of the Dominican Priory, Oxford', *Oxoniensia*, 50 (1985), 131–208. For a general review, L. Butler, 'Houses of the medicant orders in Britain: recent archaeological work', 123–65 in P.V. Addyman and V.E. Black (eds), *Archaeological Papers from York presented to M.W. Barley* (York Archaeological Trust, 1984).

71. Schofield, chapter 4, note 33, 77.

72. Unger, above, note 18; A.R. Lewis and T.J. Runyan, *European and Naval Maritime History, 300–1500* (Bloomington, Indiana University Press, 1985), 118 *seq.*

73. J.M. Steane, *The Archaeology of Medieval England and Wales* (London/Sydney, Croom Helm, 1985), 139–40.

74. R. Fox and K.J. Barton, 'Excavations at Oyster Street, Portsmouth, Hampshire, 1968–71', *Post-Medieval Archaeology*, 20 (1986), 31–255.

75. P.M. Losco-Bradley and C.R. Salisbury, 'A medieval fish weir at Colwick, Nottinghamshire', *Transactions of the Thoroton Society*, 83 (1979), 15–22.

76. R.H.C. Davis, 'The ford, the river and the city', *Oxoniensia*, 38 (1973), 258–67.

77. D.A. Hinton, *Medieval Jewellery* (Princes Risborough, Shire, 1982).

78. Atkin, Carter and Evans, above, note 29, fig. 36 no. 23, and report by S. Margeson; S.E. Rigold, 'Two common species of medieval seal-matrix', *Antiquaries Journal*, 57ii (1977), 324–29.

79. L. Butler, 'Symbols on medieval memorials', *Archaeological Journal*, 144

(1987), 246–55.

80. Beresford, chapter 4, note 9.

81. D.D. Andrews and G. Milne (eds), *Domestic Settlement 1: Areas 10 and 6*, J.G. Hurst (ed.), *Wharram: A Study of Settlement on the Yorkshire Wolds, Volume I* (Society for Medieval Archaeology Monograph 8, 1979), 17–19 and 138–39.

82. F.A. Aberg (ed.), *Medieval Moated Sites* (London, Council for British Archaeology Research Report 17, 1978).

83. Wood, above, note 39.

84. N.W. Alcock, *Cruck Construction* (London, Council for British Archaeology Research Report 42, 1981); Dyer, above, note 35.

85. E.W. Parkin, 'A unique aisled cottage at Petham', 225–30 in A. Detsicas (ed.), *Collectanea Historica: Essays in Memory of Stuart Rigold* (Kent Archaeological Society, 1981).

86. Faulkner, above, note 38, 104–07.

87. Contributions by B.E. Harris *et al.*, *Galleries which they call The Rows, Journal of the Chester Archaeological Society*, 67 (1984).

Chapter Eight
THE LATER THIRTEENTH AND
FOURTEENTH CENTURIES

1. M. Prestwich, *The Three Edwards* (London, Weidenfeld and Nicolson, 1980), especially 49 *seq.*; S.L. Waugh, 'Tenure to contract: lordship and clientship in thirteenth-century England', *English Historical Review*, 101 no. 401 (Oct. 1986), 811–39; J.R.V. Barker, *The Tournament in England* (Woodbridge, Boydell and Brewer, 1986), especially chapter two.

2. Platt and Coleman-Smith, chapter 7, note 38, 31 and 37.

3. Fox and Barton, chapter 7, note 74, 41–53.

4. Rogerson, chapter 7, note 20; J.L. Bolton, *The Medieval English Economy, 1150–1500* (London/Ottawa, Dent, 1980), 274 *seq.*; A. Saul 'Great Yar-

mouth and the Hundred Years' War in the fourteenth century', *Bulletin of the Institute of Historical Research*, 52 no. 126 (Nov. 1979), 105–15.

5. J.R. Hunter, 'Medieval Berwick-upon-Tweed', *Archaeologia Aeliana*, 5th ser. 10 (1982), 67–124.

6. An excellent typescript report was recently submitted to *Medieval Archaeology* on the work undertaken by the Cleveland County Archaeology Section.

7. M.O.H. Carver (ed.), *Two Town Houses in Medieval Shrewsbury, Transactions of the Shropshire Archaeological Society*, 61 (1983).

8. Harris *et al.*, chapter 7, note 87; H.L. Turner, *Town Defences in England and Wales* (London, John Baker, 1971), 202–03.

9. P. Dixon, 'Tower houses, pelehouses and Border society', *Archaeological Journal*, 136 (1979), 240–52; M.W. Thompson, *The Decline of the Castle* (Cambridge, University Press, 1987), fig. 10.

10. H. Clarke and A. Carter, *Excavations in King's Lynn, 1963–70* (Society for Medieval Archaeology Monograph Series 7, 1977).

11. P. Armstrong, 'Kingston upon Hull', *Archaeological Journal*, 141 (1984), 1–4 and excavation reports in Hull Old Town Report Series, in *East Riding Archaeologist*.

12. T.P. Smith, *The Medieval Brickmaking Industry in England 1400–1450* (Oxford, British Archaeological Reports British Series 138, 1984), for most of this paragraph; for kilns at Beverley, work by Humberside County Council Archaeology Unit summarized in S.M. Youngs, J. Clark and T. Barry, 'Medieval Britain and Ireland in 1986', *Medieval Archaeology*, 31 (1987), 110–91, entry 129; for floor-tiles, E.S. Eames, *English Medieval Tiles* (London, British Museum Publications, 1985).

13. J.A.F. Thomson, *The Transformation of Medieval England* (London/New York,

Longman, 1983), 125 *seq.*; J.T. Rosenthal, *The Purchase of Paradise: Gift Giving and the Aristocracy, 1307–1485* (London, Routledge, Kegan and Paul, 1972), 70.

14. J. Blair, 'Stokesay Castle', *Archaeological Journal*, 138 (1981), 11–12.

15. Barker, above, note 1, chapters three and five: M. Biddle and B. Clayre, *Winchester Castle and Great Hall* (Winchester, Hampshire County Council, 1983), 37–40.

16. Kenilworth (and all others): Brown, chapter 7, note 12, 150–52 and for the waterworks, M. Aston and C.J. Bond, 420 in Aston (ed.), chapter 7, note 9; Warwick: R.K. Morris, 'The architecture of the earls of Warwick in the fourteenth century', 161–74 in W.M. Ormrod (ed.), *England in the Fourteenth Century: Proceedings of the 1985 Harlaxton Symposium* (Woodbridge, Boydell, 1986); Okehampton: R.A. Higham, J.P. Allan and S.R. Blaylock, 'Excavations at Okehampton Castle, Devon: Part 2: the bailey', *Devon Archaeological Society Proceedings*, 40 (1982), 19–151.

17. The most recent survey of parks is by P. Stamper, 'Woods and parks', 128–48 in Astill and Grant (eds), chapter 7, note 5.

18. D. Austin, 'Excavations in Okehampton Park, Devon, 1976–78', *Devon Archaeological Society Proceedings*, 36 (1978), 191–240.

19. Beresford, chapter 6, note 1; D. Austin, 'Dartmoor and the upland village of the southwest of England', 71–80 in D. Hooke (ed.), *The Medieval Village* (Oxford, University Committee for Archaeology Monograph 5, 1985); D. Austin and M.J.C. Walker, 'A new landscape context for Houndtor, Devon', *Medieval Archaeology*, 29 (1985), 147–52; G. Beresford, 'Three deserted medieval settlements on Dartmoor: a comment on David Austin's reinterpretations', *Medieval Archaeology*, 32 (1988), 175–83.

20. Windsor: Brown, chapter 7, note 12, 209; York: P.V. Addyman *et al.*,

'Palaeoclimate in urban environmental archaeology at York, England: problems and potential', *World Archaeology*, 8ii (1976), 220–33; marginal land: M.L. Parry, *Climatic Change, Agriculture and Settlement* (Folkestone, Dawson-Archon Books, 1978) and C.D. Smith and M. Parry (eds), *Consequences of Climatic Change* (Nottingham, University Department of Geography, 1981); Battle Abbey: J.N. Hare, *Battle Abbey* (London, Historic Buildings and Monuments Commission for England Archaeological Report 2, 1985); Bordesley Abbey: P. Rahtz and S.Hirst, *Bordesley Abbey* (Oxford, British Archaeological Reports British Series 23, 1976), fig. 4.

21. West Whelpington: M.G. Jarrett and S. Wrathmell, 'Sixteenth- and seventeenth-century farmsteads: West Whelpington, Northumberland', *Agricultural History Review*, 25 (1977), 108–19; Wharram Percy: M.W. Beresford, 'Documentary evidence for the history of Wharram Percy', 5–25 in Andrews and Milne (eds), chapter 7, note 81, at 11–13; Gomeldon: J. Musty and D. Algar, 'Excavations at the deserted medieval village of Gomeldon, near Salisbury', *Wiltshire Archaeological and Natural History Magazine*, 80 (1986), 127–69.

22. Foxcotte: Russel, chapter 7, note 56; Isle of Wight: Beresford and Hurst, chapter 7, note 33, fig. 13.

23. Barton Blount and Goltho: Beresford, chapter 6, note 2.

24. Langdon, chapter 7, note 51, and *id.*, 'Horse hauling: a revolution in vehicle transport in twelfth- and thirteenth-century England', *Past and Present*, 103 (May, 1984), 37–66; Grant, chapter 7, note 5, at 177–78; J. Clark, 'Medieval horseshoes', *Datasheet 4* (Finds Research Group 700–1700, 1986).

25. Grant, chapter 7, note 5 is a new authority for this material; for residue analyses, work by e.g. J. Evans and M. Card, 126–27 in J.E. Pearce, A.G. Vince and M.A. Jenner, *Medieval Pot-*

tery: London-type Ware (London and Middlesex Archaeological Society Special Paper 6, 1985).

26. Recent discussion of these issues was initiated by H.E.J. LePatourel, 'Pottery as evidence for social and economic change', 168–79 in P.H. Sawyer (ed.), *Medieval Settlement* (London, Edward Arnold, 1976).

27. V. Bullough and C. Campbell, 'Female longevity and diet in the Middle Ages', *Speculum*, 552 (1980), 317–25; M.W. Bishop, 'Burials from the cemetery of the hospital of, St Leonard, Newark, Nottinghamshire', *Transactions of the Thoroton Society*, 87 (1983), 23–35; C. Dyer, 'English diet in the Middle Ages', 91–126 in Aston *et al.*, (eds), chapter 7, note 66.

28. W.J. White, 'Changing burial practice in late medieval England', 371–79 in J. Petre (ed.), *Richard III. Crown and People* (Gloucester, Alan Sutton, 1985); St Bees: work by D. O'Sullivan reported in *Daily Telegraph*, 15 June, 1983; de Manny: M. Jones, 'Edward III's captains in Brittany', 99–118 in Ormrod (ed.), above, note 16; Lady Audley: P.J. Wise, 'Hulton Abbey: a century of excavations', *Staffordshire Archaeological Studies*, 2 (1985), 1–142; de Hastyngs: B. Hooper *et al.*, 'The grave of Sir Hugh de Hastyngs, Elsing', *Norfolk Archaeology*, 39i (1984), 88–99; Burghersh: C. Wells, 'Report on the human bones', 285–88 in C. Green and A.B. Whittingham, 'Excavations at Walsingham Priory, Norfolk, 1961', *Archaeological Journal*, 125 (1968), 255–90; C. Burgess, ' "By Quick and by Dead": wills and pious provision in late medieval Bristol', *English History Review*, 102 no. 405 (Oct. 1987), 837–58.

29. D.A. Birkett, 'The human burials', 291–99 in R. Daniels, 'The excavation of the Church of the Franciscans, Hartlepool, Cleveland', *Archaeological Journal*, 143 (1986), 260–304.

30. Bordesley: R.F. Everton, 'Human bones', 216–22 in Rahtz and Hirst,

above, note 20; Leicester: Mellor and Pearce, chapter 7, note 70. For leprous skeletons, M. Farley and K. Manchester, 'The cemetery of the leper hospital of St Margaret, High Wycombe, Buckinghamshire', *Medieval Archaeology*, 33 (1989), 82–89.

31. Raunds: Cadman, chapter 6, note 53; Abingdon: M. Harman and B. Wilson, 'A medieval graveyard beside Faringdon Road, Abingdon', *Oxoniensia*, 46 (1981), 56–61; St Helen's, York: Dawes and Magilton, chapter 6, note 53.

32. Canterbury: J. Hatcher, 'Mortality in the fifteenth century: some new evidence', *Economic History Review*, 39i (Feb. 1986), 19–38; syphilis: A. Appleby, 'Famine, mortality and epidemic disease: a comment', *ibid.*, 30iii (Aug. 1977), 508–12; sinusitis and cancer: G.T. Hanweld, 'Medieval osteo-pathology, its possibilities and limitations: a survey', 57–61 in J.G.N. Renaud (ed.), *Rotterdam Papers IV* (Rotterdam, Stichting Het Nederlandsee Gebruiksvoorwerp, 1982); malaria: P. Franklyn, 'Malaria in medieval Gloucester: an essay in epidemiology', *Transactions of the Bristol and Gloucester Archaeological Society*, 101 (1983), 111–22; urinals: e.g. R.J. Charleston, 'Appendix 2: Vessel glass', 208–11 in P.M. Christie and J.G. Coad, 'Excavations at Denny Abbey', *Archaeological Journal*, 137 (1980), 138–279.

33. Exeter: work by Exeter Museums Archaeological Field Unit summarized in S.M. Youngs, J. Clark and T. Barry, 'Medieval Britain and Ireland in 1983', *Medieval Archaeology*, 28 (1984), 203–65, entry 28 and pers. comm. C.G. Henderson; London: W.C. Wijntjes, 'The water supply of the medieval town', 189–203 in Renaud (ed), above, note 32.

34. Norwich, Botolph Street/St George's Street site: Atkin *et al.*, chapter 7, note 29; Battle: Hare, above, note 20, 176; pottery: Vince, chapter 5, note 29,

70–73; pewter: R. Brownsword and E.E.H. Pitt, 'Some examples of medieval domestic pewter flatware', *Medieval Archaeology*, 29 (1985), 152–55.

35. T.A.P. Greeves, 'The archaeological potential of the Devon tin industry', 85–95 in Crossley (ed.), chapter 3, note 2; J. Hatcher, *English Tin Production before 1550* (Oxford, Clarendon Press, 1973); I. Blanchard, 'Industrial employment and the rural land market', 227–75 in R.M. Smith (ed.), *Land, Kinship and Life-Cycle* (Cambridge, University Press, 1985).

36. J. Blair, 'English monumental brasses before 1350; types, patterns and workshops', 133–215 in J. Coales (ed.), *The Earliest English Brasses: Patronage, Style and Workshops, 1270–1350*, with analyses by R. Brownsword.

37. Further results of the valuable programme of analyses undertaken at Coventry (Lanchester) Polytechnic: R. Brownsword and E.E.H. Pitt, 'A technical note on some 13th-century steelyard weights', *Medieval Archaeology*, 27 (1983), 158–59.

38. J. Cowgill, M. de Neergard and N. Griffiths, *Knives and Scabbards* (London, Her Majesty's Stationery Office, 1987), 17–24.

39. E.W. Moore, *The Fairs of Medieval England: An Introductory Study* (Toronto, Pontifical Institute of Medieval Studies, 1985).

40. Vince, chapter 5, note 29, 56–57 and 75–76.

41. D.M. Metcalf, 'A survey of numismatic research into the pennies of the first three Edwards (1279–1344) and their continental imitations', 1–31, S.E. Rigold, 'Small change in the light of medieval site-finds', 59–80 and M.M. Archibald, 'Wastage from currency: Long-Cross and the recoinage of 1279', 167–86 in N.J. Mayhew (ed.), *Edwardian Monetary Affairs (1279–1344)* (Oxford, British Archaeological Reports British Series 36, 1977); York; Pirie, chapter 4, note

15; E.K. Fisk, 'The response of non-monetary production units to contact with the exchange economy', 53–83 in C.G. Reynolds (ed.), *Agriculture in Development Theory* (Yale, University Press, 1975).

42. N.J. Mayhew and D.R. Walker, 'Crockards and pollards', 125–46 in Mayhew (ed.), above, note 41; A. MacGregor, 'Coin balances in the Ashmolean Museum', *Antiquaries Journal*, 65i (1985), 439–44; Oxford: N.J. Mayhew, 'Coins and jettons', Fiche 2 B 13 (another bad example of chapter 3, note 12) in Palmer, chapter 7, note 69; Exeter: Shiel *et al.*, chapter 6, note 42.

43. M. Mitchiner and A. Skinner, 'English tokens, *c.* 1200 to 1425', *Brtitish Numismatic Journal*, 53 (1983), 29–77.

44. P. Spufford, 'Coinage and currency', 788–873 in M.M. Postan and E. Miller, *Cambridge Economic History, Vol. II, Trade and Industry in the Middle Ages* (Oxford, University Press, second edition 1987); Rochester: report by M. Archibald, 27–28 in A.C. Harrison and D. Williams, 'Excavations at Prior's Gate House, Rochester 1976–77', *Archaeologia Cantiana*, 95 (1979), 19–36; Denny: S.E. Rigold, 'Appendix 7: Numismatica', 264–65 in Christie and Coad, above, note 32.

45. Bolton, above, note 4, 298.

46. Portchester: J. Munby and D. Renn, 'Description of the castle buildings', 72–119 in Cunliffe and Munby, chapter 6, note 15 at 95; J.R. Kenyon, 'Early artillery fortifications in England and Wales: a preliminary survey and reappraisal', *Archaeological Journal*, 138 (1981), 205–40; Canterbury: D. Renn, 'A note on the West Gate gunloops', 117–19 in S.S. Frere, S. Stow and P. Bennett, *Excavations on the Roman and Medieval Defences of Canterbury* (Kent Archaeological Society, Archaeology of Canterbury II, 1982); Thompson, above, note 9, 36.

47. Cooling: Kenyon, above, note 46;

Bodiam: D.J. Turner, 'Bodiam, Sussex: true castle or old soldier's dream house?', 267–77 in Ormrod (ed.), above, note 16; D.J. Cathcart King, *The Castle in England and Wales: An Interpretative History* (London/Sydney, Croom Helm, 1988), chapter 12.

48. J.R. Alban, 'English coastal defences: some fourteenth-century modifications within the system', 57–78 in R.A. Griffiths (ed.), *Patronage, the Crown and the Provinces* (Gloucester, Alan Sutton, 1981); Bramber: K.J. Barton and E.W. Holden, 'Excavations at Bramber Castle, Sussex, 1966–67', *Archaeological Journal*, 134 (1977), 11–79; E. Searle, 'The abbey of the Conquerors', *Proceedings of the Battle Conference*, 2 (1979), 154–64.

49. Cathcart King, above, note 47, chapter 12.

Chapter Nine
THE LATER FOURTEENTH,
FIFTEENTH AND EARLY
SIXTEENTH CENTURIES

1. C. Platt, *Medieval England* (London/Henley, Routledge and Kegan Paul, 1978), 211–12; reports by P.Bennett, *Archaeologia Cantiana*, 101 (1984), 299–30 and 305–06; *ibid.*, 102 (1985), 252–53; B.W. Spencer 'Medieval pilgrim badges', 137–47 in J.G.N. Renaud (ed.), *Rotterdam Papers*, 1 (1968).

2. Battle: discovery by D. Martin described in J.R. Armstrong, *Traditional Buildings – Accessible to the Public* (Wakefield, E P Publishing, 1979), 97; Tewkesbury: *ibid.*, 63; York: P. Short, 'The fourteenth-century rows of York', *Archaeological Journal*, 137 (1980), 86–137; Gloucester: R. Holt, 'Gloucester in the century after the Black Death', *Transactions of the Bristol and Gloucestershire Archaeological Society*, 102 (1984), 73–128; Lavenham: Armstrong, this note, 87–117; Halifax area: B. Hutton, 'Aisles to outshots',

145–51 in Addyman and Black (eds), chapter 7, note 70; Norton St Philip: E.H.D. Williams, J. and J. Penoyre and B.C.H. Hale, 'The George Inn, Norton St Philip, Somerset', *Archaeological Journal*, 144 (1987), 317–27; fairs: Moore, chapter 8, note 39.

3. Late-medieval urbanism has a vast literature: C. Phythian-Adams, 'Urban decay in late medieval England', 159–85 in P. Abrams and E.A. Wrigley, *Towns in Societies* (Cambridge, University Press, 1978) remains valuable; to start with J.F. Hadwin, 'From dissonance to harmony on the late medieval town', *Economic History Review*, 29iii (Aug. 1986), 423–26 and work backwards would be one possible approach, if not to enlightenment.

4. Palmer, chapter 7, note 69; J. Munby, 'A fifteenth-century Wealden house in Oxford', *Oxoniensia*, 39 (1974), 73–76; R.L.S. Bruce-Mitford, 'The archaeology of the site of the Bodleian Extension, Broad Street, Oxford', *ibid.*, 4 (1939), 89–146.'

5. J. Munby, '126 High Street: the archaeology and history of an Oxford house', *Oxoniensia*, 40 (1975), 254–308; Davis, chapter 7, note 76.

6. S.S. Frere and S. Stow, *Excavations in the St George's Street and Burgate Street areas* (Kent Archaeological Society, Archaeology of Canterbury VII, 1983), 123–30; S.S. Frere, P. Bennett, J. Rady and S. Stow, *Canterbury Excavations: Intra- and Extra-Mural Sites, 1949–50 and 1980–84* (Same series, VIII, 1987), 126–28.

7. Norwich: Atkin, Carter and Evans, chapter 7, note 29; Northampton: J. Williams, chapter 7, note 43.

8. R. Smith and A. Carter, 'Function and site: aspects of Norwich buildings before 1700', *Vernacular Architecture*, 14 (1983), 5–18; A.B. Whittingham, 'The White Swan Inn, St Peter's Street, Norwich', *Norfolk Archaeology*, 39i (1984), 38–50; J. Campbell, *Norwich* (London, Scolar Press with Historic Towns Trust, 1975), 23–24.

9. M. James, 'Ritual, drama and social body in the late medieval English town', *Past and Present*, 98 (Feb. 1983), 3–29.

10. Norwich: A.D. Saunders, 'The Cow Tower, Norwich: an East Anglian bastille?', *Medieval Archaeology*, 29 (1985), 109–19; B.S. Ayers, R. Smith and M. Tillyard, 'The Cow Tower, Norwich: a detailed survey and partial reinterpretation', *ibid.*, 32 (1988), 184–207; Southampton: Faulkner, chapter 7, note 38, 62–66 – I have learnt much about this building and about cannonry from Robert Thomson.

11. Turner, chapter 8, note 8, 27; Poole: K.J. Penn, *Historic Towns in Dorset* (Dorset Natural History and Archaeological Society Monograph 1, 1980), 78–83; Southampton: C. Platt, *Medieval Southampton* (London/Boston, Routledge and Kegan Paul, 1973), 142–46 (Beaulieu's acquisition by 1454 is odd – gift? or if by purchase, how and why?).

12. Frere, Stow and Bennett, chapter 8, note 46, 72–80; Turner, above, note 11, 59–60.

13. Dorchester: J. Draper and C. Chaplin, *Dorchester Excavations 1* (Dorset Archaeological and Natural History Society Monograph 2, 1982); Wareham: D.A. Hinton and R. Hodges, 'Excavations in Wareham, 1974–75', *Proceedings of the Dorset Natural History and Archaeological Society*, 99 (1977), 42–83 at 77–78; Devizes: J. Haslam, 'The excavation of the defences of Devizes, Wiltshire, 1974', *Wiltshire Archaeological Magazine*, 72/73 (1980), 59–65; Banbury: K.A. Rodwell, 'Excavations on the site of Banbury Castle', *Oxoniensia*, 41 (1976), 90–147.

14. Newbury: A.G. Vince, *Bartholomew Street, Newbury* (Newbury, District Museum, 1980); Alton: M. Millett, 'The history, archaeology and architecture of Johnson's Corner, Alton', *Proceedings of the Hampshire Field Club and Archaeological Society*, 39 (1983),

77–109.

15. E.g. half the chartered markets of the thirteenth-century West Midlands had ceased to trade by *c.* 1500: Rowlands, chapter 7, note 22, 73–76.

16. D.H. Evans and D.H. Heslop, 'Two medieval sites in Yarm', *Yorkshire Archaeological Journal*, 57 (1985), 43–77.

17. McNeil, chapter 7, note 32; Rowlands, chapter 7, note 22.

18. Cleere and Crossley, chapter 7, note 61; J.H. Money, 'Medieval iron-workings at Rotherfield, Sussex', *Medieval Archaeology*, 15 (1971), 86–111; R.F. Tylecote, *Metallurgy in Archaeology* (London, Edward Arnold, 1962); W.R. Childs, 'England's iron trade in the fifteenth century', *Economic History Review*, 34i (Feb. 1981), 25–47.

19. M. Rule, *The Mary Rose: The Excavation and Raising of Henry VIII's Flagship* (London, Conway Maritime, 1982).

20. M. Redknap, *The Cattewater Wreck: The Investigation of an Armed Vessel of the Early Sixteenth Century* (Oxford, British Archaeological Reports British Series 131, 1984).

21. Unger, chapter 7, note 18, chapters 4 and 5.

22. J. Hay, 'The great bullion famine of the fifteenth century', *Past and Present*, 79 (May 1978), 3–54.

23. References in chapter 7, note 43 and chapter 8, note 42.

24. M. Mellor, 'Pottery', 73–76 in D. Sturdy and J. Munby, 'Early domestic sites in Oxford: excavations in Cornmarket and Queen Street, 1959–62', *Oxoniensia*, 50 (1985), 47–94, at 75–76.

25. Astill, chapter 7, note 66.

26. Allan, chapter 4, note 35.

27. P. Mayes and K. Scott, *Pottery Kilns at Chilvers Coton, Nuneaton* (Society for Medieval Archaeology Monograph 10, 1984); A.D.F. Streeten, 'Craft and industry: medieval and later potters in south-east England', 323–46 in H. Howard and E.L. Morris (eds), *Production and Distribution: A Ceramic View-*

point (Oxford, British Archaeological Reports International Series 120, 1981).

28. Essays in P. Davey and R. Hodges (eds), *Ceramics and Trade* (Sheffield, University Department of Prehistory and Archaeology, 1983).

29. London: Vince, chapter 5, note 29; Exeter: Allan, chapter 4, note 35.

30. Wharram: J.G. Hurst, 'Imported pottery', 94 in Andrews and Milne (eds), chapter 7, note 81; Goltho: Beresford, chapter 6, note 2, 69; Foxcotte: C. Matthews, 'The pottery', 186–93 in Russel, chapter 7, note 56; marketing: Astill, chapter 7, note 66.

31. G. Astill and A. Grant, 'The medieval countryside: efficiency, progress and change', 213–34 in Astill and Grant (eds), chapter 7, note 5; Blanchard, chapter 8, note 35; D. Martin, 'Housing in eastern Sussex in the late medieval period', 93–96 in P.L. Drewett (ed.), *Archaeology in Sussex to AD 1500* (London, Council for British Archaeology Research Report 29, 1978).

32. Low Throston: D. Austin, 'Low Throston II: excavation on a deserted medieval hamlet, 1972', *Transactions of the Architectural and Archaeological Society of Durham and Northumberland*, 4 (1977), 21–30; for fields and parks generally, Astill and Stamper in Astill and Grant (eds), chapter 7, note 5.

33. Grant, chapter 7, note 5; pewter spoons: London Museum, *Medieval Catalogue* (London, Her Majesty's Stationery Office, 1940), 128–33; scabbards: Cowgill, de Neergard and Griffiths, chapter 8, note 38, 34 and 61.

34. Cat-skinning: G.C. Jones, 'The

medieval animals bones', 31–44 in D. Allen and C.H. Dalwood, 'Iron Age occupation, a middle Saxon cemetery and twelfth- to nineteenth-century urban occupation: excavations in George St., Aylesbury, 1981', *Records of Buckinghamshire*, 25 (1983), 1–60, at 38–39; rings: Hinton, chapter 7, note 77; mirrors: J. Bayley, P. Drury and B. Spencer, 'A medieval mirror from Heybridge, Essex', *Antiquaries Journal*, 64ii (1984), 399–402; portraits: J. Alexander and P. Binski (eds), *The Age of Chivalry* (London, Royal Academy of Arts with Weidenfeld and Nicolson, 1987), entry 713.

35. Thomson, chapter 8, note 13, 93, 111, 125 etc.; Thompson, chapter 8, note 9, 75.

36. Alexander and Binski, above, note 34, entry 726; Hunter, chapter 7, note 63.

37. Thompson, chapter 8, note 9; A. Emery, 'Ralph, Lord Cromwell's manor at Wingfield (1439-*c.* 1450): its construction, design and influence', *Archaeological Journal*, 142 (1985), 276–339; Stamper, chapter 8, note 17.

38. C. Coulson, 'Hierarchism in conventual crenellation: an essay in the sociology and metaphysics of medieval fortification', *Medieval Archaeology*, 26 (1982), 69–100; S. Moorhouse, 'Medieval distilling-apparatus of glass and pottery', *ibid.*, 16 (1972), 79–122; White, chapter 8, note 28; N. Palmer and C. Dyer, 'An inscribed stone from Burton Dassett, Warwickshire', *Medieval Archaeology*, 32 (1988), 216–19.

39. Cathcart King, chapter 8, note 47, chapter 14 stresses that some were habitable – but they were not for their owners' occupation.

INDEX

(For brevity, individuals' names are not separately entered. Sites etc. are entered only if referred to more than twice: others are enumerated in their counties. Numbers in bold refer to figure numbers.)

Agriculture, fields and field-systems 2–3, 6, 10–12, 16, 23, 29, 34, 38, 44, 57–9, 61, 68, 71, 80, 84, 87, 91, 95–6, 106–8, 120, 143, 145, 150, 163, 165, 171–5, 180, 191, 207–8, 210

Alfred Jewel 81, **4,6**

Amherst brooch **2,1**

Anglo-Saxon Chronicle 19, 42, 47, 65, 68, 74, 94

aristocrats, individual 61, 94, 98, 103, 109, 114, 115, 127, 137, 138, 162, 169, 170, 176, 178, 188, 190, 209, 210

Avon *see* Gloucestershire, Somerset

badges 208

Bantham 15, 16, 39, 161

Barnack 46, 71, 129

Barnstaple 115, 120, 132

Barton Blount 158, 174, 207

Barton Court Farm 11, 22, **1,2**

Bath 30, 76, 124, 129

Battle Abbey 172, 182, 190, 192, 193

Bayeux Tapestry 121–2, 126

beach markets 15, 161

Beauvais 82, 205

Bedford 63, 85, 95, 103, 105, 121, 125, 158, 199

Bedfordshire 152, 205; sites in 26

Benedictinism 99–101

Benedictional of St Ethelwold 101

Berkshire 206; sites in 179, 200; *see also* Barton Court Farm, Reading, Wallingford, Windsor

Bodiam Castle 188–90, 211

Bodleian bowl 146, **7,4**

Bolton Castle 190

bone-working 3–4, 103, 105, 118, 119, 143, 153

bones, animal 2–3, 9–10, 15, 23, 57–9, 70, 94–6, 103, 105, 119, 120, 129, 130, 136–7, 171, 172, 175, 180, 208

bones, bird 2, 136

bones, fish 15, 58, 152, 160, 175

bones, human 12–14, 21, 35, 47, 70, 118, 129–31, 176–9, **8,2**

books 211

Bordeaux 40, 56, 202, 206

Bordesley Abbey 154–5, 173, 178, 179

Boston 138–40, 156

brick 46, 168, 209, 210

Brixworth 46, 60, 69

Buckinghamshire 152; sites in 16, 32, 203; *see also* Walton

buildings 1, 2, 6, 7, 9–12, 15, 16, 18, 27–9, 31–2, 35–7, 39, 44–6, 55, 57–61, 64, 67–8, 71, 74, 76–7, 79–80, 82, 87, 89–91, 94, 103–4, 106–16, 136, 141–6, 148, 150, 152, 158–9, 161–4, 166–9, 171–4, 180, 182, 191–201, 207, 209–11, **7,3, 7,6, 7,8, 9,2**

Burghal Hidage 43, 76, 91, 103

burial, burial customs etc. 5, 7, 8, 11–19, 21–7, 30–7, 40, 42, 46–7, 52–3, 56, 57, 60, 61, 64, 69–72, 94, 97–9, 104, 108, 109, 114, 115, 119, 123, 128–33, 138, 146, 161, 162, 183, 191, 210, 211, **3,2**

Burton Dassett 211, **9,5**

Bury St Edmunds 12, 139, 186

239